To Gregory Vlastos

Preface

This book is intended for readers who have little or no previous knowledge of the philosophers of the Greek and Roman world, or of their literary and historical background. Naturally, I hope it may be useful to students and teachers in courses on Greek philosophy; these readers will get both less and more than they might expect. Chapters 2 to 4 by no means cover all 'the Presocratics', as they are normally conceived; on the other hand, they cover some authors and questions that deserve to be studied more often than (as far as I know) they are usually studied by students being introduced to early Greek philosophy. In Chapters 5 to 7 I devote a good bit of space to Plato and Aristotle; but I have tried to prevent them from dominating the picture, and in Chapters 8 to 11 I have sought to give some idea of both the variety and the continuity in philosophy after Aristotle.

Some passages from Classical authors are quoted in translation in the text. Readers should be warned that a mark of omission may sometimes indicate a considerable gap in the original. I use angle brackets, < ... >, to supply words left unexpressed, but clearly intended, in the original. I use square brackets, [...], for explanatory interpolations that are not meant to be part of the translation. Square brackets sometimes appear around authors' names in the Notes, to indicate spurious or doubtful works.

I do not provide a systematic historical outline; but I have tried to give the dates of major philosophers at reasonable intervals in the text, and they are repeated, together with the dates of other authors cited, in the index. It will be obvious that many dates of philosophers are imprecise, or unreliable, or both ('*fl.*' (= *floruit*) indicates some specific evidence of the person's being active in the year or years given). I have usually added BC or AD to dates only where there seemed to be some danger of confusion.

Since this book results partly from my own attempts at teaching in this area, I have benefited from the stimulating and thoughtful questions and comments of many undergraduates, and from

helpful discussions with people who have shared the teaching—
Jennifer Whiting, Henry Newell, David Brink, and Susan Sauvé.
Successive drafts of the book have been greatly improved as a
result of numerous and persistent criticisms and suggestions by
Gail Fine. The Press's readers have made useful comments on
later versions. It gives me special pleasure to dedicate this book
to Gregory Vlastos.

T. H. IRWIN
Cornell University
Ithaca, New York
January 1988

Note to 1996 reissue:
I have revised the Notes and Bibliography to include a few recent
publications.

Contents

I

Introduction

i. *Scope*

This book introduces some of the issues of philosophical interest in Classical thought, in the 1,100 years or so from Homer to Saint Augustine. It is therefore concerned primarily with Greek philosophy—that is, philosophical thought expressed in the Greek language—and its immediate descendants.

The choice of a starting-point for this book is not arbitrary, since Homer's poems are among the earliest works of Greek literature, and had a profound influence on later Classical thought. The choice of a place to stop is far more arbitrary. The death of Augustine in AD 430 falls in the period when the Western (Latin-speaking) Roman Empire collapsed. The Classical tradition in philosophy continued in the Eastern (Greek-speaking) Empire and in the Arab states, before being reintroduced into Western Europe; and it is in some ways regrettable to suggest that the fall of part of the Empire marks an important break in the history of philosophy. Still, it is not completely wrong to regard Augustine as the beginning of mediaeval philosophy; and if we stop with him, we have a reasonable idea of the direction in which philosophy went in the later centuries.[1]

To give a sketch of all the main philosophers and philosophical issues in Classical thought would require either a long book or a very compressed one; and I have not tried to be comprehensive. I have omitted some of the major Presocratics, most of Plato's later dialogues, much of Scepticism, the more technical aspects of Stoicism, the whole of ancient logic.[2] On the other hand, I have discussed some writers who are not philosophers. In the first three chapters I have done this to illustrate the problems and arguments from which philosophy arose. In the last chapter I have said something about Christian thought to indicate one important effect of Classical philosophy. In these cases I have kept in mind the readers who approach Classical philosophers without a background in Classical history and literature. However, I have given a very incomplete picture of the aspects of Classical thought that are not strictly philosophical. Medicine, mathematics, astronomy, dynamics, geography, history, grammar, literary criticism—all these developed in the Classical world, often in close connexion with the development of philosophy. The mutual influence—good and bad—between philosophy and these other disciplines receives only occasional glances in this book.[3]

Instead of trying to cover all these topics and philosophers, I have tried to discuss some questions in enough detail to bring out some of their interest and significance. I have picked topics that a reader can usefully consider without extensive reading of difficult texts. The best way to introduce the right questions is often to raise objections and criticisms. I have done this in order to suggest directions for readers to follow, not to tell them what to think, or even to tell them what can be said on each side of a particular issue. Comments are meant to be provocative rather than conclusive.

ii. *Periods*

With the appropriate cautions about arbitrary divisions between periods, it may be useful to mark a preliminary division into four periods:

Speculative philosophy (Chapters 2-4). Before Socrates philosophy develops through the successive speculative systems of the Presocratic naturalists. Many of these thinkers put forward very general views about the nature and origin of the world; sometimes they recall the myths about the gods, sometimes they seem to be primitive natural scientists.

Critical philosophy (Chapters 5-7). Socrates, Plato, and Aristotle construct philosophy as a discipline distinct from mythology and empirical science, concerned with the foundations of knowledge and morality.

Systematic philosophy (Chapters 8-9). The Stoics and Epicureans use Presocratic, Platonic, and Aristotelian material to construct self-consciously integrated philosophical systems, applying a single set of principles to questions about knowledge, nature, and morality.

Transcendent philosophy (Chapters 10-11). The revival of Platonism in the later Classical world turns philosophers' attention from the understanding of observable reality to the search for knowledge of the unobservable and super-sensible. Such an outlook makes later Platonism a natural companion to Christian theology.

These divisions are too crude to be taken very seriously. None of them has any explicit ancient authority except for the division between the first and second periods; Aristotle insists on this division, and (as we will see later) we have good reason to agree with him. The other divisions are much less sharp; but they give a general impression of the attitudes and assumptions of philosophers in different periods.

iii. *Questions*

This book would fail in its purpose if its themes were very closely connected. For part of the interest of Greek philosophy is the relative independence of some philosophers from their predecessors, and the wide range of questions that came within the scope of philosophy at different times. Plato and Aristotle, in particular, are important primarily because they raise new philosophical questions and find new areas of philosophical inquiry; it is true, but less important, that they also answer old questions. For this reason among others, it would be a mistake to try to define a philosophical question or argument at this stage; it is best to watch the growth of philosophical thinking to see what became characteristic of it, and why. Still, I have picked some major themes and to some degree concentrated on them, in order to display some of the connected and continuous arguments that run through the whole history of Classical thought.

Epistemology. The first philosophers seek to know and understand the world, and they soon raise questions about our resources for gaining knowledge, and about the relative importance of observation and theory, or sense-perception and reason, as sources of knowledge. Questions about sources of knowledge stimulate epistemology (theory of knowledge), while doubts about the possibility of knowledge provoke sceptical reactions.

Metaphysics. Understanding the world involves the discovery of natural laws, and forces us to ask how our conception of ourselves fits into our understanding of the rest of nature. A scientific theory of natural processes sometimes seems to leave no room for our belief in ourselves as conscious, rational, responsible agents. Questions about the place of human consciousness and agency within a universe governed by physical laws raise problems about body and mind, and about causation and free will—two central problems in metaphysics (inquiry into the nature of reality).

Ethics. Philosophers seeking a rational understanding of nature also seek a rational understanding of morality. They look for reasonable principles to guide human conduct and to justify social and political structures. Socrates and his successors argue about the correct account of a person's good; the relation between a person's own good and the good of other people; and hence about the relation between self-interest and morality. They try to formulate a critical moral system that will show us both what is true in our pre-reflective moral beliefs and how to correct them.

Theology. The concerns of the first philosophers are similar to those of religion and mythology—to understand the origin and nature of the world, and our place in it. In its different phases Classical philosophy challenges the religious outlook, develops independently of it, and seeks to absorb traditional religion into rational theology. Augustine shows how one movement in later Greek philosophy came to accept the claims of Christianity, and formed Christian theology. It is still an open question which attitude to religion counts as philosophical progress or decline— whether philosophy should try to defend, criticize, ignore, or undermine all or some of the claims of all or some religious outlooks.

While it is useful to distinguish these different areas of philosophical inquiry, it would be unfortunate to give the impression either that they are quite unconnected with each other, or that every philosopher takes the same view about how they are connected. The rest of the book should counteract any such impression.

iv. *Sources*

A reader who wants to go deeper into Classical thought than I have gone in this book should turn to the Notes. They identify some of the texts I have relied on, and should help readers in exploring the texts for themselves. I have cited the evidence not only for my account of different philosophers but also for some points about the historical or political background, so that readers can consult these sources also. All the philosophical texts I cite, and almost all the non-philosophical ones, are available in English translations.[4]

References to modern books and articles are highly selective, and cite works of quite varying levels of difficulty and specialization. They are not meant to provide a systematic survey of secondary literature; the coverage is uneven between different topics, since some topics have attracted more interesting work than others. The references are meant to introduce readers to some of the more interesting discussions of the topics covered in this book, or to points of view different from my own, or to treatments of questions that I mention only briefly.[5]

2

Homer

i. *The importance of Homer*[1]

One of the earliest Greek philosophers, Xenophanes (580–480 BC), explains that he criticizes Homer because 'from the beginning everyone has learnt according to Homer'.[2] He is right to suggest that Homer (? *c*.750 BC) acquired a unique authority. For the Greeks had no Scripture corresponding to the Bible or the Koran; but they had the *Iliad* and the *Odyssey*, the two long poems ascribed to Homer.[3] These were not an authoritative text, protected from criticism or expounded by authorized interpreters; and they did not constitute the formal doctrinal standard of any religious system. Still, they were similar to the Bible in so far as many Greeks with some education learnt the Homeric poems; over a millennium after the time of Homer, Augustine still learnt the poems. The Athenians heard them recited in public. An orator, appealing to Homer as a moral authority, remarks:

Your fathers took him to be such an excellent poet that they passed a law that every four years he, alone of all poets, should have his works performed by reciters at the All-Athenian festival.[4]

From Homer many Greeks drew central and influential, not always conscious, elements of their conception of the gods and the relation of gods to human beings, and they drew a moral outlook and ideal that remained influential long after it had been thoroughly criticized.

It is not surprising, then, that later philosophers regularly quote and allude to Homer.[5] He is not always an authority; indeed, he is sometimes a target, since thoughtful Greeks attack and challenge his views on morality and religion.[6] To see what they thought they should challenge, we too should begin with Homer.

Homer may have lived in the middle of the seventh century, perhaps 150 years before the beginning of Greek philosophical thinking; he may have lived in Ionia, where Greek philosophy began, in one of the Greek communities of western Asia.[7] He presents his views (or the views expressed in his poems) in narrative verse, not in philosophical argument; but the views are neither primitive nor unreasonable. If we see why they might reasonably appeal to common sense and experience, we will see why the earliest philosophers found it necessary to challenge common sense and experience as sources of reasonable beliefs.

ii. *The ideal person and the ideal life*

The Homeric moral outlook is most easily understood from its conception of the ideal person. The leading characters of the *Iliad* are heroes of a past age; their goodness, excellence, or virtue (three ways of rendering the Greek *aretê*) were unequalled in Homer's own time. But what Homer counts as goodness is not the sort of thing that we might most readily think of as such.

Some of a person's goodness is outside his control. A good person must have been born into a good family, and must himself be rich and strong; Homer suggests that a person loses half his goodness on the day he becomes a slave. Though Homer does not consider those who win wealth without being nobly born, those who share his outlook refuse to recognize such people as genuinely good. The hereditary, social, and material components of a person's goodness are so important that, if you have them, you remain a good person, even if you behave badly. The shirker Paris fails to perform the actions of a good man, but remains a good man because he meets the other conditions for being good. To this extent a person's goodness is not in his control.[8]

Some aspects of it, however, are in his control, and he is expected to display his excellence in his actions, characteristically and ideally the actions of a warrior and leader. A good man excels in battle, and his characteristic virtues are strength, skill, and courage. He is born into a leading place in society with a large share of its resources, and he has the virtues he needs to defend his place against attack. Hence he is expected to excel. Achilles' father sent him to Troy 'always to be best and to excel the others';

and, like the other main characters, Achilles tries to achieve pre-
eminence in the qualities and actions that make a person's excellence. Achilles is the 'best of the Achaeans', above all because
he is pre-eminent in these virtues; and these are the virtues his
father had in mind when he wanted Achilles to excel the others.
Self-defence also requires the intelligence to form plans, and the
skill to persuade others to co-operate in carrying them out. But
these virtues are secondary to those of the warrior.

The character of the excellent person is clearer from the sorts
of goals he aims at. Achilles and Agamemnon quarrel, in the
incident that begins the main action of the *Iliad*, because Agamemnon takes Briseis, who is Achilles' prize, and so slights Achilles' honour. Honour (*timê*), as Homer conceives it, includes,
primarily, other people's good opinion, and, secondarily, the material and social 'honours' that are both causes and effects of
this good opinion. The hero is individualistic, in so far as he is
concerned primarily with his own success and reputation; he does
not aim primarily at some collective goal that includes the good
of other people, or of a whole society. On the other hand, he is
also other-directed, in so far as he must attend to the good opinion
of the people who control the goods he aims at. Moreover, as
Aristotle remarks, the hero must respect, not merely manipulate
their opinion, since it defines the values that make his own aims
worth while for him.[9]

iii. *Self and others*

We may find Homer's conception of a good person rather surprising. If we think one person is better than another, or we want
to be better than we are, most of us would not have the Homeric
virtues primarily in mind. We often think a good person is one
who treats other people well. In Homeric ethics, similarly, the
hero is expected to have some concern for the interests of others;
but the nature and limits of his concern for them are not what we
might expect.

The hero is certainly not indifferent to others; indeed, much of
the action of the *Iliad* results from the concern of some people
for the interests of others. Thetis is concerned about her son

Achilles, Hector about his wife Andromache and his son
Astyanax, and Achilles about his friend Patroclus. Nor is concern
limited to concern for individuals. Sometimes people care about
the welfare of the group they belong to in some co-operative
project. For the Greek leaders this group is the Greek army,
whose collective opinion agrees that Achilles and Agamemnon
are both to blame for their neglect of the army's welfare in favour
of their private quarrel about their own honour. Similarly, Odysseus appeals to the common interest of the group in his attempt
to persuade Achilles to give up the quarrel. For the Trojans the
common good is the good of their city. Hector urges this concern
on them, and displays it himself.[10]

A hero of superior strength and power has inferiors who depend
on him, and he is expected to defend them; they normally and
legitimately expect his aid. A good king, such as Odysseus, cares
about the welfare of his people. A good husband, such as Hector,
cares about his wife. Achilles does what is expected of the greater
hero, and cares about his friend and dependant Patroclus.

Apart from these specific expectations of particular people in
special relations to the hero, people in general expect him to be
moved by common human feelings. Patroclus attacks Achilles for
his indifference to the sufferings of the Greeks, not simply because
he is part of the expedition, but because they are suffering as a
result of his action. Achilles displays the same callous indifference
in his killing of Lycaon, and in his dishonouring of Hector's
corpse. He finally outgrows this attitude when he meets Priam:
when he thinks of his own father, he understands Priam's feelings
and is moved by them. The customary practice of supplication
depends partly on these sympathetic feelings directed to someone
needing help. Someone who, like the Cyclops, lacks these feelings
for human beings acts like a wild animal rather than a human
being—indeed, even the Cyclops has such feelings for his
animals.[11]

The interests of other people, then, are important to a hero;
and he is criticized if he is as indifferent to them as Achilles is.
And yet a hero's attitude to these interests is not a prominent
part of his goodness. Achilles loses none of his heroic virtue by
being selfishly indifferent to others; he remains the best of the

Achaeans, and no one so much as suggests that his selfish indifference might damage his reputation for goodness. On the
other hand, if he had been captured by pirates and sold into
slavery, he would have lost half his virtue. Criticism of such
indifference remains rather mild; for selfish indifference is a minor
flaw, compared with the main components of a person's goodness.

iv. *Priorities*

The *Iliad* clarifies from different points of view this secondary
status of other people's interests. First, some other-regarding concerns are purely instrumental to a hero's primary aims. One warrior's success often depends on co-operation with fellow-warriors.
A hero displays his power and strength most effectively when he
can protect his dependants as well as himself. Since these concerns
for others are instrumental to his concern for his own honour, he
has no reason to care about other people's interests if they conflict
with the demands of his own honour.

Not all the hero's other-regarding concerns, however, seem to
be purely instrumental. It is easy to see how both co-operation with
fellow-warriors and protection of dependants advance a hero's
primary aims; but it is not so easy to explain or justify the attitudes
that rest on common human feelings simply by their instrumental
value. Still, even if they are not purely instrumental, they are
strictly secondary. The hero is expected to display other-regarding
concerns, but never to sacrifice any of his power or status because
of them. No one, therefore, criticizes Achilles for his first withdrawal from the battle; indeed, most of the other leading Greeks
assume that they should offer him compensation. He is certainly
criticized for his rejection of the offer made by the delegation of
Greek leaders (in Book ix); but no one suggests that he is less
good or less deserving of honour than he was before. When he
returns to the battle, it is not because he cares about the rest of
the Greeks, but because Patroclus has been killed. He is not even
concerned about the death of Patroclus for Patroclus' own sake;
he regrets the weakness that he has himself displayed by failing
to protect his own dependant.

Hector is the Homeric hero who is most conscious of the claims of others, and specifically of his family and his city; none the less, his primary motives are exactly the same as Achilles'. Twice Hector chooses to avoid shame and dishonour for himself, even if his action harms his family and his city. He concedes that Troy will benefit if he retreats, but he takes it for granted—and no one contradicts him—that honour and shame require him to stand his ground, to face Achilles, and to die. When he has to make the most crucial choices, Hector shows that he is moved by the primary Homeric motives and virtues.[12] We may hesitate to say he is selfish, if we think selfish people are out to preserve themselves at the expense of others; but he is none the less strikingly indifferent to the interests of others.

For a Homeric hero, then, the interests of other people are often important, but always strictly secondary. Indeed they count for so much less than the primary virtues that a man's goodness or badness is finally measured by the primary virtues alone, not at all by his concern for others.

v. *Difficulties in Homeric ethics*

The Homeric outlook creates conflicts for those who accept it. Some of the conflicts arise for the individual himself. He has to adjust his conception of his aims and interests to the demands of those who can honour or dishonour him. This may not create a conflict if other people endorse his aims. But the different aims of different individuals may create a conflict between the aims of one individual and the actions approved by others. In such a conflict the individual cannot claim to be following his own values against the expectations of others; for his values attach most importance to the approval of others, and he violates his own values if he fails to be guided by their opinions.

Achilles illustrates just this sort of conflict between self-assertion and conformity to the demands of others. He competes for honour with Agamemnon, and Agamemnon wins the first round by taking Briseis; but Achilles would have won the second round, had he accepted Agamemnon's offer of compensation. At this point Achilles seems almost to free himself from the normal heroic dependence on other people's opinion. He claims to be content with the prospect of an obscure life without honour, since honour is unstable and transitory, and in any case does not matter much to someone when he is dead. It turns out, however, that Achilles is not as independent and self-directed as he claims to be. His shame at the dishonour he suffers from the death of Patroclus forces him back into the battle, even though he knows his own death will be the result.[13]

Homeric ethics creates these conflicts within an individual, but it also creates them within a society. For it gives each member a reason for doing actions that are bad for the society as a whole. Since each hero wants his own honour, and sees a reasonable chance of winning it in competition with others, he is unwilling to refrain from competition; but when everyone tolerates this system, it may be bad for everyone.

If heroic morality is bad even for the heroes who have most to gain from it, it is still worse for their social inferiors. They can expect protection from a hero, within the limits imposed by the hero's pursuit of his own honour; but these limits make the hero rather an unreliable protector. If I am a hero judging a legal action involving a poor dependant of mine and a rich man of my own social position, I may see no point in giving the verdict to the poor man, if an alliance with the superior man will do more for my status and honour. I will be an unreliable protector, just as Achilles was of Patroclus, and Hector of his family and community; for it is easy to think of situations where the duties of a protector have to come second to the overriding claims of honour. The hero's pride and self-esteem require the pursuit of the heroic virtues, and make him ashamed to fail in them.

Homer does not expose this consequence of Homeric ethics in the *Iliad*. It is closer to the surface in the *Odyssey*, in the conduct of Penelope's suitors. Their selfish and parasitic behaviour is bad for the whole community; and yet, from one point of view, it is eminently heroic, since it promises considerable rewards in honour and status for the lucky one who marries Penelope. But Homer's near contemporary, the poet Hesiod, exposes the anti-social aspects of Homeric morality. Like Homer, he recognizes a heroic age in the past; but in his own day he sees 'bribe-eating kings' who cheat the poor at law. The distance between the Homeric heroes and Hesiod's bribe-eating kings is quite short; even if Homer does not advocate the corrupt behaviour attacked by Hesiod, his own moral outlook seems to justify it.[14]

Homer largely ignores the effects of the observance of Homeric morality on the non-heroic classes who are its victims. He attends to them in just one episode in the *Iliad*. Thersites—a brash, obstreperous, and (for good measure) ugly rabble-rouser, corresponding to some people's prejudices about trade-union leaders—presents a good argument against the kings and their outlook, denouncing them as selfish parasites wasting the resources of the community. He is answered by the skilful debater Odysseus; this time, however, Odysseus relies not on his debating skill, but on forcible suppression. Homer is not the last conservative to approve of this treatment of subversive arguments presented by unmannerly people who do not know their place. Nor is he the last to represent the lower classes as agreeing with such treatment for those who complain about their betters.

A defender of Homeric morality might argue that, despite its inconvenient results for some people, it is on the whole best for an unstable society exposed to external attack; as a warrior and protector, the Homeric hero may seem to perform a service useful to his community. This is a weak defence; its weakness exposes a general flaw in explanations and defences of social institutions that appeal to their positive function in society. Even if some defence is needed, why should the Homeric hero be the only, or the preferable, means of defence? And would his services be needed so much if he were not so devoted to quarrels and wars? His own values help to create the social conditions for which those values seem appropriate.[15]

vi. *Gods and the world*

Some of the most striking aspects of the myths of contemporary Western Asia—and of Greek myths—are rarely displayed in the Homeric poems. In these myths gods correspond very closely to natural forces, and indeed sometimes seem to be identified with them; they are partly human, partly animal, often monstrous, and

they are propitiated by sacrifice and magic. We can see some of
this outlook (though in a fairly sophisticated form) in Hesiod;
but there is very little of it in Homer. Even the giants, witches,
and other creatures of myth and folktale in the *Odyssey* are rather
human and familiar.[16]

Homer makes the gods human because he wants to make them
intelligible, and so to make events intelligible. If we are dealing
with a half-human, half-bestial monster, we hardly know what to
expect of it, or how it will react to different sorts of treatment.
Human beings, generally speaking, are easier to understand. If
we know that someone is brave, jealous of his honour, devoted
to his family, and so on, we expect that, in normal conditions, his
behaviour will be more or less appropriate for someone with this
outlook in this situation. Fairly rational agents with fairly stable
aims are predictable and reliable.

This is how Homer conceives the gods. They are not mech-
anisms to be manipulated by magic or sacrifice. Though they
certainly care about sacrifices, they are not rigidly or mechanically
controlled by them. When Athena's purpose is firmly fixed against
Troy, she is not swayed by sacrifice, as she would be if it had
some automatic mechanical effect. Zeus decides how much of
Achilles' prayers he will grant. Hera, Aphrodite, Poseidon, and
Athena, as they appear in both poems, have fixed and intelligible
purposes. Natural forces, therefore, do not strike at random, but
as a result of the steady purposes and intentions of the gods. In
looking for regularity, laws, and order in natural processes,
Homer begins a search that dominates Greek—and not only
Greek—philosophical and scientific thinking.[17]

It is equally important, however, to notice the limits of order
and regularity in Homer's conception of the world. Though the
gods are fairly constant, they are also fickle and variable in the
same way that human heroes are, and for similar reasons. Moreover, their control over the natural order is not complete. Homer
sometimes, though not characteristically, comes close to identifying the gods with the natural processes that (in his more usual
view) they control. But he never suggests that every earthquake or
storm, for instance, reflects some steady and intelligible long-term

purpose of the god Poseidon who is sometimes said to be responsible for them. The Hebrew prophet Amos sees God's hand
in every natural disaster: 'If disaster falls on a city, has not the
Lord been at work?' But Homer makes no such general assumption. Some things happen in the Homeric universe by chance, at
random, for no particular reason.[18]

vii. *Gods and moral ideals*

For someone who accepts Homeric morality the gods present a
definite and attractive ideal; indeed, it is such an attractive ideal
that a human being cannot achieve it unless he is lucky enough
to become a god, as Heracles did. But he can recognize it as an
ideal to aim at as far as he can.[19]

The gods have their recognized honour and status, and are
secure in the possession of them; and though they suffer some
disappointments, these do not affect the character of their lives.
Gods who are angry usually get some satisfaction, and no gods
described in Homer are so frustrated and dissatisfied that they
find their lives as a whole miserable. Often they are feasting and
laughing; and on the whole they enjoy their immortal lives. Hence
they are regularly called 'blessed' or 'happy'.[20]

For human beings this god-like existence of success and enjoyment in the secure possession of honour and power is the ideal
to be pursued. The hero who pursues it aims at honour and power
for himself, but discovers that these are insecure, and in any case
transitory. For a while Achilles seems to prefer the security of the
divine life, even if he has to sacrifice honour and power to get it;
but in the end he chooses the other elements of the divine life
over security, and Homer leaves no doubt that this is recognized
as the right choice for a hero to make.[21]

Like other aspects of Homeric ethics, the ideal of divine happiness forces a conflict on the human individual. He must sacrifice
security for the dangerous pursuit of precarious honour, or he
must choose security with the certainty of failure in his other most
important aims. If we face such a conflict in our aims, we might
reasonably ask if we are right to pursue all these aims. Seeing this

conflict, not all Greeks remained satisfied with the ideal offered by the Homeric gods.

viii. *Zeus and the world order*

Zeus holds a special place among the Homeric gods and in the Homeric conception of the universe. He reflects some oppositions and potential conflicts that are never explicitly faced in the Homeric poems.

In some ways he is one god among many, though the most powerful of them. He shared power with Poseidon and Hades, the other sons of Cronus, after they had violently overthrown their father (the harsh details of this story are told, significantly, by Hesiod, not by Homer). He is scolded and cajoled by the other gods; he is even distracted and seduced by his wife Hera for a whole book (xiv). It seems to be a matter of luck and chance that Zeus takes charge again before it is too late and his plans have gone completely astray.

But this is not the whole truth about Zeus. He is stronger than all the other gods together. His will is fulfilled in the Trojan War and the sack of Troy. Homer insists on this at the beginning of the poem, and refers, though not often and not prominently, to the will of Zeus in the vicissitudes that follow. The beginning of the *Odyssey* suggests that the supremacy of Zeus depends on the consent of the other gods, but that none the less his design is carried out.[22]

And yet it is not always clear that Zeus's own will is fulfilled. He is rather obscurely connected with the 'fates' (*moirai*, meaning 'parts' or 'portions'). A person's 'fate' or 'portion' determines the time of his death; and when two heroes are fighting, Zeus weighs their two fates to see which hero has to die. Sometimes Zeus considers whether to save a particular hero from his fate; but he never actually violates the fates. Nor is he forced to follow them against his considered decision; his considered decision always turns out to conform to the fates.[23]

These fates do not constitute a single fate, a necessary order that determines each event in the universe. Homer's fates reflect only the vague belief that some events, and especially the time of an individual's death, are determined inevitably by previous events beyond our control, perhaps beyond the control of any rational agent, human or divine. Since order and regularity in the Homeric universe are only partial, the fates determine only some events in it.[24]

Homer suggests, none the less, that Zeus's will is in control. The suggestion is perhaps more prominent in the *Odyssey*, but the *Iliad* accepts it no less firmly. Moreover, Zeus, unlike the other gods, seems to have wider concerns than his own honour and success. He is also concerned with justice in human societies. Eventually he punishes the Trojans for condoning Paris's breach of the proper relations between host and guest. He is angry at the breaches of justice that easily tempt Homeric heroes in their treatment of their social inferiors. He seems to be ready to enforce the other-regarding moral requirements that seemed to be secondary in the Homeric ethical outlook.[25]

Zeus and the fates display two tendencies in Homeric thinking that potentially conflict both with each other and with the primary Homeric ethical outlook. The primary outlook recognizes a partially ordered universe; Homeric gods act like human beings, and care about some things that happen, while other things just happen, for no reason and in no definite order. Zeus and the fates, however, suggest two different types of order. The fates suggest an impersonal, amoral order, independent of the choices of gods or human beings. Zeus, on the other hand, suggests a moral order, embodying an intelligence and will that transcend normal heroic values, but still recognizably belong to an intelligent moral agent. In these two different ways Homer points to possible lines of thought that go beyond the limits of his own outlook.

ix. *The main difficulties in Homer*

It is easy to see that the Homeric poems appeal to the imagination and the emotions. It is perhaps less obvious that the Homeric outlook appeals to common sense and observation; but this point is worth stressing, since, surprisingly, some of the aspects that especially appeal to common sense are those that later Greeks found most open to criticism.

Homeric ethics appeals to common sense because the Homeric hero aims at clearly desirable goals, and aims at them realistically. Success, social status, power, wealth, and honour are readily intelligible goals, and the hero aims at them without apology. He has no illusions about the dangers he faces, but the hazards of his life do not lead him to despair. He pursues his interests vigorously, and does not take his duties to others so seriously that they interfere with his pursuit of his own interests.

The Homeric gods appeal to common sense and observation because they avoid fantasy and exaggeration. They are not monsters, and they are not unimaginably superhuman. Since they are like us, they explain some aspects of the universe in terms that we can readily understand. Moreover, Homer wisely does not appeal to the gods to explain everything in the universe; some of it remains random or uncontrolled. Homer's view of the world does not include natural or divine laws that imply specific predictions about what will happen in specific conditions (e.g. that if there is a natural disaster, some god is punishing you); indeed, it is hard to think of any disorder or disaster in the world that Homeric theology could not accommodate. Belief in the Homeric gods is to this extent rather undemanding; nothing that can happen seems to give us positive grounds for disbelief.

The criticisms of Homer focus especially on the presence of disorder and conflict. Homeric ethics gives each person an interest in supporting a system whose effects harm everyone. It is harmful enough for those who benefit from the system, since the aims of each hero cause damaging conflicts with other heroes; and it is still more damaging, with still less compensating benefit, for the non-heroic people who will never win in the competition for honour.

Moral criticism may arise from reflexion on conflicts within a prevailing moral system, or from awareness of its conflicts with the requirements of a human society; and Homeric ethics is open to both sorts of criticism. Individual pursuit of honour conflicts with the legitimate claims of others—in this case, with the claims of Achilles' fellow Greeks and Hector's fellow Trojans. Unrestrained heroic ethics tends to threaten the co-operative relations in any tolerable form of society, since non-heroes cannot trust heroes and heroes cannot trust one another.

Homeric ethics did provoke criticism, along these lines among others, from later Greek thinkers. But it also proved remarkably resilient, and remained influential in practice even when it faced theoretical criticism. Its clarity, intelligibility, and appeal to common sense help to explain its survival.

Homeric cosmology is no less full of conflicts. Homer's picture of the world displays a mass of actually or potentially conflicting forces; and the different forces embody conflicting attempts to understand the world. The many gods and natural forces suggest that the world is only partly predictable, and only partly under intelligent control. The primacy of Zeus suggests total intelligent control. The role of the fates suggests total determination, but perhaps without intelligent control. To expose the potential conflicts in Homer, a critic need only press some of the questions that are raised by Homer himself. How far could the other gods frustrate the will of Zeus or the fates? If the sea were left to itself, could it frustrate the will of the gods, or violate the fates? Could Zeus violate the fates if he wanted to?

Rational cosmology begins with these questions about Homer; for Homer shares the interests of the rational cosmologist far enough to raise some of the right issues. He wants to discern some regular, predictable pattern in the workings of the universe. But in trying to describe the pattern he exposes some of its difficulties; the roles of the gods, the fates, and partially random natural forces are never made clear. A critical reader might reasonably be dissatisfied with Homer's description.

These questions about Homer are the starting-points for Greek scientific and philosophical thinking.

3

The Naturalist Movement

i. *The naturalist outlook*

Between the age of Homer (mid-eighth century) and the age of
Socrates (late fifth century), the Greeks began systematic rational
study of the natural order and the moral order. Aristotle distinguishes those who talk about gods and offer poetic or mythological accounts from those who offer rational accounts that can
be seriously studied:

The school of Hesiod and all the theologians considered only what was
persuasive to themselves, and thought little of us . . . But it is not worth
seriously examining the sophistries of mythology, whereas we must in-
terrogate those who present a rational demonstration.

He calls the second group 'students of nature' or 'naturalists'
(*phusiologoi*), as opposed to Hesiod and his followers, because
they abandon mythology to ask a new question, about the nature
(*phusis*) of things. Aristotle's comments on the 'mythologists' are
unsympathetic, indeed unfair; but he has good reason to believe
that a new movement began with Thales (*c*.625–*c*.545), 'the ori-
ginator of this sort of philosophy'. He rightly thinks it is worth
his while to conduct a rational discussion with these thinkers.[1]

Many have followed Aristotle in taking the naturalists to be
the first philosophers and scientists.[2] To see if this judgement is
right, we ought to see what is distinctive of these thinkers. This
chapter will consider the main naturalist doctrines; the next chapter will turn to some of the criticisms, reactions, and further
developments that they provoked.

ii. *Nature as matter*

Aristotle claims that the naturalists identify the nature with the
'matter' (*hulê*) or 'basic subject' (*hupokeimenon*) of things:

Most of the first philosophers thought the only origins of everything were material. For, they say, there is some <subject> that all beings come from, the first thing they come to be from and the last thing they perish into, the substance remaining throughout and changing in its attributes; and this is the elementary <basis> and the origin of beings. And for this reason they think nothing either comes to be or perishes, since they assume that in every change this nature [i.e. the subject] persists. For just as we say Socrates does not come to be unqualifiedly whenever he becomes good or musical, and does not perish <unqualifiedly> whenever he loses these states, since the subject, Socrates himself, remains, so also, <they say>, nothing else <either comes to be or perishes unqualifiedly>, since there must be some nature, either one or more than one, that persists while the other things come to be from it.[3]

We can also recognize a continuing subject in more extensive changes: if we make a square lump of bronze that was one centimetre wide into a round coin that is two centimetres in diameter, the very same lump of bronze is the continuing subject, its dimensions and shape alone having changed. The continuing subject may not be continuously observable as easily as the bronze is: if we cook oats and water to make porridge, the result may not look much like oats or water, but still they are what it is, and they are continuing subjects that have undergone change.

If we find the continuing subject of change, we seem to find the nature of things. If we take an ordinary subject (Socrates, the coin, the porridge), we can ask what its nature is, or what the subject really is; and a reasonable answer will tell us what its basic, underlying subject is. It is not Socrates' nature to be tanned or pale, since he could lose these properties and still exist; but we might say it is his nature to be a man, and the man is the basic subject. Similarly, we can say that porridge is oats and water that have been cooked together; this is a better answer than 'Porridge is a sticky mess' or 'Porridge is light grey', because it allows us to say how the porridge came into being. It also allows us, in principle, to explain the properties and behaviour of the porridge; if we know what oats and water are like and how they interact, we can predict what will happen when porridge is eaten by someone with a specific type of body. In Aristotle's view, the naturalists want to explain the world as a whole in the same way. They want to find the nature of things by finding their basic matter.

In Homer the nature and constitution of things does not play the primary role in explaining what happens to them. He often explains events by some external divine agency affecting the sea to produce a storm, or affecting human bodies to produce a plague. In so far as they appeal to the nature and constitution of things, the naturalists assume that this Homeric view is mistaken. In their view, things seem random, or to require divine intervention, only because we do not know enough about the constituent stuffs and processes.

iii. *Conceptions of nature*

Anaximander (*c*.610–*c*.540) assumes an original stuff that is 'unbounded' (or 'undefined', *apeiron*), because it is qualitatively indeterminate. It does not itself have the characteristics of ordinary things (rocks, rivers, and so on) or even of their constituents (earth, water, and so on), but it has the basis of all these in it. To give a rough and partial illustration, we might say that the coal in the earth is neither gas nor coke nor soap nor tar, but it is the basis of them all. Anaximander's 'Unbounded' stands in this relation to familiar observable things and stuffs. The ceaseless movement of the Unbounded produces a 'generative source', which is separated from the Unbounded, and in turn produces the four basic opposites—hot and cold, dry and wet—that constitute the different things in the world and underlie all observable processes and changes.[4]

Eventually the opposites perish again and return to the Unbounded, which has existed all along, being 'everlasting and ageless'. In the present state of the world Anaximander sees mutual destruction of the opposites: water chills and dampens, while heat warms and dries; hence rivers silt up, while coastlines erode, so that in one place the dry encroaches on the wet, and in another the wet advances on the dry. If one or other of these processes continued too long, it would destroy the world we know. The Unbounded, however, 'seems to be the original principle of the other things, and seems to surround and govern all things . . .

and this is the divine, since it is immortal and indestructible, as Anaximander and most of the naturalists say.' The Unbounded maintains the order of the opposites, so that they 'pay the just penalty and retribution to each other for their injustice, in accordance with the order of time (as he says in somewhat poetical words)'. The Unbounded exacts the just penalty for encroachment, and so maintains the stability of the present world order, for the finite time that the present order lasts.

The Unbounded has neither beginning nor end, because Anaximander rejects coming to be from nothing and destruction into nothing as violations of basic laws governing coming to be and perishing; neither of them is explicable unless both of them are from something and into something. Unless there is something ungenerated and never destroyed, being would have come to an end in the past, or would do so in the future. The Unbounded is needed 'because only in this way would coming to be and perishing not fail—if the source from which the things coming to be are removed is unbounded'.[5]

These claims about the Unbounded show that Anaximander is concerned with law and regularity in the universe. He does not want to say that the world order began for no reason at some particular time. He fails to say, however, what caused the separation of the generative source at some particular time; presumably the cause must have been some previous change in the Unbounded, and he seems unable to explain that change. Nor does he explain why the opposites return to the Unbounded. At both points he seems to appeal to uncaused change. If so, he must leave an element of the randomness he wants to escape. Anaximander's main principles and general scheme express clearly the aims of naturalism; his imperfect execution of these aims suggests that a rigorous naturalist must go further.

iv. *Change and stability*

Heracleitus (*c*.500) presents a new form of naturalism that both extends and criticizes Anaximander. He states his naturalist aims clearly and self-consciously:

This world order [*kosmos*], the same for all, was made by no god or man, but always was and is and will be an ever-living fire, being kindled in measures and quenched in measures.[6]

In saying that the cosmos never came into being Heracleitus disagrees with Anaximander; he recognizes no generation of an ordered world out of the Unbounded, and no destruction into the Unbounded. He probably sees that Anaximander's belief in a beginning of the ordered world requires uncaused changes; and so he believes that a more consistent application of Anaximander's naturalist principles requires an ingenerable and everlasting ordered world. The world is kindled and quenched 'in measures', in so far as every change within the world order is 'measured', that is, determined by some regularity and natural law.

Heracleitus does not believe in the usual sort of basic subject or matter. We speak of a basic subject as something persisting through change (e.g. Socrates becoming pale). But a bonfire is made of wood, grass, paper, leaves, etc. in the right proportions, and it keeps burning as long as more of the right stuff is added, and the same physical laws are observed. There seems to be no continuing subject at all, since none of the wood, leaves, and so on survives; but there is a continuous process, since the fire still burns. The continuity of the process and the discontinuity of the subjects suggest to Heracleitus that the world order is suitably compared to a fire. The process replaces Anaximander's continuing subject, the Unbounded.

Heracleitus thinks we must admit that the world as a whole and the allegedly stable, persistent things in it are really not continuing subjects any more than fires are. His argument is this:

(1) The fire yesterday and the fire today are not the same subject, because they are composed of different stuff.

(2) In general, if x at time t1 and y at time t2 are composed of different stuff, they are not the same thing.

(3) But even allegedly stable things are composed of different stuffs at different times.

(4) Hence they do not really persist.

The compositional principle of identity stated in (2) is illustrated in the particular case of fire in (1). Once we see that we already presuppose the principle, we must apply it equally to rivers: their water is always flowing away and being replaced, and since loss of constituents means destruction, they are always being destroyed and replaced by other rivers. Heracleitus infers that we cannot step into the same river twice; there is no continuous subject that is the same river on two days, any more than there is a continuous subject that is the same fire: in both cases there is simply a continuous process.

He uses fires and rivers to defend a general claim about reality and persistence. As Plato says:

Heracleitus says somewhere that everything passes away and nothing remains, and in likening beings to the flow of a river says that you could not step into the same river twice.

Each apparently stable thing grows and decays and interacts with others; it is being transformed all the time, and so passing out of existence to be replaced by something else. If the compositional principle of persistence is true, this conclusion is true. The naive belief in persisting subjects with opposite properties at different times turns out to be confused. For though we accept this view, we also accept the compositional principle, and therefore have to admit that ordinary things are not stable after all. Heracleitus dissolves things into processes.[7]

Heracleitus' rejection of a continuing subject also explains his belief in the 'unity of opposites'. The road up and the road down, he says, are one and the same. The same water is both good (for fish) and bad (for human beings). The strung bow is held together in being pulled apart. God is both day and night, summer and winter, war and peace, satiety and hunger. 'War is the father and king of all', because everything depends on a ceaseless struggle between opposites.[8]

Heracleitus does not mean that the opposites are indistinguishable—we can distinguish the crooked from the straight parts of a line of handwriting. But he thinks there is no subject beyond the pair of opposites. Since there are no persistent subjects, there is nothing beyond the opposites. In the simple-minded view that is challenged by the compositional principle of identity, the opposites are properties of a single persistent subject; but we have found no reason to believe in any such subject.

Instability, however, is not Heracleitus' main concern. The
stable features of the universe, in his view, are not the rocks, trees,
and other ordinary objects that appear to common sense—for
these objects undergo ceaseless change—but the processes of
change that these ordinary objects undergo. Ceaseless changes
may seem to imply instability in the universe; but in fact they are
stable because, contrary to the belief of common sense and
Homer, changes conform to regular and stable laws of nature.
Heracleitus recognizes no conflict or disruption upsetting the
usual and proper order. 'War is common, justice conflict, and all
comes to be according to conflict and how things must be.' For
Heracleitus, 'the hidden order is stronger than the apparent'; there
may be apparent disorder, since there are no stable objects, but
there is hidden order, since they conform to regular and ex-
ceptionless laws. The whole cosmic process is regular and orderly,
with no gaps.[9]

v. *Nature and history*

The naturalists apply their claims about nature to the understanding of the world as a whole and to the processes in the
natural world. But our knowledge of their physical theories is
fragmentary; and in some ways we can more easily grasp the
importance of their views by seeing how they affect the writing of
history, and the theory and practice of medicine.

In many ways the history of Herodotus (? *c*.484–*c*.420) is like
an epic poem in prose. He says in his Preface that his purpose is
to record the great and remarkable deeds of Greeks and non-
Greeks so that they win the renown they deserve. The motive is
familiar in Homer; and Herodotus' history would be intelligible
and enjoyable for an audience who enjoyed Homer.[10]

However, Herodotus goes beyond the outlook of epic. He examines at length the customs, beliefs, and institutions of the main
non-Greek peoples who enter his history. He contrasts the political systems of the Greeks and the Persians, of different Greek
states, and of the same state at different times. He appeals to these
social, cultural, and political differences to explain the conflicts
and interactions between different peoples, and their results. In

appealing to them he appeals to general laws, to principles about how people in a given society with particular customs in a particular environment can be expected to act in certain given circumstances. These principles transform Herodotus' work from purely epic narrative into historical analysis and explanation.

In explaining the success of Athens he refers not simply to the actions of individual Athenians, but also to the growth of democracy at Athens and the resulting sense of individual concern and responsibility for the state. He is the first to describe the collective actions of the Athenian democracy, not simply the individual actions of aristocrats. Again, he explains the bravery of the Spartans not by their individual heroism, but by their collective moral and political outlook:

The Spartans as individual fighters are inferior to no man, but together they are the best of all men. For they are free, but not free in every way; for they have law as their ruler, and they fear it far more than your subjects fear you [the Persian king]. For they do what it commands, and its command is always the same, never to flee from any mass of people in battle, but to stand firm in the line and either to overcome or to be killed.

The collective Spartan training and upbringing is a general explanation of their action.[11]

Still wider and more general laws about human societies and their environment appear in Herodotus. He associates the Egyptians' unusual norms and customs with their unusual climate; and he perhaps suggests that the natural poverty of Greece provokes the Greeks to develop appropriate laws and institutions to overcome it. At the very end of the history he relies on a general principle about the natural environment and the human response to it. He attributes to Cyrus, the founder of the Persian royal house, a decision to keep the Persians in rough country, not to migrate to a fertile plain, since 'soft country produces soft men'.[12]

Herodotus implies that historical events and changes are not all explained by reference to individual decisions, whims, or quarrels, or by sudden and unpredictable interferences by the gods, or by unaccountable chances. Some are explained by general regularities about types of societies, about the effects of social

and political institutions on action, and about the relation between human beings and their environment.

vi. *Nature and medicine*

During the fifth century some Greek medical theorists and prac-
titioners ceased to rely on magic; they were influenced by the
naturalist search for general laws.[13] The doctor who attends to
the basic constituents of bodies sees regularity where the layman
sees unpredictable and inexplicable variation.

> The following were the circumstances of the diseases from which we
> made our diagnosis; we learnt from the common nature of all things
> and the special nature of each thing, from the disease, the patient, the
> treatment applied and the one applying it—these make a diagnosis easier
> or harder . . . From these we must also consider the results that come
> about through them . . .
> All diseases have the same manner; but their places differ. And so
> diseases seem to be quite unlike each other because of this difference in
> their places, but in fact they all have a single character [*idea*] and cause . . .
> It may seem that all this is concerned with the heavens; but if we
> consider it afresh we will find that study of the stars makes no small
> contribution, but an extremely large one, to medicine. For with the
> changes in the seasons, men's diseases and digestive organs change too.[14]

The naturalist medical theorist assumes that he can find general
laws about the constitution of the body to show that the wide
variety of symptoms can all in principle be predicted from knowledge of their constitution and the environment.

 The Hippocratic treatise (ascribed to Hippocrates of Cos
(? *c*.470–*c*.400) 'On the Sacred Disease' attacks the traditional
attitude to epilepsy. This was called 'sacred' because it seemed to
be a spectacular interference by the gods, disturbing the ordinary
course of things; but the author thinks it has no right to this
name:

> The truth about the so-called 'sacred disease' is as follows. It seems to
> me no more divine and no more sacred than other diseases. Rather, it has
> a nature [*phusis*] and an explanation, but men have supposed [*nomizein*] it
> is something divine because they are inexperienced and prone to amaze-
> ment, because it is not at all like other diseases.

Magicians and charmers insist that it is divine because their treatment rests on no rational explanation:

Being at a loss and having no treatment that would help, they sheltered themselves behind the divine and counted this disease sacred so that their lack of knowledge should not be exposed.

When a rational explanation is found, we no longer think the 'sacred disease' is any more sacred than any other disease; 'they are all divine and all human'.[15]

The naturalistic doctor denies that any disease results from extraordinary divine intervention, or from inexplicable chance:

Each of these <diseases> has its own nature, and none comes about independently of nature . . . For when chance is examined it turns out to be nothing; for everything that comes to be is found to come to be for some cause, and in this cause chance turns out to have no reality but to be an empty name.[16]

In claiming that everything is determined by causes conforming to general laws, the writer implies his disbelief in events that happen because of divine intervention independent of natural laws, and in purely random occurrences that happen for no reason at all. In his claim about general laws he assumes the determinist principle, that everything is determined according to natural laws by previous events. As we have seen in discussing Heracleitus, this determinist principle is widely (though not universally) applied to cosmology by the naturalists.

vii. *The problems of method*

The naturalists could not have reached their views by traditional methods. The poets appeal ultimately to divine authority, to the Muses who are the source of the poet's song, and who transmit to him a true memory (when they choose to). They appeal more directly to memory and tradition.[17] If the naturalists had accepted this method of discovery and confirmation, they would never have reached their views, let alone persuaded anyone else to agree with them. That is why naturalists attack tradition and authority. Hecataeus (*fl.* 500), a historian and geographer from Miletus, says at the beginning of his history: 'I write these things as they seem true to me; for the stories of the Greeks are many and ludicrous, as they appear to me.' Xenophanes (580-480) recognizes that 'from the beginning everyone has learnt according to Homer'; and so he has to criticize Homer and the tradition. Heracleitus criticizes the poets for their false view of the universe.[18]

We might say—rather naïvely—that Homer's mythological world view cannot be justified by appeal to observation and experience. Hence, we might suppose, if we observe things more closely, we can see why things happen as they do on different occasions, and why Homer is wrong to describe them as he does. Such a simple-minded appeal to the value of observation could hardly vindicate the naturalists against Homer. For many naturalists do not study the phenomena they can observe. They speculate about the unobservable—the origin and destruction of the world, the nature of the heavenly bodies, and in general about how things might happen. They do not characteristically argue from observation and experience about how things actually do happen. The relatively small role played by observation may seem to us to be surprising and regrettable. But if we examine the naturalists' attitudes to observation, we will see why their caution in appealing to it is more reasonable than we might think.

Many of their actual appeals to observation are fairly speculative. Anaximander may have appealed to the erosion of land by water and the silting-up of harbours to illustrate the conflict of opposites. At least Xenophanes appeals to these observed processes, and to the evidence of fish fossils far from the current seashore.[19] Anaximander speculates more boldly about the explanation of observed phenomena, in his account of the origin of the human species. Appealing to the prolonged helplessness of the human infant, he argues that human beings must originally have been born from creatures of a different and more self-sufficient species, and suggests that they were born from fish-like creatures.[20]

Herodotus ridicules some early maps for showing Asia and Europe equal in size and the Ocean running round the outside. These maps reflected their authors' limited experience, and probably also their idea of symmetry and appropriateness; fuller acquaintance with the relevant phenomena might have resulted in less simple and less tidy maps. But the diplomatic and military importance of maps must have stimulated criticism and improvement. Aristagoras of Miletus (the home of the early naturalists and of Hecataeus) brought a map with him to Sparta, to encourage the Spartan king to undertake an expedition against the Persian capital, Susa; the map was useful until Aristagoras had to admit that it would be three months' journey.[21]

These are examples of naturalistic speculation rather loosely connected with observation. Some medical writers, however, collect observations more systematically. Some of the Hippocratic works (the 'Epidemics') are case histories, detailed reports of the course of a disease in particular patients. At a more theoretical level some of the Hippocratics profess to be empiricists, decrying theories that are based not on observation but on 'assumptions' (*hupotheseis*) about the elements—the sort of assumptions that the more speculative naturalists make:

All those who have undertaken to speak or write about medicine and have assumed for their argument some assumption, either the hot or the cold or the dry or the wet or whatever else they like . . .—these people clearly go wrong in many of the things they say . . . Therefore I have supposed that medicine needs no empty assumptions such as the unseen and confusing things need, about which it is necessary to use an assumption if anyone tries to say anything, as for instance about the things in the heavens or the things under the earth.

Other writers disagree; some apply naturalist theories to medicine in the way that their empirically minded colleagues deplore. Even the appearance of concern with observation is sometimes misleading: though many claims could be observationally tested, very few observational tests are mentioned. Still, many naturalists agree that systematic empirical inquiry and observation are important.[22]

Such inquiry and observation are no less important in history. Indeed, the name 'history' for Herodotus' work (and hence for the work of other historians) is derived from his first sentence 'This is the exposition of the *historia* of Herodotus', where '*historia*' means 'inquiry'—the sort of methodical investigation that Herodotus carried out in preparation for writing his narrative.

Herodotus also illustrates the difficulty of finding full and reliable
observations as a basis for theory. He sees the importance of
first-hand observation, and tells us the extent of his own travels
and first-hand knowledge; but he often has to rely on hearsay,
and realizes it is not all reliable: 'I am obliged to say the things
that are said, but not obliged to believe them all; and this remark
is to apply to my whole account.' He reports stories without
vouching for their truth. He reports a story of a voyage around
Africa that he wrongly believes to be geographically impossible.
He sees the importance of empirical evidence, but he does not
collect it uncritically, and recognizes the weakness of his own
critical equipment.[23]

viii. *General laws*

It should now be easier to see why, as I suggested earlier, the
naturalists were right not to defend their arguments by a simple
appeal to the evidence of observation. If they had attended too
closely to observations, without relying on naturalist principles
not derived from observation, they would never have formed
scientific theories. Those who look at the world in a Homeric way
will find it easy to reconcile their outlook with their experience
and observation. If I get caught in a storm at sea, perhaps I have
offended Poseidon and it will blow over if I make a sacrifice to
him. If the storm does not blow over, my belief is not refuted,
since I have other explanations ready. Perhaps Poseidon was too
angry to be appeased, or my sacrifice was too small, or another
god intervened, or this particular storm 'just happened' with no
particular divine cause. If I hold this sort of view, it will be
difficult to refute me by observation; indeed, I may well claim that
naturalist assumptions about general laws violate the evidence of
observation.[24]

A more reflective attitude to observation suggests that our use
of observation actually relies on theoretical principles of the sort
that the naturalists discover. We think observation and ex-
periment are informative because we expect that if we have once
observed something we should be able to observe it again in the
same circumstances. It would be pointless for us to attempt to

confirm experiments by replicating them, if we did not agree with the naturalists' determinist assumption—that natural processes conform to general laws, and that apparent exceptions to these laws are to be explained by further general laws.

The importance of this assumption is underlined by Hume (1711-76):

The vulgar, who take things according to their first appearances, attribute the uncertainty of the events to such an uncertainty in the causes as makes the latter often fail of their influence; though they meet with no impediment in their operation. But philosophers, observing that, almost in every part of nature, there is contained a vast variety of springs and principles, which are hid, by reason of their minuteness or remoteness, find, that it is at least possible the contrariety of events may not proceed from any contingency in the cause, but from the secret operation of contrary causes . . . A peasant can give no better reason for the stopping of any clock or watch than to say that it does not commonly go right: but an artist easily perceives the same force in the spring or pendulum has always the same influence on the whole; but fails of its usual effect, perhaps by reason of a grain of dust, which puts a stop to the whole movement.[25]

The philosophers appeal to their experience of the 'vast variety of principles' elsewhere in nature, to argue that there is no genuine irregularity in this case. But in arguing in this way they assume that this case will be like the rest of nature; they assume the very sort of regularity that they appeared to be arguing for. They cannot therefore appeal to observation to support their view of this case; and the vulgar can fairly claim that observation supports their belief in irregularity.

The determinist assumptions of naturalism imply that systematic observation is important, in so far as it should help us to find the general laws in natural processes. But observations apparently cannot themselves support the naturalist against the Homeric outlook; and the naturalists therefore need some other defence of their outlook.

ix. *Reason and argument*

Heracleitus raises some of the right questions in the theory of knowledge (epistemology; Greek *epistêmê*, 'knowledge'). He rejects the traditional appeal to the Muses, and does not want to be accepted as an authority. 'Don't listen to me', he says, 'but to the *logos*.' Grasp of the *logos* ('reason', 'account', 'argument' are all aspects of the meaning) is not the mere accumulation of information. Heracleitus criticizes excessive trust in the senses: 'The eyes and ears of those who have the souls of barbarians are bad witnesses for human beings.' Unquestioning confidence in the senses is like children's trust in what their parents tell them, reflecting failure to make a deeper inquiry.[26]

Heracleitus contrasts sleeping and waking, to explain the contrast between the senses and the *logos*; and he suggests that the senses are good witnesses, if properly understood. We know that we live in a world that is common to all, and that we see bodies— external realities that continue to exist even when we do not see them. If we rely on our apparent sensory experience, we must believe all our dreams and hallucinations, but if we do that, we will never reach any conception of a common world. In deciding that my dreams are unreliable, I assume that the world conforms to the general laws that seem to be violated in my dream experience.

Naturalist cosmology applies the same *logos* that underlies our common-sense contrast between the objective world and our dreams. Cosmology seeks to discover regularity, law, and order in the world. We cannot, in Heracleitus' view, reject this demand for regularity unless we also reject our common-sense conception of an external objective world. Some claims of naturalist cosmology appear to conflict with experience and observation. But the appearance of conflict is misleading, and deceives only people with 'barbarian souls', those who refuse to apply critical intelligence to their experience. Heracleitus defends his views on the instability of things and the stability of processes, by general principles that we already apply to familiar situations (e.g. the compositional principle of identity applied to fires).

If Heracleitus is right, he has a strong argument against Homer and against Hume's 'vulgar' outlook. He could not defend determinist principles by appeal to observation; and any other argument might seem to be circular, by relying on the principles themselves. He argues, however, that Homer and common sense are really committed to naturalist principles already, in drawing the ordinary distinction between dreaming and waking; Homer fails to see that the ordinary distinction supports naturalism. Heracleitus' rational principles are the common *logos*, not merely his own preferences; they are not merely the product of authority or tradition, but we can all discover them if we understand the assumptions we already accept.

x. *Ethics*

The Homeric world is an unstable and disorderly system, and Homeric society is also unstable and disorderly. A society is fairly stable in so far as it maintains some agreed rules and practices, and the members of that society observe them. But in Homer the prevailing moral outlook provokes competition, conflict, and aggression.

Homer is not indifferent to law and justice. Odysseus contrasts justice with savagery; and the Cyclopes who lack justice lack the basic institutions of social and political life. For Hesiod justice and law are the distinctively human institutions that prevent us from preying on each other like beasts; they give human beings their best hope of preservation. In Homer and Hesiod, however, the prospects for justice are insecure and precarious. The naturalists agree in looking for order in the world as a whole; and some of them probably also share a distinctive ethical outlook that especially values law and justice.

The direction of naturalist criticism is easiest to see in a particular example. Xenophanes attacks the general admiration for strength and athletic prowess, because it expresses the Homeric outlook; athletics, war, and political activity are different ways of displaying and advancing power, honour, and status. Pindar (518-438) wrote poems in honour of the winners in athletic contests, and his extravagant praise of the winner in a chariot race, for not disgracing the hereditary virtue of his ancestors, illustrates the widespread esteem of the athletic virtues. Solon (*fl.* 594) saw their danger and tried to limit the scale of prizes and honours for athletes. Xenophanes sees that respect for law and justice will always be weak where admiration for the Homeric virtues is strong.[28]

Xenophanes' attacks on Homeric competitions are one aspect of a wider struggle against the Homeric outlook at the social and political level; and at this level the influence of naturalism is important. In sixth-century Athens, as in Victorian Britain, social and political reform would have been inconceivable without some belief in social laws and regularities. Conscious institutional reform requires the belief that certain changes can be relied on to produce regular effects. We can see from Homer that such a belief does not seem self-evidently true to everyone. The political reformers who hold it show that they stand with the naturalists and with Herodotus against Homer and Hesiod.

Athenian political institutions were largely the work of two innovative legislators, Solon (594) and Cleisthenes (508), who reformed the constitution with the clear aim of changing the nature of the governing class and of political life. Solon was a poet and politician, later remembered as the founder of the Athenian democracy, and the first 'champion of the common people'. He believed that the cause of civil conflict was unrestricted and unchecked power in the hands of a hereditary upper class. He formed a new deliberative Council to assume some of the traditional powers of the hereditary Council of the Areopagus. He formed jury courts with jurors probably chosen by lot, and so allowed the common people a crucial role in the supervision of the government. Solon's reforms were intended to prevent the Homeric virtues from destroying the community.

Solon's convictions about the effectiveness of deliberate action rest on his views about the operations of justice and injustice on a social level. In explaining why justice should be pursued and injustice avoided Solon does not appeal to divine rewards or punishments, but strictly to the effects—injustice is an 'inescapable plague' producing civil conflict and civil war. 'My spirit', he says, 'urges me to teach the Athenians these things, how bad laws produce the most evils for a city. ' Bad laws produce these results unavoidably, according to general principles with uniform and predictable results.[29]

A Homeric outlook encourages me to advance my interests, or those of my family or my supporters, at the expense of the rest of the community. Solon's successor Cleisthenes saw that these narrow loyalties threatened the Solonian constitution. Herodotus suggests that Cleisthenes won the struggle for power against other aristocratic factions by 'co-opting the people into his faction'; and his complicated institutional reforms were designed to make it harder to exploit the traditional loyalties supporting the aristocratic factions.[30] To undermine them he introduced democratic local government in Attica (the whole area, urban and rural, governed from the city of Athens), with newly created district assemblies controlling admission to citizenship—an important function previously confined to aristocratic bodies.

But institutional reforms alone may still fail in their aim if they conflict with unchallenged Homeric assumptions and aspirations; as long as some people try to excel in Homeric virtues, the demands of justice and of the community will threaten to conflict with the overriding aims and values of individuals. Moreover, naturalist ethical assumptions are themselves not always clear or beyond criticism; views about law and justice will indicate some of the difficulties.

Heracleitus agrees with Solon that the people should defend and maintain law, and he urges the repression of the wanton aggression that Solon held responsible for lawlessness and disorder. The city's law is the rational order in the city, just as natural law is the rational order in the universe. Indeed, for Heracleitus, the relation is closer than mere analogy, since all human laws are nourished by the single divine law of the universe. In some way that he does not explain, the city conforms best to natural law when it observes its own laws.[31]

In this very general defence of law, Heracleitus seems not to distinguish law from justice; and sometimes, admittedly, the distinction may not be clear. If powerful people can violate law and custom when it suits them, stricter observance of law may secure more justice; people will not be cheated of the benefits due to them by law. Initially it is important to urge the acceptance of some system of law—universally accepted and impartially interpreted rules. But it soon becomes clear that not every law is equally just, and that some are capable of improvement in the interest of the people affected by them.

Once we see a difference between *positive* law (the law currently in force in a particular state) and the principles that might require changes in positive law, Heracleitus' position seems unhelpfully simple. Solon's defence of law is a defence of the common interest against the greed of the few. But a defence of law might also defend the status quo against questions and reforms. When Heracleitus claims that all human laws are nourished by the one divine law, he assumes that the divine law is just. But it is hard to agree that all positive law is just, and so hard to agree with Heracleitus' uncritical support of law. He might distinguish (as others have) positive from natural law, identifying natural law with divine justice; but then it becomes harder to claim that every positive law accords with natural law, or that all positive laws should be accepted.

In any case, the naturalists seem not to have answered a more elementary question. The Homeric virtues seem to be qualities that benefit the agent himself, advancing his honour, power, and status. Why should someone reject these virtues for the good of the community? Apparently he is asked to sacrifice his interest for the good of others, and has been given no clear reason for doing so.

xi. *The gods*

The naturalists' determinist principles conflict with Homer's belief in arbitrary and unpredictable interference by the gods in natural processes.[32] Naturalist moral and political doctrines also conflict with the traditional functions of the gods. In Homer and Hesiod Zeus punishes injustice; but for Solon injustice brings its own penalty in the harm it causes to the public interest. Xenophanes finds the Homeric gods no more credible than the black gods of the Ethiopians or the equine gods whose images horses would carve if they could. He also finds the Homeric gods immoral, since their morality is the very outlook that the naturalists reject. Similarly, Heracleitus vilifies the traditional view of the gods and the gross and indecent ceremonies of their public cult, including ritual slaughters and phallic processions.

Herodotus combines traditional with naturalist beliefs, and, unlike Homer, has a fairly clear conception of a natural explanation; for he regards an event as especially divine if it seems to have no ordinary rational explanation. We might suppose that Herodotus has room for the gods only if he is not a complete naturalist, and allows, as a complete naturalist would not, some events that breach ordinary natural regularities. Apparently, then, we might suppose, a complete naturalist, believing that everything is determined by the nature of the constituent stuffs and their interactions, will have no need and no room for gods.[33]

This supposition, however, is far too simple to capture the naturalists' attitude to the divine. For in fact they say quite a lot about gods. Thales apparently said everything is full of gods. Xenophanes seems to identify the one god with the world. The Hippocratic writer argues that all diseases alike are both divine and human. Heracleitus says that the sun will not overstep its measures because the Furies, the helpers of justice, will find it out. The Furies are traditionally recognized as goddesses; and Heracleitus speaks, though cautiously, in similarly theological terms in saying that the one and only wise thing is both unwilling and willing to be called Zeus. Like Xenophanes, he seems not to separate the god from the world order, since god is taken to be day and night, summer and winter, and the other opposites, and to change as fire changes. Naturalists in general seem to claim that everything is divine and that the divine order is nothing more than the natural order.

Such claims might seem to eliminate the divine in favour of the natural. Someone who says witches are simply hysterical women does not really believe in witches; and when Xenophanes says the goddess Iris is simply the rainbow, he recognizes only a natural phenomenon and rejects any belief in a goddess. Though naturalism is expressed in theological terms, it seems to replace gods with nature, and therefore to reject belief in gods.[34]

But it is a mistake to suppose that the naturalists are atheists. To reject an inappropriate conception of a god is not to reject belief in the divine. Heracleitus thinks the cosmic wisdom is unwilling to be called Zeus, because it is not the Zeus of the anthropomorphic, mythological conception, or the Zeus of popular religious ceremonies. But these views do not make Heracleitus an atheist; indeed, Christian writers endorse naturalistic criticisms of traditional religion.[35] Criticisms of the Homeric gods do not imply rejection of belief in some intelligent reason controlling the events in the world.

Herodotus expresses the basic naturalist assumption about gods. He suggests, rather fancifully, that the earliest inhabitants of Greece called them 'gods', *theoi*, because 'having arranged (*thentes*) all things in order (*kosmos*), they maintained them and all their due assignments'. He even maintains that these earliest inhabitants had this conception of the gods long before they had assigned them distinct names and personalities; the Homeric and Hesiodic gods were recent accretions, and have no monopoly on the title of gods. These historical and etymological speculations also explain why naturalists claim to believe in a god, in so far as they believe in a world order and its arranger.

Naturalists reasonably claim that their conception is more suitable for a god, because it does not limit him by human imperfections. A proper god need not exert himself, need not struggle with other gods, to achieve his will. Nor need he interfere with the natural order if, as Heracleitus insists, it already conforms to his laws; he is not so incompetent that he must interfere in the world order he ought to have arranged well in the first place. The god has wisdom superior to human wisdom, and sees the justice in the whole world order; and since he is supreme in the universe, there is only one god.[36]

The naturalists develop some aspects of the Homeric conception of Zeus into a new conception of god. We might usefully compare developments in Hebrew thinking. Some Hebrews conceived Yahweh as a tribal god fighting for his people against other gods. But critics argued against the existence of other gods. For Hebrews as well as Greeks the regularity and order of the universe proclaim the unity and power of God. Sometimes God seems to share human limitations; but some writers protest at any attempt to limit his powers or to make him dependent on human favour. The Hebrew prophets, like the Greek naturalists, want an adequate conception of a god free from human limitations.[37]

The naturalists' tendencies towards monotheism result from their basic determinist principles. They believe the universe is a world order; it displays laws and regularities. Homer's conception of the universe requires a number of competing gods; but, in the naturalists' view, the order, law, and justice of the universe manifest a single intelligence. Divine law and cosmic justice keep the sun in its place and nourish human laws and justice. This is why Heracleitus thinks that if we recognize law and order in the universe we must seek law and justice in human society.

Since the naturalists do not clearly distinguish law from justice, they do not see a dilemma arising for their claims about divine justice. If any regularity at all constitutes justice, then we can see justice in the world if we can see regularity. But mere regularity does not seem to require a divine intelligence, unless intelligence is needed to explain any sort of regularity.

It is more plausible to claim that divine intelligence explains the existence of cosmic justice if cosmic justice works in ways that we would expect an intelligent and just designer to work—if, for instance, it seems to be designed for the benefit of those affected by it. Solon and Heracleitus perhaps accept such a claim about cosmic justice; but it seems far harder to defend than the claim about mere regularity.

Herodotus is an incomplete naturalist, and his conception of the gods shows the difficulties a naturalist has to face. Sometimes the gods seem to be Homeric, interfering on particular occasions to pay off particular scores. Sometimes they seem to follow more general principles. Solon tells Croesus, 'everything divine is envious and disruptive', always destroying the prosperous people despite all their efforts. Such a god 'allows no one to think lofty thoughts except himself'. The god's actions seem rather impersonal. People in Herodotus remark that human life has its ups and downs and that prosperity tends to cause its own downfall; divine envy may be intended to explain this regularity, or perhaps simply to describe it. In nature Herodotus ascribes wise foresight to the divine, since it makes timid and weak creatures more prolific than their predators; but it is less obvious that divine 'envy' indicates foresight and wisdom. Divine action seems rather rough justice if it disrupts and destroys without any previous fault.[38]

At one critical moment in Herodotus' history the gods appear in a complex role. The Persian king Xerxes is moved by bad advice, pride, and over-confidence to invade Greece; but when he begins to change his mind, a dream comes to warn him to maintain his original plan, and a further dream eventually persuades his sceptical adviser Artabanus that Xerxes' invasion is something that 'has to happen' and 'a divine impulse'. The gods clearly intend to punish Xerxes for his pride and arrogance; and they intervene to make sure he does not escape his punishment. But at the start he makes his decision for intelligible reasons, and the gods make sure he sticks to it. Herodotus assumes that the god does not simply cut down the tall stalks or strike the tall trees with lightning just because they are tall. The divine order is just, punishing injustice through the laws of nature and human society, not cancelling or violating those laws.[39]

In trying to show how the order of nature is also an order of divine justice, Herodotus draws out some of the consequences of naturalist assumptions about the gods. He equally shows how many difficulties arise in trying to apply the naturalist assumptions to human life and history. In theology as in ethics, naturalist claims raise questions that the naturalists do not answer. Questions raised but unanswered in Homer provoke the naturalist movement; and similarly questions about the naturalist outlook provoke later movements in Greek thought.

4
Doubts about Naturalism

i. *Tendencies*

The naturalists offered rational arguments against the traditional Homeric outlook, and sketched an alternative conception of the world and an alternative method of inquiry into it. During the fifth century BC, and especially in its second half, in the lifetime of Socrates (469–399), some of the naturalist outlook was itself criticized. Some of the critics are themselves naturalists, seeking to state naturalist doctrines in more defensible forms; Aeschylus (525–456), Democritus (? *c*.460–*c*.360), and Thucydides (*c*.460–*c*.400) illustrate this critical naturalism. Others, however, argue that the difficulties in naturalism point to some error in its basic assumptions; Protagoras (? *c*.485–*c*.415) reaches this anti-naturalist conclusion, and so, in very different ways, do Plato and Aristotle.

The critics of naturalism are not all later than the naturalists we have already discussed. Herodotus lived until the 420s, in the lifetime of Democritus, Thucydides, and Protagoras. Sophocles (*c*.496–406), in some ways close to original naturalism, outlived Euripides (*c*.485–*c*.407), a critic. The two movements overlap and interact.

Each critic rejects some claim of Heracleitus, and their criticisms raise serious questions about all his main naturalist principles. He identifies law and justice; Aeschylus attacks him. He believes in cosmic justice; Democritus attacks him. He believes that justice guides human history; Thucydides attacks him. He believes science is continuous with common sense; Democritus attacks him. He thinks there is an objective world that we come to know in scientific inquiry; Protagoras attacks him.

ii. *Tragedy and naturalism*

Tragedies were performed at a public religious festival in Athens, where the audience probably included many inhabitants of Athens—women, children, resident aliens—who were not present in the Assembly. Though the tragedians were not primarily moral philosophers or political propagandists, they consider moral and political issues. Though they usually begin from stories of the heroic age, especially from Homer, they often criticize the Homeric outlook. Aeschylus' trilogy the *Oresteia* (three connected plays presented successively on a single day) criticizes both Homeric and naturalist views, and comments sharply on recent political developments in Athens.[1]

The legislation of Solon, Cleisthenes, and their successors confirmed the democratic character of the Athenian constitution. The most important (and many unimportant) political and administrative decisions depended on the Assembly, consisting of all the citizens. A Council of Five Hundred, chosen by lot from and by all the citizens, prepared the business for the Assembly; Athens had no cabinet, no organized political parties, and no whips. The most important officials were the ten 'generals', with both military and civil functions, elected annually, re-eligible, responsible to the Assembly, and open to the scrutiny (often close, vigorous, and partisan) of the same citizens sitting in the jury-courts.

In 462 Ephialtes and Pericles introduced reforms that reduced the power of the traditionally aristocratic 'House of Lords', the Council of the Areopagus. They wanted to confine it to its 'original' function as a court to try cases of homicide, curbing its allegedly 'usurped' political functions. The reforms were passed; but Ephialtes was mysteriously murdered. About the same time war broke out between Athens and some allies of Sparta, and in 458 some disaffected Athenians invited the Spartans to invade Attica to overthrow the Athenian democracy. The *Oresteia* was produced in this tense situation, in 458. The first two plays (the *Agamemnon* and *Choephori*) make no overt political comments; but they prepare for the political themes of the third play (the *Eumenides*).[2]

The Homeric element in the plays is obvious. The *Agamemnon* begins with the Trojan War and with the anger of Artemis that delayed the Greek fleet. The human characters—Agamemnon, Clytaemnestra, Orestes, and Electra—are moved by the Homeric motives of honour and shame. These are all familiar from the *Iliad*. But they are controlled by a naturalist conception of cosmic justice. In Homer the supremacy of Zeus is spasmodic, but in Aeschylus it is constant. Heracleitus said that the sun will not overstep its measures because, if it does, the Furies, servants of justice, will find it out; and the *Oresteia* displays the Furies maintaining the inexorable laws of justice.[3]

Clytaemnestra and Orestes are avengers vindicating divine justice, but they are also human agents, moved by intelligible human motives. A Homeric agent could try to excuse his action by attributing responsibility to some god. Agamemnon tells Achilles:

The cause lies not in me, but in Zeus, and my fate, and the Fury that walks in mist, who threw savage infatuation into my spirit in the council, on the day when I myself took the prize from Achilles.

Achilles neither accepts nor rejects this disavowal of responsibility. In the *Agamemnon* the Chorus reject a similar attempt by Clytaemnestra to shift responsibility for Agamemnon's death from herself to some supernatural spirit avenging the crimes of Agamemnon's ancestors; but they do not deny supernatural influence, and they regard it all as the work of Zeus. Just as Herodotus does not intend 'the divine' to replace human decisions and responsibility, Aeschylus insists both on human responsibility and on divine causation.[4]

Aeschylus does not believe cosmic justice works in the mechanical way described by some of his naturalist predecessors. Nor does he agree that prosperity by itself provokes divine jealousy; only unjust prosperity leads to downfall. Aeschylus sees the same pattern in contemporary history; in the *Persians* he describes the defeat of the Persian empire, setting the pattern for Herodotus.

In this, as in other cases, the effects of divine justice are destructive. At the end of Sophocles' *Trachiniae*, Hyllus is about to take his father Heracles to his funeral pyre, and remarks: 'You have seen new and terrible deaths, many woes and new sufferings, and there is none of these that is not Zeus.' For similar reasons, Aeschylus' Chorus remark that the favour of the gods is 'violent'. At the end of the *Choephori* they admit that justice has been done, but wonder whether the cycle of destruction will ever end. These tragedians agree with the naturalists' view that the world is not disorderly and that justice is not sporadic; moral law is a natural law and natural law has no exceptions.[5]

iii. *Beyond naturalism*

Still, when Sophocles' Hyllus sees Zeus's design in everything, what he sees may not seem very creditable to Zeus; at the end of the play, as at the end of Aeschylus' *Seven against Thebes*, the main characters are dead or dying, having paid the penalty for their crimes and errors. In the *Eumenides*, however, Aeschylus urges that such destructive sequences of crime and punishment cannot be genuine justice.

Orestes has to choose either to kill his mother or to let his father's murder go unavenged and to leave Argos under the tyrannical usurper Aegisthus. The Furies fasten on the crime of killing his mother; but he replies that he had to choose between that and the worse crime (he supposes) of failing to avenge his father. The Furies agree that he would have been punishable for that crime too; but they do not count that as a justification or excuse for what he did.[6] The Furies want Orestes and Athens to suffer no less than Agamemnon, Clytaemnestra, and Aegisthus suffered. But they overlook an important difference: the other three showed no hesitation, reluctance, or regret at their choice, whereas Orestes chose an injustice only because he thought it was the only way to avoid a worse one. The Furies seem indifferent to this distinction of motives.

A conception of injustice as simply the breaking of law, requiring inflexible punishment, leads to disaster. The arguments of Apollo, the Furies, and Athena, in the trial of Orestes, are implausible and inconclusive. Athena's argument only provokes the Furies to threaten retribution on Athens, until she introduces an altogether new type of argument. She appeals to the bad

consequences of the threatened retribution, and to the good consequences of a reconciliation that allows them to use their powers
for the good of the whole city. The solution that is reached does
not abandon the principle of retribution—the Furies retain this
function; but it regulates and tests the operations of this principle
by appeal to the common interest of those affected.[7]

Aeschylus presents the Areopagus as a homicide court, with
only those powers left to it by Ephialtes. The appeal to the Furies
to forgo the exercise of their traditional prerogatives in the interest
of the whole community is equally an appeal to Athenians who
might resent the democratic reforms. While Solon had left the
Areopagus intact, Aeschylus argues for acceptance of the democratic reforms that seriously weakened its political role.

In criticizing the Furies' conception of justice Aeschylus criticizes the Heracleitean conception too. Heracleitus conceives
justice as advance and retreat, law-breaking and retaliation, disturbance and counter-disturbance; he sees no distinction between
positive law and natural or cosmic justice. Aeschylus suggests
that Heracleitean justice is no real justice; the *Oresteia* displays
sharply and disturbingly the injustice of some positive law, and
the hazardous but necessary task of reforming it.[8]

Aeschylus separates justice from mere observance of positive
law at the human level. He also raises the standard for divine and
cosmic justice. Aeschylus' gods are more just than the Homeric
gods and the Heracleitean Zeus. But if they exist, it seems harder
to explain the apparent injustice in the universe. Homer can explain these aspects easily; and nothing violates Heracleitean justice; but a believer in Aeschylus' gods will be puzzled. Naturalists
might reasonably reconsider their grounds for belief in Aeschylean cosmic justice; and Democritus' reconsideration leads
him to disbelief.

iv. *Appearance and nature*

Democritus (? *c*.460–*c*.360) agrees with Heracleitus' view that 'the
hidden order is superior to the apparent', and that the senses are
bad witnesses if they are not interpreted correctly. But Democritus
thinks the senses are far worse witnesses than Heracleitus took

them to be, and argues that they are deeply misleading guides to reality.[9]

If my hand is heated and yours is chilled, the same water may appear warm to you when you put in your chilled hand and cold to me when I put in my heated hand. From this Democritus argues as follows:

(1) Either (a) both my appearance and yours are correct, so that the water is both warm and cold; or (b) both are incorrect, so that the water is neither warm nor cold; or (c) one appearance is correct and the other is incorrect.

(2) There is no reason to prefer either your appearance or mine.

(3) Hence (c) is false.

(4) But (a) is self-contradictory.

(5) Self-contradictory statements cannot be true.

(6) Hence (a) is false.

(7) Hence (b) is true.

Now Democritus sees that the same form of 'argument from conflicting appearances' applies to all colours, sounds, smells, tastes, temperatures, and therefore that things cannot really have any of these properties.

He must defend (2) against the objection that sometimes one perceiver (e.g. the healthy one as opposed to the sick) is better at detecting the real colour or taste of things. To know that some people are better than others at detecting perceptible properties of things, we must rely on some beliefs about what the real properties of things are; these beliefs rely on the senses; but the senses offer conflicting appearances. We are back where we started; and if we try some further criterion to resolve the conflict, the same difficulty will arise. To avoid an infinite regress, we must accept (2), agreeing that the appearances are equipollent (i.e. equally reliable).[10]

The rest of the argument depends on the Principle of Excluded Middle (either p is true or not-p is true, with no third possibility) and the Principle of Non-Contradiction (p and not-p cannot both be true). Democritus rejects Heracleitus' solution to the problem of conflicting appearances. Heracleitus' doctrine of the unity of opposites suggests that both conflicting appearances are true (as in (1a)); but if he means to violate the Principle of Non-Contradiction, he leaves us unable to say anything definite about the world.

This argument applies to every perceptible quality that allows conflicting and equipollent appearances. Democritus

undermines the things appearing to the senses, and says that none of them corresponds to the truth, but only to belief, and the truth is that there are atoms and void. For he says: 'By convention [*nomos*] there is sweet, bitter, hot, cold, colour, but in reality atoms and void.' He means: perceptibles are conventionally supposed and believed to exist, but in truth none of them, but only atoms and void, exists.

In Democritus' view the senses offer a 'bastard' form of judgement, and only reason offers genuine knowledge.[11]

Democritus believes reason can discover the hidden order that is inaccessible to the senses. Rational argument, independent of the truth of sensory appearances, shows us that reality must allow the possibility of change. For even if our appearances are misleading, they change; their changes must have some cause, since an uncaused change violates the determinist assumptions of naturalism; hence reality must include some cause of change. A further argument shows us that the basic reality must, like Anaximander's Unbounded, have neither beginning nor end. Democritus argues:

(1) It is impossible for something to come to be from nothing or to perish into nothing.

(2) If everything comes to be, something must come to be from nothing (otherwise not everything would have come to be), and if everything perishes, something must perish into nothing.

(3) Therefore not everything can come to be or perish.

(4) Therefore there must be some things that neither come to be nor perish.

This argument is unsound, since (2) is false. While (1) implies that not everything can come to be or perish at the same time, this weaker conclusion does not support (4).

Democritus believes that though he rejects the senses, he can justifiably assume that ultimate reality is everlasting and undergoes change. The basic realities are permanent, indivisible atoms (Greek *atomos*, 'undivided' or 'indivisible'), which have size, shape, and weight, but no other perceptible qualities, and are always in motion. Their temporary combinations form the apparently solid objects that appear to us. The apparent perceptible qualities—colour, taste, smell—of tables and cabbages appear to us to belong to external bodies, but are really only our appearances, resulting from the interaction between us and the atoms.[12]

To show how the atoms might cause these appearances, Democritus uses analogies from observation; he commends Anaxagoras for his claim that 'things that appear give us a sight of things that are not clear'. Just as pins make a sharper impression on us than blunt objects, so also, we may assume, atoms of different shapes cause sweet or sharp sensations on the tongue. Democritus does not claim that these macroscopic analogies prove the atomic theory; but they show us how the theory might explain our observations.[13]

v. *Nature and purpose*

Democritus' atomism rigorously pursues the naturalist aim of explaining the observed variety of natural processes by means of deterministic laws about the basic underlying matter. This outlook conflicts with our common-sense view of plants and animals. We often want to explain their behaviour by mentioning purposes, goals, or ends. We say a heart functions as it does in order to pump blood, and that the dog is running in order to catch the cat, because it wants to catch the cat. But from Democritus' point of view the only explanations refer to movements of atoms, and atoms have no goals or purposes, but just move because of their properties and the forces exerted on them. Hence the view that animals, or parts of them, have goals or purposes must surely be an error of common sense. Once we accept naturalism we are not tempted to believe that the designs and purposes of particular gods cause thunderstorms or plagues; we explain these events by the basic constituents and their movements. When we understand organisms better, we can also refer to their constituents with no reference to design or purpose. Common-sense talk of purposes seems as ill-founded as talk of Homeric gods.

If we agree with Democritus so far, we must apparently also think differently about ourselves. Human beings and their minds are part of nature; they are composed of atoms, conforming to the same laws as other atoms. Though we often say we act because we have chosen or decided to act, we must apparently be wrong; these explanations belong to 'convention', and cannot describe the reality that consists only of atoms and their interactions.

We sometimes suppose that we differ from rocks, trees, and dogs because we have free will; we choose freely and are morally responsible, open to praise or blame, for what we have freely chosen to do. We don't blame a rock for falling on us, or a bee for stinging us, because we agree they have no free choice. But if we agree with Democritus, we may easily conclude that we are no different from rocks and bees; they are just collections of atoms and so are we, since we are determined by the same laws. The atomist Leucippus (mid-fifth century) strongly asserts naturalist determinism: 'Nothing happens at random, but everything for a reason and by necessity'; and the necessity derived from the atoms seems to remove individual responsibility. In later anecdotes Democritus was presented as the laughing philosopher, laughing at the meaninglessness and pointlessness of human lives: 'There is nothing in them to be taken seriously, but they are all vain and empty, a movement of atoms and infinity. ' To the extent that we attach meaning and significance to our actions because we believe they are the result of responsible choice, we can see some justice in this picture of Democritus.[14]

But which of Democritus' views implies the challenge to responsibility? Three different doctrines may be relevant: (1) determinism—every event is necessitated by a previous event; (2) constitutive atomism—everything is composed of atoms and of no other constituents; (3) eliminative atomism—only the atoms are real, and the appearances are matters of convention and illusion. Democritus accepts all three doctrines. But it is not clear that the second requires the third; and while it is clear that the third challenges beliefs in human responsibility, the implications of the first two are far less clear. These distinctions become important in discussion of the different replies to Democritus by later philosophers.[15]

vi. *Nature and cosmic justice*

In Democritus' universe everything is the necessary consequence of the movements of atoms conforming to general laws. Heracleitus does not distinguish regularity, law, order, good order, and justice. But Democritus, like Aeschylus, does distinguish them, and sees no room for cosmic justice. The movements of the atoms depend only on their nature and their previous state; Democritus assumes an original movement of the atoms, and explains the later stages by reference to that alone, without reference to any intelligence.

Even if mere regularity does not imply cosmic justice, we have some grounds for belief in cosmic justice if the world appears to be designed for the benefit of its inhabitants. The growth of civilization was traditionally ascribed to gods revealing particular skills to human beings. Democritus argues that, on the contrary, external conditions affecting human nature necessarily produce particular responses, with no previous design by gods or human beings. The first human beings lived a 'disorderly and bestial life'; fear, not intelligence, taught them to collect in groups, and their first attempts to communicate were indistinct mumblings. Only experience and gradual development taught them what to do; 'and in general need itself was the universal teacher for human beings'. Neither free choice nor design, but inevitable reaction to circumstances, caused human beings to form their characteristic way of life.[16]

Prehistory and anthropology serve the atomist argument against purposive and goal-directed explanations of human action, whether the purposes are divine or human. Democritus does not speak, as Heracleitus does, of a cosmic wisdom that is unwilling, but also in a way willing, to be called Zeus. He recognizes no cosmic wisdom at all.

vii. *Naturalism and human nature*

Just as Democritus seeks to explain natural processes by the basic laws of atoms, Thucydides (*c*.460–*c*.400) seeks to explain social and historical processes, and especially the disturbances caused by wars and revolutions, by the basic laws of human nature.[17] Just as an atomic theory will be unconvincing if its laws are too few or too simple to explain the complexity of observed phenomena, a theory of human nature must show that it can cope with the variety of observed social and historical phenomena. Thucydides tries to show that his theory passes this test—that it explains, without over-simplifying, the variety and complexity of social and political conflicts. He examines the major war in the Greek world of his time, the Peloponnesian War (431–404), which involved Athens and Sparta, and the many cities allied with one or the other. He intends his account to illustrate tendencies and processes that remain the same 'as long as human nature remains the same'. That is why his work is a 'possession for ever', not merely of passing interest.[18]

Thucydides assumes that, since we compete for limited resources that we all want, each of us has desires that tend to conflict with the desires of other people. I therefore want to prevent interference by others; I fear others who threaten interference; and so I want power over them, to prevent their interference. Hobbes (1588–1679) develops Thucydides' point:

So that in the first place, I put for a general inclination of all mankind, a perpetual and restless desire of power after power, that ceaseth only in death. And the cause of this is not always that a man hopes for a more intensive delight, than he has already attained to; or that he cannot be content with moderate power; but because he cannot assure the power and means to live well, which he hath present, without the acquisition of more.

Coexistence with someone else of roughly equal power is inherently unstable, since it will always be in the interest of each to dominate the other; hence freedom and security for oneself seem to require rule over others. But if I am free to attack others of roughly equal power, and they are free to attack me, I will be worse off than if none of us attacks any of the others. We must therefore constitute some authority with the power to keep the peace and to compel us to stand by the agreement.[19]

Such an account offers a naturalist explanation of the state as the result of a 'social contract', an agreement neither to commit nor to suffer aggression. Glaucon in Plato's *Republic* describes the basis of the agreement:

Those who are unable to do injustice while avoiding suffering it think it expedient to make an agreement with each other neither to do nor to suffer injustice . . . And this is how justice came into being, and what it is; it is intermediate between the best condition, of doing injustice without penalty, and the worst, of suffering injustice without being able to retaliate.

As a speaker in Thucydides says, 'What is just in the human way of thinking is judged from equal compulsion, but the stronger do what they can and the weaker submit to it.' A stable practice of justice needs equal compulsion exerted on the self-interested individuals who will break the rules if they are not compelled to keep them. Equal compulsion makes it reasonable to obey rules of justice.[20]

When equal compulsion is missing, human nature inevitably abandons justice. In relations between states there is no equal compulsion, because there is no superior authority over, say, Athens and Sparta, that can enforce non-aggression. It is therefore often in the interest of one side or the other to commit aggression in order to exert its power, or to try to remove a source of fear. These are the motives Thucydides mentions to explain the events resulting in the outbreak of the Peloponnesian War; the Athenians grew powerful, aroused fear in the Spartans, and compelled them to go to war.[21]

In the Peloponnesian War Athens generally supported democracies and Sparta oligarchies; and so each party within a state could count on external support for a violent revolution. If the external support for one party was stronger, that party would be able to dominate the state, and to crush its opponents. The 'equal compulsion' securing obedience to the established regime was removed, and revolution became an attractive option. In these conditions no one had reason to observe rules of justice any more, and so they were not observed. Thucydides describes a bloody revolution in Corcyra to illustrate the violence, ruthlessness, and abandonment of moral scruples which, he claims, became typical of the Greek world at this time. Human nature shows itself to be 'dominated by its impulse, stronger than justice, hostile to any superior power'.

War reveals human nature by 'removing the ease of daily life and fitting the impulse of the majority to the prevailing circumstances'. It is a 'violent teacher', because it forces its lessons on us, irrespective of our choice, by removing the stable system of equal compulsion. If we did not study both peace and war, we might suppose that observance of justice and morality rests on something more than advantage; but study of human nature in different conditions assures us that it is moved only by the basic motives concerned with power and fear.[22]

viii. *Questions about naturalist history*

If Thucydides' account of human nature is correct, those who claim to be moved by moral considerations, and not simply by their desire for their own power and security, are either insincere or self-deceived. And he believes that in fact many people are prone to such insincerity or self-deception about morality. Some Greeks expected the Spartans to liberate them from Athenian domination, and were inevitably disappointed to find that the Spartans, no less than the Athenians, were out for domination, not liberation. For Thucydides as for Democritus, the unchanging reality is very different from what we naively expect; and the theorist's task is to show how the laws governing the underlying reality explain the familiar appearances. Thucydides shows how to account for phenomena that appear to conflict with his theory, and how he can understand them better than we understand them through common sense.[23]

Thucydides' version of human nature, however, is suspiciously similar to the self-assertive character of the Homeric hero. The hero reflects the moral assumptions of his society, whereas in Thucydides human nature often violates accepted moral assumptions; but the character itself seems to have changed rather little. Thucydides identifies a persistent, though no longer un-controversial, cultural ideal with the basic and inevitable expression of human nature.

His acceptance of this cultural ideal encourages him to describe political life through the eyes of Pericles, whose alleged views turn out to be close to those of Thucydides himself. The democracy, in Thucydides' view, was well off when it was guided by the scientific politician Pericles, and badly off when it refused to listen to any single authority.[24]

Thucydides' conception of human nature and his bias against democracy probably distort his history. After the attempted revolt of Mytilene from the Athenian empire, the Athenians at first decided to execute all Mytilenean citizens, but then changed their mind because 'it seemed a terrible and cruel decision, to destroy a whole city, rather than just those responsible for the revolt'. Thucydides describes a long debate over this decision, but he never again mentions Athenian aversion to cruelty and injustice. Since it has no place in Thucydides' account of human nature, he largely ignores it in his treatment of human motives; but in this case at least he has probably distorted the truth. As Hobbes remarks of Thucydides, 'for his opinion touching the government of the state, it is manifest that he least of all liked the democracy'.[25]

Thucydides' political outlook seems to have influenced his ostensibly scientific theory of human nature and historical explanation; and he is not the last theorist whose theory suffers from such influence. Hobbes, Rousseau, Social Darwinism, and recent theories of race, heredity, and intelligence offer other examples. The influence of highly dubious moral and political views is often a reason for doubt about the scientific character of the theory.

ix. *Some effects of naturalism*

Thucydides does not himself advocate the rejection of justice and other-regarding morality; he merely describes some of the conditions in which people tend to violate it. But in so far as his naturalist account of morality seems to explain why we sometimes

have good reason to observe moral principles, and sometimes
have good reason to violate them, naturalism seems to imply
some criticism of attitudes to morality regarded as conventional
in Thucydides' time and in our own.

Democritus eliminates Aeschylean cosmic justice, and Thucydides excludes it from his history. The will of the gods provides
a reason for human beings to take justice and morality seriously,
as an expression of the divine will; Democritean naturalism removes this reason.

Aeschylus, however, does not defend justice simply because it
is the divine law; he also refers to the good of the community. But
this second defence is open to naturalist criticism. Thucydides'
Corcyreans in a time of civil conflict apparently see no alternative
to breaking ordinary moral restraints; observance of these restraints rests on absurd simple-mindedness. I seem to have reason
to observe principles of justice only as long as they benefit me; if
I advance my power and security by violating them, then I seem
to have good reason for doing so.[26] My observance of ordinary
moral rules—prohibiting lying, cheating, and so on—seems to
benefit other people, not myself. Justice benefits a weak person
who cannot defend himself, and restrains the stronger person who
would benefit from freer competition in attack and defence. In so
far as any of us may be in a weak position, each of us benefits
from living under a system of justice. Still, each of us may also
benefit from cheating, and apparently Thucydides' principles justify me in doing so when it is in my interest.

Naturalist criticism, therefore, readily suggests a sharp contrast
between nature and conventional moral norms (*nomos*), to the
disadvantage of the latter. The sophist Antiphon (*c.*480–411) calls
the provisions of conventional morality 'fetters binding
nature'. The agile young Alcibiades is presented as persuading
Pericles that there is no reason to respect a law passed by a
democratic assembly, since such a law is simply the product of
force. The understanding of human nature seems to show that
the trustworthy, honest, and reliably just person simply does not
know what is good for him.[28]

x. *Radical doubt*

The rigorous naturalism of Democritus and Thucydides argues for a sharp distinction between appearance and reality; it claims to undermine our common-sense view of the world, and to replace it with a true account of the underlying reality. But the very first steps of Democritus' argument are open to objections.

Democritus relies on the equipollence of conflicting appearances to show that perceptible qualities are not real. He infers that the atoms which constitute reality have only weight, shape, size, and motion. But these qualities themselves seem to be open to the argument from conflicting appearances; an argument that works for colour seems to work for shape and size, implying that they too are not real. Moreover, it is on the strength of sensory evidence that Democritus claims that (e.g.) sharp atoms produce bitter tastes; but if sensory evidence is totally unreliable, his claims are worthless. The argument from conflicting appearances seems to destroy his naturalist system.

If Democritus is forced to accept this extension of his argument from conflicting appearances, and also maintains his further assumptions, including the Principle of Excluded Middle and the Principle of Non-Contradiction, then he is driven to conclude that reality has none of the qualities he ascribes to it; for the problem of conflicting appearances can be raised about each of them. But this nihilist conclusion depends on the further assumptions; and why should we accept them? The problem of finding some indisputable criterion arises again for them, and we apparently cannot avoid an infinite regress.

In that case, the argument from conflicting appearances should lead us not to nihilism, but to the admission that neither sense-perception nor reason has reached any justified belief about the nature of reality. This is a sceptical conclusion. The Greek Sceptics (*skeptikos*, 'examiner') examined the grounds for believing claims about reality, found no adequate grounds, and hence suspended judgement about the nature of reality. In appealing to conflicting appearances, Democritus seems to have forced himself into scepticism. Probably he sees this himself. For he makes the senses protest to reason: 'Wretched mind, do you take your proofs from us and then overthrow us? Our overthrow is your downfall. '

If neither sense-perception nor reason leads him to the truth, he must admit that we have no access to how things really are. As Aristotle says, 'And this is why Democritus . . . says that either there is no truth or to us at least it is not evident.'[29]

The sceptical argument seems to challenge not only Democritus, but naturalism in general. If naturalism relies on the senses, it is open to the argument from conflicting appearances; if it appeals to this argument to reject the senses, it seems to destroy itself. Democritus introduces the argument from conflicting appearances to defeat Heracleitus; but he appears to have defeated naturalism. He probably does not accept the sceptical conclusion, but he does not show how he can avoid it.

xi. *Convention, truth, and reality*

Protagoras (? *c*.485-*c*.415), unlike Democritus, thinks he has a good argument against scepticism. But the argument is unlikely to appeal to Democritus or to any other naturalist, since it involves the rejection of naturalism. Protagoras uses sceptical arguments against Democritus to undermine naturalism, but thinks he can avoid the sceptical conclusion. Both naturalists and sceptics assume that how things really are is how they are objectively— independently of how they appear to any perceiver or thinker; and similarly that what is true is what is true objectively—apart from how it may appear to anyone. Democritus assumes this objectivist conception in contrasting conventional belief (*nomos*) with reality. Protagoras thinks the objectivist assumption is mistaken, and therefore that scepticism is unjustified. Against it he defends his own Measure doctrine:

A human being is the measure of all things—of things that are, how they are, and of things that are not, how they are not.

Different examples, referring to different sorts of properties, show how Protagoras might defend the Measure doctrine as a reply to the argument from conflicting appearances.

First, some of Heracleitus' examples of compresence of opposites might be taken to challenge the objectivist assumption. If we say that Socrates is tall and short, or that sea-water is healthy

and unhealthy, our claims may seem to conflict, but they need
not. Socrates is tall compared to the shorter Cebes and short
compared to the taller Phaedo; and, as Heracleitus says, sea-water
is healthy for fishes and unhealthy for human beings. In these
cases the truths depend on a standard of comparison. Once we
allow relativity, we remove the appearance of contradiction, and
Democritus' appeal to the Principle of Non-Contradiction leaves
us untouched. The standard of comparison provides the 'measure'
that Protagoras seeks.[30]

Other cases of apparent conflict might be supposed (though
not uncontroversially) to yield to similar treatment. Herodotus
describes Greeks and Indians apparently disagreeing about
whether it is pious or impious to bury or to eat the dead. But
perhaps they do not really disagree, since one practice is pious in
Greece and the other is pious in India. Herodotus himself remarks
that this example shows how 'convention (or 'law'; *nomos*) is king
over all'. He is right, in Protagoras' view, if he means that human
convention is the measure of how things really are.[31]

Protagoras suggests that the same analysis will work for other
properties; we can make true judgements about how things are if
we realize that their truth is 'measured' by our conventions and
assumptions, not by any objective reality. Democritus thinks conflicting appearances cannot both be true because he holds that
true judgements must be objectively true. But he is wrong, in
Protagoras' view, to oppose convention to reality; for Protagoras'
examples suggest that how things really are is itself a matter of
convention. This solution may be regarded as an adroit escape
from scepticism—or as a useless subterfuge that concedes everything important to the sceptic.

xii. *Scepticism, conventionalism, and morality*

Naturalist assumptions and arguments raise some questions
about justice and morality. Scepticism and conventionalism undermine naturalist reasons for attacking morality, but raise
difficulties of their own.

It is easy to begin a sceptical attack on morality if we consider
the similarity between a moral norm and a law or convention

(Greek uses *nomos* for all three). Moral norms seem to show variation across societies; and if they create conflicting appearances, it is not clear how the conflict is to be resolved. Such arguments from variation may convince us that moral norms are merely a matter of convention with no claim to truth.

The sceptic finds no reason for choosing one moral outlook over another. He has no reason to violate the generally recognized morality of his society, since he has no truer principles to offer. On the other hand, if he feels inclined to change his views, he has no reason not to change them, since he has no reason to think they are true. Scepticism leaves him powerless to make a rational estimate of the truth of any conflicting moral beliefs, and so unable to make a rational decision between them.[32]

In moral questions as elsewhere Protagoras offers his conventionalism as an escape from scepticism. He maintains that the Athenians' agreement about justice constitutes what is really just—in Athens; similarly, the Persians' agreement constitutes what is really just—in Persia.[33] But if some Athenians think it is right to break the laws of Athens, their belief is also true, on Protagoras' standards, in their subgroup of Athens. Protagoras cannot tell us which belief we should accept, or how we should change our beliefs.

Neither scepticism nor conventionalism gives us a reason to prefer one moral outlook over another. But they may still influence our moral outlook. They make us less likely to resist moral views that are urged on us with enough vigour by other people. If the dominant people around us are eager for our acquiescence in their moral views, we have no reason to resist; and if we find conventional views irksome and feel like deviating, we have no reason to conform. Though scepticism is consistent with strict conformity to conventional morality, it leaves the sceptic's moral outlook vulnerable to pressure that others see reason to resist.

xiii. *Political tensions*

Critical reflexion on moral and political questions was not confined to small groups of speculative theorists. Political developments in Athens (the city for which we have the best evidence) in the fifth century combined to force these questions on the attention of many Athenians.

The Athenian democratic system, as it developed in the fifth century, was rule (*kratos*) by the people (*dêmos*), and '*dêmos*' in Greek (like 'the people' in English) may refer either to the whole body of citizens or to the lower class—indeed Aristotle insists that democracy is essentially rule by the lower class. The democratic regime allowed real power and responsibility to the poor (though not to slaves or women), and the constitution protected and advanced their interests. The rich and well-born had less exclusive control in Athens than in Greek cities with oligarchic constitutions.[34]

The Athenian democracy persisted, with modifications and interruptions, from Cleisthenes in the sixth century until the Romans destroyed it in the first century. The upper classes accepted it partly, no doubt, because they had a privileged position; the poor did not abolish inequalities of wealth or status, and the rich occupied the public offices of responsibility and profit. But their loyalty cannot easily be explained by this sort of motive alone; it is reasonable to assume that many felt some loyalty to democracy as a just and fair system in the interests of all the citizens.

Such convictions, however, conflict with a Homeric outlook. Someone pursuing his own honour and status might sometimes be content with a position of honour in a democracy. But at other times he might reflect that he could do better for himself and his social class in a regime designed for the benefit of the upper classes. In this frame of mind he might agree with Alcibiades' comment (according to Thucydides) on democracy, that 'there is nothing more to be said about such acknowledged foolishness'. Revolutionary efforts might be futile in peacetime under a strong democracy. But war, 'the violent teacher', gave more opportunities—to the opponents of Ephialtes in 462, and to the opponents of democracy late in the Peloponnesian War.[35]

xiv. *The growth of political debate*
The situation of the upper classes in the Athenian democracy encouraged reflexion on their grounds for loyalty to the democracy. The processes of democratic government encouraged their reflexion to take a particularly self-conscious form.

In the Athenian democracy, success depended on ability to speak, argue, and persuade in large public meetings. While any member of the Assembly was entitled to address it, it is likely that the only people who addressed it regularly and effectively were the political leaders. Even after it became a democracy Athens continued to draw these leaders from the traditional ruling class— the well-born, rich, and leisured. These rich Athenians sought help from rhetoricians and sophists, two groups of professional teachers; indeed, the demand for such teaching probably helped to create the two professions.

Rhetoricians taught the art of effective public speaking—how to marshal arguments, present them clearly, and raise the audience's emotions. In Plato's *Gorgias* the rhetorician Gorgias (*c.*483–376) boasts of his ability to control and sway public meetings on all sorts of issues. He was a delegate from his native city (Leontini in Sicily) to Athens in 427, and his rhetoric is reported to have impressed the Athenians, since they were people with quick wits and a taste for speeches.[36]

Sophists were less specialized teachers; some of them boasted of their expertise in all areas of knowledge. Hippias was ready to speak on astronomy, geometry, arithmetic, grammar, literary criticism, music, and history. Sophists often used the results of naturalist inquiry; they ensured that naturalist speculations and theories were not confined to a few theorists but became, to some degree, the common property of an educated class. But the aim of all this was general education that would equip a man for success in public life.[37]

The sophists aroused both enthusiasm and suspicion. They claimed to add something useful to the gentleman's traditional upbringing, based on Homer, the poets, and the laws of the city. Their claims aroused suspicion that their teaching would be subversive. Many sophists fully accepted conventional norms and moral beliefs; and to this extent suspicion was unjustified. But the claim to improve traditional education implied scope for criticism; and to this extent social and political conservatives were right to be suspicious.

Democracy encouraged the development of the argumentative and rhetorical skills that could present a persuasive case to a mass

audience. But persuasive argument has to persuade its hearers by
appeal to some principles that they can be presumed to share.
Persuasive speakers in democratic Athens had to appeal to democratic principles; and in the course of appealing to such principles,
they came to articulate them, and also began to examine them.
Examination of democratic principles might well raise questions
about their justification; and for the upper classes, using their
sophistic training to reflect on their role in a democracy, these
questions became urgent.

xv. *Practical results*

For many Athenians questions about justice and conventional
morality were not merely speculative. Democracy required some
concern for law, justice, and the common good from the richer,
better-born citizens. Why should they not act illegally and violently to win power for themselves? In the last quarter of the
fifth century Athens was one of the cities in which the upper
classes saw an opportunity for political revolution.

One oligarchic revolution, of the 'Four Hundred' in 411-410,
was led by, among others, the sophist Antiphon. He was a radical
critic of law and conventional justice, attacking them as violations
of nature. Thucydides describes him as 'second to none in excellence' (virtue; *aretê*). Another of the Four Hundred, who eventually moved the decree prosecuting Antiphon, was Andron,
companion of the radical critic Callicles. We know of Callicles'
views from Plato's *Gorgias*; they are similar on important points
to Antiphon's views, and also to the views of the rhetorician
Thrasymachus, as they are presented in Book i of Plato's *Republic*.
We have some reason to believe that such views were quite widely
accepted among Athenian oligarchs.[38]

The Four Hundred fell; but after six more years of democracy
a still narrower oligarchic clique, the 'Thirty', took over with
Spartan help, at the end of the Peloponnesian War. Among the
Thirty was Critias, a relative of Plato and associate of Socrates;
one of their allies was Plato's uncle Charmides. Critias himself
wrote a play in which a speaker describes the gods as an invention
of legislators wanting to frighten people into obeying the laws.

Chaerephon, another of Socrates' associates, was a leader of the democracy restored (with the help of the Spartans, now under a king more favourable to Athenian independence) in 403.[39]

Probably philosophical views and political aims were connected. Democratic spokesmen urge young oligarchs to be just and law-abiding. Some defenders of conventional law-abiding morality try to show that justice is the best and most expedient policy. But not everyone was convinced. A supporter of Callicles or Thrasymachus or Antiphon or Critias might dismiss arguments about justice as attempts to deceive the stronger, more able people into acting against their own interest. From this point of view, the appeal to nature appears to justify pursuit of one's own selfish, non-social, and anti-social desires and aims; for appeals to the interests of others appear to rest on mere convention. As Callicles says in the *Gorgias*:

Those who lay down the laws are the weak creatures, the many. And so they lay down the laws and assign their praise and blame with an eye on themselves and their own advantage. They terrorize the stronger people who have the power to get more . . . and tell them that taking more for themselves is shameful and unjust . . . But I think that if a man is born with a strong enough nature, he will shake off and smash and escape all this.

On this view, the weak behave as Thucydides' account of human nature predicts; they try to make themselves stronger, and to restrain the strong. But if the strong have exposed the merely conventional character of appeals to justice, and follow the overriding claims of human nature, they will not be deceived by the conspiracy of the weak.[40]

These critics of ordinary morality examined nature and convention with some definite biases. Self-seeking Homeric morality kept its hold on them; and their class interest made principles of justice unequal competitors with Homeric ideals. They were already predisposed to challenge the principles that upheld loyalty to democracy; and naturalist, sceptical, and conventionalist arguments showed how convincing these challenges could be.

xvi. *The unsettled questions*

The naturalist outlook did not answer every reasonable question. We have seen how unanswered questions led to doubts, and how doubts raised further serious questions about the whole naturalistic outlook.

Naturalism rested on the division between appearance and objective reality, and on the assumption that we can argue from reason and appearance to justified conclusions about objective reality. But when Democritus divides appearance from reality, he makes knowledge of objective reality impossible (if we accept his other assumptions), and forces us into scepticism. Protagoras frees us from scepticism if we give up any hope of knowing an objective reality.

Naturalism in ethics seemed to defend justice and morality. Heracleitus and Aeschylus both try to connect cosmic with human justice. But Democritus and Thucydides raise doubts about cosmic justice. Study of human nature raises doubts about human justice. Justice and morality may be conventionally accepted; but, unless we agree with Protagoras, we will not be satisfied with that defence.

During the last third of the fifth century, covering the Peloponnesian War, much of Socrates' adult life, and Plato's earlier life, conventional morality was under attack from these different directions. Some tried to defend it. One writer says that law is not contrary to nature, but actually required by nature as a protection against human weakness; someone trying to overthrow the law will make everyone his enemies. These arguments rightly challenge the simple assumption that whatever is to some degree conventional must be rejected as contrary to nature. Particular languages include conventional elements, but language itself is an expression of human nature; and a parallel observation may rightly be used to dispel confusions about the conventional character of laws and moral practices.[41]

Still, such arguments scarcely refute sceptics or naturalists. Even if human societies all have some law, so that the existence of law is not a matter of convention, this agreement fails to resolve the disagreement between laws, and leaves the sceptics room for their argument. The fact that others will suspect and hate me if they know I am unjust simply shows that I should not let my injustice be widely known, but should benefit from secret injustice.

So far, the critics seem to have a strong case against conventional morality.

The naturalists thought they could do better than custom, authority, myth, and tradition; they expected that someone who compared them with Homer and Hesiod would become a naturalist. The problems in naturalism might make us unsure about this. If naturalism leads to the rejection of common sense and eventually to scepticism, what is the point of it? And if naturalism leads to the rejection of morality, should we be naturalists?

Those who refuse to give up rational inquiry and its claim to reach objective truths must show either that naturalism does not lead to these unacceptable results, or that rational inquiry can reach objective truths without relying on the naturalist assumptions that are most vulnerable to criticism. Socrates, Plato, and Aristotle try a combination of these two approaches.

5
Socrates

i. *Socrates' trial*

Socrates (469–399) cross-examined other people on moral and political issues. Though he claimed to know nothing about these issues himself, his questions reduced his interlocutors to such confusion and puzzlement that their firmest and most cherished beliefs seemed to waver under Socrates' patient, polite, but insistent and irritating scrutiny. In the *Laches* the Athenian general Nicias warns his friends that a discussion with Socrates will involve an examination of their whole life:

> You seem not to know that if you meet Socrates in discussion, you are bound to find that even if you begin by discussing something else, before you are done you will be led around in argument by Socrates, until you are trapped into giving an account of yourself—of how you are living your present life and how you have lived your life in the past. And once you are trapped, Socrates will not let you go until he has tried and tested you thoroughly on each point.

In the *Gorgias* Callicles sees that the results of a Socratic examination may be uncomfortable:

> Tell me, Socrates, should we take you to be joking or in earnest? If you're in earnest, and what you say is true, doesn't it follow that our human life is upside down, and that everything we do is the exact opposite, it would seem, of what we ought to do?

Nicias is an admirer of Socrates; Callicles is an articulate and vigorous opponent; but they both expect radical criticism from him.[1]

He was well known for his strikingly ugly face and for his eccentric austerity in dress and habit; that was part of the reason why the comic dramatist Aristophanes (? *c*.450–*c*.385) found him useful as a typical sophist to be caricatured in the *Clouds* (produced in 423). Socrates claimed not to be a sophist; he did not offer to teach anything, wrote no books, and took no money as payment (he does not claim to refuse gifts from his friends). But he discussed the moral and political issues that concerned the sophists and their audiences; and the suspicion that the sophists aroused in some conservative Athenians fell on him.[2]

Socrates also aroused suspicion because of the company he kept. He was himself neither rich nor well-born, but he found rich and aristocratic young men to be both sexually attractive and suitable partners in philosophical discussion. They became his disciples, and at the same time his patrons; and some of them were bitter and ruthless conspirators against the democracy. The orator Aeschines (*c*.397–*c*.322) reminds the jury, representing the Athenian people, of an incident that he takes to be a matter of common knowledge: 'You put to death Socrates the sophist, because he was exposed as the educator of Critias, one of the Thirty who overthrew the democracy.' They were quite right to hate Critias, and justifiably suspicious of the anti-democratic tendencies of Alcibiades, another companion of Socrates.[3]

In 403, after the overthrow of the Thirty, the restored democracy was anxious to unify the city, and declared an amnesty for supporters of the Thirty. This meant that Socrates' opponents could not legally attack him for his well-known relations with enemies of the democracy. But in 399 they prosecuted him none the less, on grounds that explain their distrust of him.[4]

Their first charge was religious, and it made two complaints. Socrates was accused of speculations about the heavens that resulted in rejection of the city's recognized gods; and he was accused of introducing new divinities. The first complaint was the more important. Even though some naturalists had claimed to describe, not to deny, the gods and cosmic justice, Democritus eliminated them from control of the universe; and such denial of the gods' power could be expected to provoke their anger.[5]

The second charge against Socrates was moral; it also included two complaints. Socrates was accused of 'making the inferior argument superior' and of 'corrupting the young men'. The first complaint implies that a skilled orator could make the inferior argument (the one that deserved to lose) superior (the actual winner) by his rhetorical skill; and the accusers assume that Socrates taught his own brand of rhetorical tricks. The second complaint suggests that Socrates' disciples were taken in by his tricks. Since he could apparently refute any argument in support of any conventional moral rule, his followers concluded that the conventional rules had nothing to be said for them. The behaviour of Critias or Alcibiades was simply (in the view of Socrates' prosecutors) the natural result of Socratic argument.

It is easy to understand the combination of a religious and a moral charge. The two charges are combined in Aristophanes' crude and malicious attack on sophists in the *Clouds*. Many Athenians probably agreed with Aristophanes, and found both the main currents of Greek speculation—naturalism and the sophistic movement—offensive and dangerous to religion and morality. They found their fears confirmed in the apparent results of Socrates' teaching.

ii. *Socrates' defence*

Plato's *Apology* (i.e. *apologia*, 'defence', ostensibly made at Socrates' trial) represents Socrates as rejecting both the charges against him. He claims that none of the audience has ever heard him discuss cosmological speculations (he does not deny that he engaged in them); and he argues that once the Athenians realize he is not a naturalist, they will see that the religious charges rest on a misunderstanding. Against the moral charge, he denies that he *consciously* corrupts the young men. He protests that his cross-questioning seeks only to expose his own and other people's ignorance, not to win any rhetorical victory for him. He urges his interlocutors to inquire into morality, and he expects inquiry to result in moral improvement.[6]

To show his own moral seriousness Socrates asserts his uncompromising commitment to justice, affirming that he will face death before he will commit injustice. He implies that such firm moral convictions make it unthinkable that he would corrupt the young men.

And yet his moral convictions do not always lead to actions that everyone would endorse. He refused to help the Thirty in their illegal actions, because he thought it would be unjust. He refuses to give up his philosophical activity, because that would be unjust, since it would violate a divine command he claims to have received. He will defy the Athenians themselves if they release him on condition that he stops his philosophical activity. But though he is ready to defy the law and the state, he argues strongly that the citizen has an obligation to obey the law; and in the *Crito* he gives this as his reason for refusing to escape from prison and from the death sentence that he regards as unjust.

These attitudes to the law and to public morality are self-confident. Socrates betrays no doubt about whether he is doing the right thing on different occasions, even though he is out of step with the views of his fellow-citizens. But we might well think he ought to be in some doubt about his views; for they might easily seem to be inconsistent. On some occasions he does not hesitate to disobey the authorities, and he even implies his willingness to break the law; but on other occasions he insists on the citizen's duty of obedience. Socrates himself, however, sees no inconsistency:

For I am, and always have been, the sort of person who is convinced by nothing else of mine than the argument that appears best to me on rational reflexion. And so I cannot, now that this chance has befallen me, repudiate the arguments I used to put forward, but they appear about the same as they always appeared.

He claims to find contradictions in other people's beliefs, but none in his own. He believes that his refusal to disobey the law when it condemns him to death is quite consistent with his threat to disobey a ban on his philosophical activity; but he leaves it to others to discover why his views are consistent.[7]

In claiming that his views rest on argument Socrates seems to contradict two other key points in his defence: first, that he knows nothing about the questions he discusses; and second, that his cross-examinations reveal ignorance in the interlocutor, but do not advocate Socrates' own views. What sort of argument is supposed to lead him to his moral convictions, and does it support his convictions about justice? If his defence is true, how could his opponents believe he was a threat to public morality and religion?

iii. *Socratic assumptions*

Plato shows us how Socrates 'tried and tested' his interlocutors, as Nicias said; the shorter dialogues show how the interlocutor is gradually led to question some of the principles on which he leads his life. Socrates asks the interlocutor for the definition of some virtue, asking 'What is bravery (piety, etc.)?' The interlocutor answers confidently with a general definition. Socrates convinces him that this attempted definition leads to consequences that conflict with the interlocutor's other initial beliefs about the virtue in question. The interlocutor agrees that his beliefs conflict; he decides (for reasons that we must explore later) that he has better reason to retain his other initial beliefs than to retain his attempted definition of the virtue; and so he abandons his attempted definition. The process is repeated for one or more further attempts, until eventually Socrates and the interlocutor agree that neither of them knows what this virtue is. Socrates believed all along that he did not know, but the interlocutor thought he knew, and is unpleasantly surprised to discover that he does not.

Socrates assumes that to settle some practical and urgent moral questions we need knowledge of the virtues, and that we should test claims to such knowledge by seeking definitions of the virtues. The *Laches* begins with a discussion of the sort of training that makes someone a brave soldier (a question of obvious importance for an Athenian citizen, who could expect to be called for military service). Socrates suggests that if they are to decide on the appropriate way to cultivate bravery, they ought to know what bravery is; and to see if they know, he asks for a definition. In the *Euthyphro* a moral dispute raises the problem. Euthyphro is prosecuting his father for impiety; but popular feeling regards prosecution of one's father as a scandalously impious action. Euthyphro despises popular feeling and is confident that the sort of thing he is doing is perfectly pious and required by religious duty. His confidence leads Socrates to ask him what piety is.[8]

Socrates wants a definition that gives a single account of, say, bravery that applies to all and only brave people and actions, and shows what is brave about each of them. This account will provide a 'standard' or 'pattern' by reference to which we can judge whether someone's actions display the virtue or not. We do not give the right sort of answer if we simply list recognized examples of brave or pious actions. Socrates wants not 'the many piouses', but the single 'form' or 'character' (*eidos, idea*) they all share.⁹

We may be surprised that Socrates chooses to cross-examine a person's life and moral outlook simply by asking him to define a virtue; this seems too abstract and theoretical a question to show that our ordinary morality is 'upside down'. Acting morally and learning to be a good person do not seem to require knowledge of definitions. If we want to teach sewing or carpentry, we must be able to recognize the sorts of competence to be expected from the expert; but can we not recognize these without a general definition? Surely the same is true for moral training and learning; should we not just imitate recognizably admirable people? Nor do we seem to need Socrates' 'standard' to make true judgements. Surely we can often grasp and use a word properly without a general definition. Words for colours, for example, are hard to define, but even so we can tell blue things apart from red.¹⁰

To see why Socrates wants a definition, we should consider the questions that arose for his contemporaries. The Corcyreans in the civil war described by Thucydides were in new situations and faced new demands; they therefore faced doubts and disputes about which actions were or were not brave:

In their justifications of actions they reversed the customary evaluations conveyed by names. For unreasoning daring was counted as bravery in support of one's allies; provident delay was counted as fair-seeming cowardice; temperance was regarded as a pretext for cowardice; and understanding everything was regarded as good for nothing in action.¹¹

It seemed that bravery required unscrupulous determination to ignore any sanction of law or morality to advance one's own cause, and that justice, as normally conceived, would be mere cowardice. We could not hope to resolve this sort of dispute by appealing to recognized examples of bravery; for the dispute arises precisely because some people reject conventional views about which actions are genuinely brave. The dissident claims we are wrong to think that bravery never conflicts with our other moral obligations. Socrates seeks to resolve this dispute by asking Laches to describe the appropriate standard for brave action.

In seeking a definition Socrates is not asking what the word 'bravery' means, and the disputes that concern him are not merely verbal. Thucydides' Corcyreans might agree that 'bravery' means (say) 'fearless resolution in a worthy cause'; but they do not agree about the sort of action that this virtue requires. They need a clearer grasp of the standard they apply in regarding actions as brave. Socrates is right to look for a standard to explain and correct judgements about bravery.

Socrates thinks he does not know the definition of any of the virtues; and he convinces his interlocutors that they do not know either. But he assumes that both he and his interlocutors make true judgements. We might learn the answer to an arithmetical problem even if we cannot work it out for ourselves; but when we can work it out ourselves, we know that this is the right answer, and do not simply get the answer right. This is the knowledge that Socrates thinks he lacks and wants to find. He lacks the explicit justification that will show the truth of his beliefs in disputed cases.[12]

Socrates is concerned with an urgent and important dispute about moral beliefs; and if he can answer the questions he asks, he will resolve some of the disputed issues. Moreover, the search for a definition quite reasonably forces the interlocutor to examine his life; he has to decide if he really understands the principles he acts on, and whether his life really conforms to the principles that he finds he accepts on reflexion.

iv. *Socratic arguments*

It is all too easy to see how Socrates' cross-examination might expose the confusion, imprecision, and superficiality in our moral thinking. But Callicles claims that if Socrates is right, our life is proved to be upside down; and Socrates claims that his arguments justify his positive moral convictions. How can his cross-examinations lead an interlocutor beyond the admission of ignorance to further moral discovery?

Socrates' questions expose a conflict in the interlocutor's beliefs; Laches, for instance, finds that he cannot both define bravery as standing firm and admit that sometimes a tactical retreat is the brave action. He agrees that he must reject the proposed definition. After further questions, Laches finds himself agreeing that fearlessness and resolution are always brave; that bravery is a virtue; that a virtue is always fine and beneficial; and that fearless resolution is sometimes disgraceful and harmful.[13]

These beliefs together raise difficulties. Someone who does not scruple or hesitate to harm other people in the pursuit of his own amusement may be fearless and resolute; in that case he will be brave, if that is all it takes to be brave. But this trait is not 'fine and beneficial', and we may well hesitate to admit that someone who displays it is (to that extent) a good person. Since we think bravery is a virtue—that it tends to make someone a good person—we cannot count mere fearless resolution as bravery; Thucydides' Corcyreans must be wrong. Socrates shows us that our first conception of bravery conflicts with some simple, but basic, principles about moral virtues.

Socrates seeks to amend and improve an interlocutor's beliefs, not to destroy them. Some interlocutors feel their firm convictions being undermined. He is compared with a jellyfish that numbs the victims it stings, and with Daedalus, who could make statues move as Socrates makes beliefs move and wander away. Such a reaction might lead to scepticism. But Laches' confusion does not result in scepticism. Though cross-examination reveals inconsistencies in his beliefs, reflexion shows him how to improve them. Confused and sceptical reactions reflect only part of the truth about Socrates. He deserves to be taken seriously when he claims to be searching for the truth.[14]

v. *Morality and religion*

Do Socrates' methods result in any conclusions of moral importance?

Euthyphro is sure he is doing the correct and pious thing by prosecuting his father. But he has little success in explaining what is pious about the action, and finds no satisfactory account of piety. His most promising effort identifies the pious with what the gods love. Socrates agrees that this account covers all and only the right cases; but he rejects it as a definition. He requires Euthyphro to distinguish different claims:

1. x is pious if and only if it is loved by the gods.
2. x is pious because it is pious.
3. x is loved by the gods because it is pious.
4. x is pious because it is loved by the gods.
5. The pious is what is loved by the gods.

Socrates argues that while (1) to (3) are true, (4) is false, and hence (5) must also be false. If (5) were true, then we could correctly replace (2) with (4); but Socrates argues that if (2) and (3) are true, then (4) must be false. The truth of (2) implies that x's being pious must be the explanation of x's being loved by the gods; whatever property piety turns out to be, it should explain why the gods love pious things. But the truth of (4) implies, contrary to (3), that being loved by the gods is the explanatory property. Since (4) does not state a genuine explanatory property, we cannot correctly replace (2) with (4); and hence, once Euthyphro has accepted (1) to (3), he must reject (5).[15]

We might think that (5) simply says the same as (1); and if Socrates thought so, he would have to agree with Euthyphro. But he insists that (1) only states something that is true of piety, not what piety itself is (it may be true of human beings that they are the only animals who laugh, but that is not what it is to be a human being). An answer to his demand for a definition must provide a standard, and so must explain why something is pious. But (5) cannot do this, since Euthyphro has agreed (in (3)) that x's being pious explains why the gods love x, not the other way round.

Euthyphro could consistently reject (3), if he said that religious morality depends wholly on the arbitrary will of the gods. On this view, the gods do not approve of a pious action because of any features that make it pious apart from its being approved of. Nothing about murder, then, causes the gods to disapprove of it; they have no reason not to approve of murder, and it is simply an arbitrary choice of theirs to condemn it.

Socrates' questions to Euthyphro focus attention on the role of (3) in Euthyphro's and Socrates' beliefs. In doing so, they also throw some light on a trend in Hebrew, no less than in Greek, thought about God and morality. Like Aeschylus, the Hebrew prophets distinguish God's moral demands from the ritual observances normally associated with religion. They reject the view, widespread though not universal in Homer and in later Greek religious thought, that religion is a contract, with human beings offering sacrifices and other ritual attentions as payment for divine favour. The prophets insist that God's favour cannot be bought by a fixed schedule of actions, and that God requires moral integrity. Many Hebrews, like many Greeks, believed that they could atone for past misdeeds by offering extra sacrifices. But the prophets reply that moral corruption cannot be wiped out or outweighed by lavish observances. Socrates makes explicit this assumption that underlies the prophetic conception of religion and morality.[16]

But why do they distinguish the moral law so sharply from the ritual law? Do they simply insist that one arbitrary divine command matters more than another? Socrates' questions allow us to see more clearly what the prophets assume. They assume that God expresses a moral ideal because he knows what is morally good and demands it. He knows the principles that we can also know to be morally good. His demands are not arbitrary, but reflect truths about moral goodness that are true independently of his choices.

Though naturalist views about the gods reject the assumption that they can be influenced by sacrifices, Socrates' examination of Euthyphro applies to them also. Socrates implicitly asks Anaximander and Heracleitus what makes cosmic justice *just*; it cannot be just simply because it is the way the world actually is. To show that it is really just is a more demanding task than they had realized.[17]

Socrates exposes some of the difficulties that face someone who wants to make God's will the ultimate standard of what is morally right. His own position has its apparent difficulties too (it might, for instance, appear to make God superfluous or irrelevant as a source of moral principles or moral guidance); but it presents a reasonable alternative to a traditional view of religion and ethics. Kant (1724–1808) accepts and expresses the Socratic demand:

Each example of morality which is exhibited to me must itself have been previously judged according to principles of morality to see whether it is worthy to serve as an original example, i.e. as a model. By no means could it authoritatively furnish the concept of morality. Even the Holy One of the Gospels must be compared with our ideal of moral perfection before he can be recognized as such.[18]

Socrates' argument extends beyond piety to morality in general; for it extends beyond divine authority to other claims to moral authority. If someone says that what is right is what the laws require, we can ask the question Socrates asks Euthyphro. Those who maintain this view make morality an arbitrary creature of law, and free law from moral criticism. Protagoras' conventionalist view, treating morality and justice as a matter of convention, also makes them immune to rational criticism. Against him Socrates implies that in fact we apply some further standard in judging whether a norm or convention is just or not, and that this standard makes conventional norms open to rational criticism.

These implications of the discussion with Euthyphro should assure us that Socrates' questions have significant moral consequences. They force us to see that a consistent reply to his questions may be quite implausible. We have seen that if consistency were all that mattered, the interlocutor could easily avoid defeat by rejecting one of Socrates' crucial assumptions. But when we count the cost of rejection, we can see why we have good reason to agree with Socrates.

vi. *The unity of morality*

The argument with Euthyphro suggests that piety is less separable from the other virtues than Euthyphro initially thinks. If the gods approve of pious actions simply in so far as they are morally right, then piety imposes no special duties beyond the duties imposed by morality in general. Euthyphro finds no acceptable way to distinguish piety from justice, and hence no acceptable way to distinguish it from other-regarding morality as a whole.

The argument about bravery leads more explicitly to the same conclusion. At first we suppose, as Laches does, that we can imagine someone being brave, fearless, and intrepid in battle, but cruel, thoughtless, and stupid; we might even think these vices are often the price of bravery. Socrates suggests to Laches that we must be wrong. A beast can be fearless because it is ignorant of the danger; a fool can be fearless because he lacks the sense to see what is frightening; someone else can be fearless because he sees nothing to live for, and does not mind if he dies. These cases do not display the virtue we recognize as bravery; and hence bravery cannot be mere fearlessness.[19]

Socrates, Laches, and Nicias eventually agree that the genuinely brave person's fearlessness must rest on his knowledge of good and evil as a whole; but this very same knowledge of good and evil is also necessary and sufficient for each of the other virtues; hence bravery turns out to be indistinguishable from virtue as a whole. This conclusion makes some practical difference. For the discussion began by asking about the sort of training suitable for developing bravery; but now we find there is no point in trying to make someone brave without teaching him the rest of virtue as well. We can perhaps make someone fearless and resolute, but if he is also cruel and thoughtless, he has not acquired genuine bravery.

The dialogue reaches no explicit result; it ends in puzzlement, designed to provoke reflexion. But reflexion suggests an answer to Thucydides' Corcyrean partisans. They assume that one virtue can conflict with another, and especially that bravery can conflict with justice. In reply Socrates suggests that deeper reflexion about the unity of morality will shake our belief in this conflict. His belief in the 'unity of the virtues' appears to be a harsh paradox. But he thinks we will find, on reflexion, that we really believed it all along; Socratic interrogation is an aid to constructive reflexion.[20]

vii. *The problem of justice*

Socrates implies in the *Crito* that his inquiries support positive moral conclusions, and that in particular they support his un-wavering adhesion to justice. He is right to claim that his method has positive moral results. The result of systematic and repeated inquiry may well be, as Callicles saw, a change of moral outlook and priorities. But is Socrates right about the actual direction of the change? Is he right to claim that his arguments support justice?

He insists that my own self-interest always gives me my overriding reason for action:

Do all we human beings want to fare well? But perhaps this is one of the ridiculous questions that I was afraid to ask. For surely it's senseless to ask questions like that; for what human being does not want to fare well?

Socrates accepts an *egoist* assumption about reasons and motives—that my own welfare is the ultimate aim of all my action. He identifies my welfare with my happiness (*eudaimonia*; 'happiness' is a conventional, though not completely satisfactory, rendering; nothing more determinate than a general notion of welfare is intended). Our question, then, is not 'Should I pursue my own happiness or some other end?', but 'Given that I want my happiness, how am I to get it?'

Socrates believes in the unity of the virtues, since he believes that they are all to be identified with knowledge of good and evil. The egoist assumption implies that the relevant good and evil must be good and evil for the agent; hence all the virtues must ultimately be ways to promote the agent's own interest. In the *Crito* he applies this general egoist assumption about virtue to justice. He claims that the moral obligations imposed by justice cannot conflict with his own self-interest:

Do we still agree or not, that what we should value most highly is not merely living, but living well?. . . And do we still agree that living well, living finely, and living justly are the same thing?

Crito agrees; but Socrates does not explain why we should assume that the just and moral life ('living finely and living justly') is the same as the happy life achieving the agent's own interests ('living well'). He claims, very surprisingly, that the virtuous person can suffer no harm at all; however badly everything else may seem to go, he never suffers any loss of happiness and welfare.[21]

Socrates is right to say we cannot consistently maintain these beliefs:

1. Justice is a virtue.

2. A virtue must always benefit its possessor.

3. Justice sometimes harms its possessor.

Socrates assumes that we must retain the first two claims and reject the third. But why is this the right resolution of the conflict? If we accept this resolution, what actions will be just, and can justice impose the other-regarding obligations commonly associated with it?

We readily assume that the obligations of justice require us, for instance, to keep agreements with other people, to respect their rights, and to consider their interests, in cases where we seem to gain some benefit by cheating or exploiting them. Socrates claims that we are wrong to suspect a conflict between self-interest and obligation in such cases. His own adhesion to justice is clear in the *Apology* and *Crito*; if he is to justify himself, he must show that his just action is actually in his own interest. But he does not present arguments to justify his confidence and resolve our doubts. We might expect him, for instance, to remove some doubts in some people by appealing to the rewards that the virtuous person can expect in an after-life—a familiar device for proving the convergence of morality and self-interest. Such an appeal, however, requires belief in the immortality of the soul. In the *Apology* Socrates conspicuously forgoes any appeal to immortality; he never suggests that belief in immortality and in post-mortem rewards and punishments is necessary to justify acceptance of justice.[22]

viii. *Intelligible misunderstandings of Socrates*

We may now try to resolve the apparently sharp opposition between Socrates' picture of himself and other people's picture of him.

He is right to deny that he deliberately or willingly corrupts the young men. His interrogations try to provoke reflexion, self-examination, and self-knowledge. An interlocutor or hearer who thinks about Socrates' methods and claims will reach moral beliefs that are derived from reasonable principles, and are themselves both more consistent and more defensible. Socrates does not encourage injustice and immorality; on the contrary, he seeks to expose the errors in some prevalent and specious arguments against justice.

Still, his method makes the charges against him more plausible. We might easily learn Socrates' techniques for causing confusion and perplexity, without learning his constructive method of systematic interrogation. We might then use these Socratic techniques as rhetorical tricks, not for constructive inquiry. Plato himself suggests that some young men learnt no more than this from Socrates:

And so, when they have refuted many people themselves, and undergone refutation by many, they fall intensely and quickly into believing nothing that they previously believed. And this is why both they and everything to do with philosophy get a bad name with other people.

This is an unreasonable, but not an unnatural, reaction to Socrates' questions.[23]

Even more can be said in support of the case against Socrates. His method is not necessarily comforting or reassuring. It forces us into puzzled confusion and leaves us to our own reflexions. His questions raise serious doubts about some aspects of conventional morality. Though he might say he wants a clearer statement of the true principles underlying some of conventional morality, his inquiry leads him to unconventional results, and conservatives might argue that the moral status quo is best left undisturbed. Such conservatives might even appeal for support to Aristophanes' *Clouds*, which might seem to suggest that ordinary people's conventional moral views are easily upset by the slightest argumentative challenge, and that it is safer not to think or argue about them at all. (This is an easy conclusion to draw from Aristophanes' portrait of Socrates, not necessarily the one that Aristophanes intended to be drawn.)[24] More radical disciples of Socrates might argue that his inquiries justify a sharper break with the status quo. From both sides it is easy to argue that Socrates is a danger to conventional morality.

For similar reasons, suspicions of Socrates' attitude to religion are not unfounded slanders, even though they miss the main point about Socrates. He does not intend his questions to Euthyphro to be attacks on religious belief or on genuinely religious practices.

But they might well lead to serious doubts about accepted religious practices. The Hebrew prophets do not claim to be inventing a new religion, but to defend and to justify belief in the same God that their fellow-Hebrews believe in; still, they might plausibly be accused of threatening widespread assumptions about religion. Socrates' accusers were right, whether they knew it or not, in some of their suspicions.

Socrates' accusers missed the main point, but they did not completely misunderstand him. Even when we correct the misinterpretations of him, we should not accept his views—nor would Socrates want us to—without further challenge and argument. Some of his claims about the connexion between his arguments and his positive moral conclusions are highly disputable; but his method shows us how we can test his views and look for the necessary arguments. This is where Plato begins his own critical reflexions on Socrates.

In Socrates Aristotle sees the beginning of moral philosophy, succeeding the study of nature. Cicero says he called philosophy down from the heavens into human life and human society. Milton rightly points to Socrates as the source of controversy and debate in later Greek philosophy:

> To sage Philosophy next lend thine ear,
> From Heaven descended to the low-rooft house
> Of Socrates, see there his Tenement,
> Whom well inspir'd the Oracle prounounc'd
> Wisest of men; from whose mouth issu'd forth
> Mellifluous streams that water'd all the schools
> Of Academics old and new, with those
> Surnamed Peripatetics, and the Sect
> Epicurean, and the Stoic severe . . .

Though Socrates does not begin philosophical argument, he displays its method and powers more clearly than his predecessors ever did.[25]

Socratic moral inquiry is philosophical, not rhetorical, because it is concerned with truth, not persuasion, and appeals to rational argument, not to custom, tradition, or authority. It is a discipline in its own right, because it does not rely on premises derived from natural speculation but on moral principles that all of us

can discover and examine for ourselves. It was easy to mistake
Socrates for something else; hence his accusers treated him as
partly a naturalist, partly a rhetorician, and altogether a public
menace. In fact he is something new, a moral philosopher.

6

Plato

i. Socrates and Plato

Plato (428-347) was born early in the Peloponnesian War, and was a young adult during the last years of the war, when pro-Spartan oligarchic sentiment grew into open disloyalty to the democracy, and eventually resulted in the rule of the Four Hundred and of the Thirty. Plato's own loyalties were divided; for he was a relative of Charmides, a member of the Thirty, but he was also a disciple of Socrates, and approved of Socrates' dissent from the lawlessness of the Thirty. The Thirty were deposed; but the restored democracy put Socrates to death, and Plato gave up any ambitions he might have had for a political career. He founded his philosophical school, the Academy, in Athens, and remained as its head until his death.

Plato wrote dialogues presenting Socratic philosophy in conversational form; and we have already drawn on his earlier dialogues for our account of Socrates. But in Plato's middle and late dialogues, the character 'Socrates' discusses questions of metaphysics, epistemology, and political theory, on which the historical Socrates was silent.[1]

Plato begins from Socratic problems, and implicitly claims to find the best arguments for Socratic convictions. But a defence of one Socratic view may imply a challenge to another. Socrates' interlocutors have to give up some of their cherished views in order to defend others. Plato finds that he has to do the same with Socratic views; he discovers that he cannot be Socrates' disciple without being his critic. Even if he does not openly disagree with Socrates, Plato implies that Socratic convictions are justified only if we accept further doctrines that would have very much surprised, perhaps even repelled, Socrates himself. As far as we can tell, Socrates never realized that his convictions about

ethics and philosophical method committed him to the elaborate
and controversial theories and speculations about knowledge and
reality that occupy Plato. But surprising though Plato's development of Socrates may seem, it is, in Plato's view, inescapable
for a serious defender of Socrates.

Plato believes he defends the central Socratic convictions; probably this is why 'Socrates' remains the main character in most of
the middle and late dialogues. But to some readers, both ancient
and modern, his defence of Socrates has seemed more like a
betrayal, a disastrous perversion of the Socratic outlook.[2] To see
if the critics are right, we must examine Plato's defence.

ii. *The theory of Socratic argument*

For all his emphasis on self-examination, and for all his confidence in his method of cross-examination, Socrates never asks
how his method works, or why he is entitled to rely on its results.
In the *Meno* Plato raises and answers these questions.[3]

At the outset Socrates explains why he insists on asking what
virtue is before he answers Meno's question about whether it can
be taught. How, he asks, can he know that Meno is short or fat,
or know anything else about Meno, if he does not know who
Meno is? Similarly, how could Euthyphro know, as he claimed
to, that it is pious to prosecute one's father for impiety, if he did
not know what piety is? Socrates asserts the priority of definition,
assuming that we can know the answer to our practical question
only if we know the definition of the relevant virtue.

Socrates wants to find what virtue is, but admits from the start
that he knows nothing about virtue. But how then, Meno asks
him, has he any reasonable basis for his inquiry? He seeks to
test a proposed definition of, say, bravery by comparing it with
examples of brave action. But if he and his interlocutor do not
know what actions are brave (since they do not know what
bravery is), how can they correctly identify examples? The priority of definition seems to make Socrates' cross-examinations
self-defeating.[4]

Socrates answers Meno indirectly, by conducting a simple geometry lesson with a slave. He draws a square with sides four feet

long, and asks the slave how long a side is needed for a square with double the area of the original square. The slave at first answers that we need a side double the length; like Socrates' other interlocutors, he is confident, unhesitating, and wrong. But further questions change his mind. He is puzzled and confused about the original questions; but still more questions show him how to find the right answer. At each stage the slave says what he believes, and Socrates does not force him. He is free to give a wrong answer (and at first he does). But if he insists on it, he must accept some very odd and difficult geometrical beliefs; and he rightly prefers to avoid these extreme consequences.[5]

Socrates' interlocutor must often decide, as the slave does, how to resolve a conflict between his beliefs (e.g. between the belief that courage is resolution and that courage is always fine and beneficial); but how does he make the right choice about which of his old beliefs to reject? If we believe that the angles in a triangle add up to 150 degrees, and find individual cases where they seem to add up to 180 degrees, we could quite consistently reject these cases, and retain our original belief. But this would clearly be an absurd way to adjust our beliefs to avoid inconsistency; for the assumptions that we need (e.g. that our instruments were defective, or that we suffer from some visual defect) will conflict with some of our more basic, well-entrenched, and strongly supported beliefs (e.g. about the accuracy of our instruments and the reliability of our senses and of other people's testimony). The reasonable way to modify beliefs is to reject those that conflict with better-supported beliefs. This is what Meno's slave does; and this is what Socrates' interlocutors do.

The slave lacks knowledge but 'has in himself true beliefs about the things he does not know'. He begins with some true and some false beliefs; but he has the capacity to make reasonable choices among his conflicting beliefs, and to sort out the true from the false. In so far as he has this capacity, he helps us to answer Meno's doubts about our capacity to inquire fruitfully through Socratic cross-examination. For even though we lack knowledge of the relevant Socratic definition, we have the capacity for intelligent choice among different possible beliefs.[6]

iii. *Inquiry and recollection*

Plato offers a speculative explanation of our capacity for intelligent and selective revision of our beliefs; he suggests that we actually recover knowledge that we knew before we were born, but then forgot. In Socratic inquiry we find the right answer from within ourselves, without external authority or new empirical information. We might compare the process with our attempts to recollect something we once learnt and have now forgotten. I may try and fail to remember the name of someone I met at a party, until I remember that the host said 'I'd like you to meet someone with a famous Russian name'; then I may remember that the person was called Tolstoy. My own thoughts and inferences lead me to this further belief; and to this extent the process is similar to a Socratic interrogation. Plato, however, sees more than a mere similarity here; he thinks the two processes are really the same. The slave's ability to answer questions he had not previously thought of, without being told the answers, is taken to show that he is really recollecting the answers that he knew in a previous existence.[7]

This argument relies on a disputable assumption. An interlocutor is capable of the self-examination, reflexion, and inference that allow him to modify his beliefs without any direct stimulus from authority or experience. But if this capacity is not learnt, why must it be further explained, by beliefs acquired without any process of learning and later recollected? Plato rightly draws our attention to our capacities for reflexion and inference. But he does not fully understand their importance; if he had, he would not have appealed so readily to pre-natal knowledge.

iv. *Knowledge and belief*

Plato believes that Socratic inquiry can lead from mere belief to knowledge:

At the moment < the slave's > beliefs are newly aroused, as though in a dream. But if someone asks him these same questions over again on many occasions and in many ways, you know that in the end he will have knowledge as accurate as anyone's about them.

The early dialogues did not draw a clear and explicit distinction between knowledge and true belief. But they relied on some distinction; for Socrates disavowed knowledge of the virtues, but did not disavow true belief about them. Plato now draws an explicit distinction:

> True beliefs . . . are not in the habit of staying put for a long time, but run away from a person's soul, so that they are not worth much, until one ties them down by reasoning about the explanation. And this, Meno my friend, is recollection, as we agreed previously . . . And this is why knowledge is more valuable than true belief, and is superior to it in having this bond to tie it down.

If we have knowledge, our beliefs will be tied down, not shaken by questioning as Euthyphro's beliefs were, because they will rest on a reasoned justification giving us some rational ground for our convictions.[8]

Plato's view of the difference between true belief and knowledge, and of the possible progress from the one to the other, disagrees with a prevalent naturalist view about the unreliability of common sense. Democritus argues from the alleged unreliability of common sense to the truth of his naturalist theory. But his argument shows how easily the rejection of common sense can support scepticism about both common sense and naturalist theory. If common sense disagrees with itself, we may conclude that the disagreement is irresolvable; in that case we are confronted with conflicting and equipollent appearances, and cannot choose between them. Similarly, if naturalist theories disagree with each other and with common sense, we may conclude that this is another irresolvable disagreement forcing us into scepticism. If we accept these arguments from disagreement, then apparently we cannot trust either common sense or naturalist theories, but must resort to scepticism.[9]

Against naturalist and sceptical views Plato insists on the continuity between common sense and knowledge. Socratic inquiry criticizes common sense from its own resources. Plato assumes that we have the capacity to sort the true beliefs from the false, and to find the justification that vindicates the true beliefs.

v. *The theory of Socratic definition*

To see if Plato is right to claim that Socratic inquiry can lead to knowledge, we need to see what kind of explanation or justification is needed for knowledge. To know about virtue we must be able to say what virtue is; and we can say this only if we find the single 'form' (*eidos*) or 'character' (*idea*) that is present in all its instances. An account of this form will give us knowledge, not mere belief, because we can use it as a 'pattern' or 'standard' (*paradeigma*) to explain why a particular action or person is, say, just or pious. Just or pious things have a common property that makes it correct to apply the same name to them. Greek-speakers apply '*dikaion*', Latin-speakers '*iustum*', German-speakers '*recht*'; but they all speak of the same thing, and it would exist even if none of them spoke of it.[10]

Plato follows Socrates in affirming the reality of the 'just itself' and the other things we try to define in a Socratic inquiry. He agrees with Socrates in recognizing the 'one pious' (etc.) besides the 'many piouses', and in looking for an account of this universal form. His further claims about Forms, however, lead him beyond Socrates (hence it is convenient to speak of 'Forms', as opposed to 'forms', to mark Plato's special claims about the entities that, in his view, Socrates had already recognized). From the dialogues, and from Aristotle's account of the Theory of Forms, we can reasonably infer that Plato ascribes these features to Forms:

1. Each Form is free of the compresence of opposites belonging to other things. Ordinary just or equal things are both just and unjust, both equal and unequal, whereas the Forms of justice and equality cannot be.

2. The Forms are completely stable and unchanging, whereas other things suffer ceaseless change and flux.

3. We cannot know about the Forms through the senses; for anything accessible to the senses suffers from compresence of opposites and from ceaseless change, and so cannot be a Form.

4. The Forms exist separately from sensible things; while sensible things change, grow, decay, come to be, or perish, the Forms are unaffected, and would exist even if sensible things did not.

Aristotle picks these features of Forms as the distinctive mark of the Platonic, as opposed to the Socratic, view. He claims that Plato believed, under the influence of the Heracleitean Cratylus, that sensible things are in ceaseless flux, and therefore cannot be known; since the Forms are objects of knowledge, they cannot be sensible things, and cannot suffer the same ceaseless flux. In Aristotle's view, Plato also takes Forms to be separated from sensible things. If these views are indeed distinctive of Plato, why does he hold them?[11]

The most important claim, partly explaining the other three, is the first. The Socratic dialogues show why the compresence of opposites is important. The form of justice is supposed to provide a standard for judging whether or not something else is just; but we have not found the right standard if the property we take to be justice turns out to be no more just than unjust, since that cannot be what makes things just. If, for instance, we define justice as returning what we have borrowed, some of our judgements about particular actions will be right, but some will be wrong. I will correctly judge, for instance, that it is just to return the lawn-mower you lent to me yesterday; but I will wrongly judge that it is just to return your gun, though you gave it me for safe keeping, and now you are insane and threatening to shoot your children. In general, if we look for the form of F, any property that is both F and not F cannot be the one we want.[12]

vi. *The senses*

In his third claim Plato agrees with the Heracleitean judgement that the senses are bad witnesses for people who do not use reason to interpret them. He believes that if we try to define the properties that concern Socrates, the senses do not focus on suitable properties; for in these cases the senses discover properties that display compresence of opposites, and we cannot rely on these properties to find Socratic definitions.

Plato argues that for some properties the senses by themselves give us the wrong sort of information. They tell us, for example, that the same thing is both big and small, or both heavy and light, in different comparisons; and if we rely on these observations alone, we will have no consistent conception of what largeness, smallness, and so on are. We may observe that two sticks of equal length are both three feet long, and if we rely incautiously on this observation, we will say that being equal is being three feet long; but in fact we have found a property that is both equal and unequal. Being equal or large is not a property of the observable object by itself; to know whether an object has it we must know what it is being compared to, and what the relevant standard of comparison is (are we looking for big mice or big mammals?). For similar reasons, we cannot define beauty or justice by simply appealing to sensory observations of beautiful or just things (suggesting, for example, that beauty is bright colour, or that justice is paying back what we have borrowed). For we never find anything beautiful or just or equal that is not also ugly, unjust, or unequal.

Socrates' interlocutors looked for definitions by relying on sensory observations of virtuous behaviour, not realizing that observable properties could not be identical to moral properties. Hence their attempted definitions mentioned properties displaying compresence of opposites. In Plato's view, there is no reasonable prospect of defining a virtue by reference to purely observable properties, avoiding mention of other virtues, and of the good promoted by the virtues. Socrates' interlocutors failed because they sought definitions involving only these observable properties; it is more reasonable, in Plato's view, to assume that each virtue must be defined in terms that mention the other virtues and the good they are all supposed to promote.

Plato takes his second claim—that Forms are unchanging, and sensibles are in ceaseless flux—to follow from the compresence of opposites. A length that is long in one comparison and short in another 'changes' from being long to being short. Platonic flux, no less than Heracleitean flux, includes the sort of instability that is implied in compresence; and for the purposes of the Theory of Forms compresence is the type of instability that explains Plato's contrast between Forms and sensible things.[13]

vii. *Questions about Forms*

Though we have explained the first three of Plato's claims about Forms, the fourth is more difficult, both because it is harder to see whether Plato accepts it, and because his grounds for accepting it, if he does, are not clear. He certainly shows, if we accept the previous arguments, that Forms cannot be sensible objects; justice, for instance, cannot be the same as types of actions that are both just and unjust (since some particular actions of that type—returning what we have borrowed, say—are just and others are unjust). Nor can Forms be sensible properties; justice cannot, for instance, be the same property as the property of returning what has been borrowed, since the latter property makes actions both just and unjust (by making some just and others unjust). But some further arguments are needed to support the conclusion (attributed to Plato by Aristotle) that Forms are separated, and therefore would exist even if no sensible objects existed. Though Plato may indeed believe in this independent existence of Forms, he does not argue for it, and he does not appeal to it in his contrasts between Forms and sensible things.[14]

The question about separation indicates one obscurity in Plato's conception of Forms. A further obscurity is his view of the relation between a Form and the property it corresponds to. We might suppose that the Form (e.g. the Just Itself) and the property or universal (justice) are the very same thing; for this is what Socrates seemed to be looking for in his search for an account of the 'one pious' and so on. On the other hand, some of Plato's remarks suggest to many readers (including Aristotle) that he cannot consistently identify the Form with the property. For he claims that the Form of F is not both F and not-F, as sensible Fs are; and sometimes seems to believe that the Form is itself perfectly F. On this view, the Form of justice is perfectly just, not also unjust, the Form of large perfectly large, the Form of equal perfectly equal, and so on. This doctrine of 'self-predication' (or, more strictly, that every Form bears the predicate that it corresponds to) is hard to apply to every Form: how large must the Form of large be, and what is the Form of equal equal to?

The fact that these questions arise suggests that self-predication rests on a mistake. And indeed Aristotle argues that in accepting self-predication Plato makes a basic mistake, treating properties as though they were further particulars (as though tallness were a tall thing, white had some colour, and so on). It remains an unsettled question, however, whether, and how far, Plato actually commits himself to self-predication in the first place.[15]

Despite these difficulties and obscurities, the Theory of Forms is a reasonable defence of Socrates' search for definitions. If we look for definitions in sensible terms, we will find that justice is both paying debts and not paying them, and so on. A Heracleitean embraces this conclusion as an example of the unity of opposites, and claims that this is what justice is. The sceptic will argue that if we cannot resolve the apparent conflict between our claims about justice, we have no knowledge of what justice really is. The conventionalist will maintain that if these conflicting claims both tell us what justice is, we should identify justice with what appears just to different people. Plato thinks these different views rest on errors about the compresence of opposites.[16]

In Plato's view, Heracleitus is wrong to think that this compresence could give us a true account of the underlying nature of justice. For it is equally true that justice is keeping and not keeping promises, inflicting pain and giving pleasure, and so on. An account of justice demands an account of the underlying principle that generates and explains the list of opposites. If we find this principle, we may forestall any sceptical or conventionalist argument. A critical attitude to Socrates' own approach to definitions suggests a better way to look for Socratic definitions.

viii. *The theory of Socratic knowledge*

We might agree with Plato that *if* we can have knowledge and *if* correct Socratic definitions are possible, then there must be Forms that are non-sensible, stable, and perfect (without compresence of opposites). To accept this conditional claim, however, is not to agree that there are Forms; for we may still doubt the possibility of Socratic knowledge and definition. Even if we agree that there are non-sensible Forms, we may think they are unknowable; for if Forms are non-sensible, and the senses are our only source of knowledge, how can we know Forms?

In *Republic* vi and vii Plato faces some of these questions. He presents the complex triple image of the Sun, Line, and Cave to describe our progress from uncritical acceptance of observational beliefs to reasoned and justified claims to knowledge. The Sun contrasts seeing in the darkness, indicating the cognitive state of examining sensible things without reference to the Forms, with seeing in the sunlight, indicating the cognitive state of being guided by knowledge of the Forms. The Divided Line subdivides each of these cognitive states into two, identifying two states of belief without knowledge (not involving Forms) and two states of knowledge (involving Forms). The allegory of the Cave presents our progress through these four stages, as a progress from the darkness to the sunlight (recalling the Sun image).[17]

We begin this progress by realizing that beliefs based on simple observation, and the moral rules based on these beliefs, are inadequate. We may initially believe (as some of Socrates' interlocutors do) that standing firm is bravery or that returning what we have borrowed is justice; but Socratic examination shows that these rules do not fully specify the relevant virtues. The allegory of the Cave describes this process of criticism and discovery. It begins with prisoners looking at reflexions cast by dummies on the wall of the cave. (If he had known of films, Plato might have described the prisoners as seeing a rather poor and dim film of the dummies, without realizing that it is only a film.) At first the prisoner thinks these sensible appearances are the whole of reality, not realizing that some other reality underlies and explains them. But suddenly he is forced to turn to the dummies (images of horses, trees, men, and so on) whose reflexions he has seen, and eventually to the fire that has been his source of light. At first he is puzzled and at a loss when he is asked to say what each of the dummies is; but gradually he acquires firmer and sounder beliefs.

Plato reasserts a major claim of his theory of recollection, that our own capacity for reasoned and self-critical reflexion can approach the truth if it is stimulated in the right way, without being fed the answers. He insists that the growth of knowledge is not like putting sight into blind eyes, but more like turning a person's eyes to face in the right direction:

Then there must be some technique for turning the soul around, for changing its direction as easily and effectively as possible. The aim is not to implant sight in us, but, assuming that sight is already there but has been turned the wrong way, to get it to turn the right way.

The technique is Socratic inquiry; it turns the interlocutor in the right direction, by making him see that sensible properties cannot give adequate definitions of the properties he wants to understand. With this step we pass from the first to the second stage of the Line.[18]

This step also suggests the method for further progress. The former prisoner in the cave is led out into the sunlight, but at first cannot look at it directly. The corresponding third stage of the Line involves the use of 'hypotheses' or 'assumptions' (Greek *hupothesis*, 'laying down'), to reach a reasonable, though incomplete, answer to Socrates' demand for definitions:

I assume on each occasion whatever account I judge to be the strongest, and whatever seems to me to agree with this I take to be true . . .

And if someone attacks the assumption itself, you will pay no attention to him, and will not answer, until you have examined the consequences of the assumption, to see if they agree or disagree with each other.

An assumption that (e.g.) justice always seeks the benefit of the people affected may conflict with our initial belief that it is always just to return what we borrow. But we should reject the initial belief, if it conflicts with still further beliefs that seem reasonable; if so, the assumption is to that extent vindicated.[19]

Since we have now reached the third stage of the Line, we have a type of knowledge, because we have an account that justifies our well-founded beliefs; we are better off than Socrates and his interlocutors were. Still, our assumptions do not yet count as complete knowledge; to reach that Plato requires a fourth stage. At the fourth stage of the Cave allegory we are able to look directly at the sun, the source of the light that lets us see other things; at the corresponding stage of the Line we reach knowledge of the Good through dialectic (i.e. Socratic cross-examination), since our knowledge of the Good is the source and basic principle of our knowledge of other Forms. At this stage dialectic discovers a genuine first principle underlying the assumptions. If we have reached the third stage, our assumptions are mutually consistent, so that one gives us no conclusive reason to reject another. But at the third stage we have only examined the consequences of the assumptions, and the consistency of the assumptions with each other; we have not yet considered whether the assumptions also support each other. If they do support each other, they are no longer mere assumptions; each gives us further reason to accept the others, and we are fully justified in accepting them all. This condition of mutual support is to be achieved at the fourth stage of the Line.[20]

The further justification and mutual support are to come from the Form of the Good. The different virtues should all contribute to some good; if an allegedly just action turns out to have consequences that we would regard as worse on the whole, then, in Plato's view, it is not a just action after all. Our conception of the good that is promoted by the virtues will regulate our conception of each of the virtues; and we will have correct accounts of the virtues when the accounts are all related to an account of the Good.

ix. *Plato's reply to scepticism*

Plato argues that if we trust some of our beliefs and reflect on them, we can make a coherent, mutually supporting structure of reasoned beliefs. If we can go this far we can answer the sceptical and conventionalist (Protagorean) arguments that rest on appeals to conflicting appearances. The first stages of inquiry reveal conflicts; but the progress of dialectic replaces conflict with mutual support.

Still, the sceptic might ask if mutual support is good enough reason to claim knowledge. Mutually supporting beliefs might still be false, since they might fail to correspond to a reality external to them—if, for example, they are just a consistent hallucination. To remove this doubt we would have to compare our beliefs to the reality they are supposed to be about; but we have no access to reality apart from our beliefs about it, and so we apparently cannot claim knowledge of things as they really are. If this sceptical doubt disturbs us, we will have to agree with Democritus that 'there is no truth, or to us at least it is not evident'.[21]

The sceptic assumes that if we cannot compare our beliefs directly with reality, we cannot justifiably claim to know their truth, and that therefore comparison with other beliefs cannot support a claim to knowledge. But why should we accept the sceptic's assumption? Plato can fairly turn this question back to the sceptic. If we apply Plato's tests of consistency and mutual support to the sceptical assumption itself, it seems implausible.

The sceptic may object that to assess the sceptical assumption by Plato's standards is merely begging the question, since the sceptic raises questions about these very standards. In reply to this objection, Plato should admit that his method of justification involves some degree of circularity; he appeals to his standards of coherence and mutual support to defend the methods and standards that the sceptic challenges. But he might fairly argue that the circle need not be vicious. To convince us that Plato's circle of justification is vicious, the sceptic might try to persuade us that all circular argument is vicious, and confers no justification. The prospects of convincing us to reject all circular argument are dim; and if we are not convinced, the sceptic seems to be trying to impose conditions for justification that we have been given no good reason to accept. It is fair to ask the sceptic for some reason to accept the assumptions that lead to scepticism, and the sceptic does not offer a reason that Plato needs to take seriously.[22]

x. *Soul and body*

Plato's account of recollection claims that our souls existed before they were incarnate in our bodies; and in the *Phaedo* he argues more fully for the claim that souls are ungenerated and immortal. This claim is important, in his view, because it both supports the possibility of pre-natal knowledge, and turns our attention to what is most important about ourselves and our welfare.

Socrates urges the Athenians to care about themselves and the welfare of their real selves, not about their external possessions. To care about ourselves we must care about our souls, to make them as virtuous as possible; no other benefit can possibly compensate for the harm we do ourselves by having vicious souls, and our welfare is secured if and only if our souls are virtuous. Socrates assumes that his soul is himself; and he contrasts virtue, as the health of the soul, with the health of the body. He assumes without explanation that my beliefs, choices, aims, and character are parts of myself more properly than my heart, arms, or weight are.[23]

Plato tries to explain and justify Socrates' assumptions. He argues that each person is to be identified with his reason and capacity for thought, and that since the rational intellect is immortal, each person is immortal. He defends a strongly dualist doctrine; body and soul are two different things, and the soul is immaterial, imperceptible, and immortal, while the body is material, perceptible, and mortal. The soul can know the Forms without the senses, and like the Forms, is imperceptible and indestructible.[24]

Plato argues at length for the immortality of the rational soul. His belief in 'recollection', as described in the *Meno*, requires belief in pre-existence; and in the *Phaedo* he offers further arguments to show that the soul survives any and all of the bodies that may ever belong to it. These arguments for immortality also support the philosopher's way of life. In coming to know the Forms and in cultivating the virtues, we prepare ourselves for the state we will finally reach when we are free of the body. Some people do brave or temperate or just actions only when they see some further material advantage coming from them; these people have a mere 'facade' of virtue. The philosopher, however, is unreservedly committed to the virtues, because he does not care about any worldly loss they may involve.[25]

xi. *The soul and the self*

In examining Plato's case for personal immortality we must ask two questions. First, is the soul, as Plato conceives it, immortal? And second, is the soul the person? In the *Phaedo* Socrates insists that *he* will not have perished when his soul is separated from his body; and we must agree with him if we are to take the interest Plato expects us to take in the first question.

Plato appeals to our capacity to know non-sensible Forms. This capacity implies that we have reason and intellect as well as senses; for we come to know Forms by rational reflexion and reasoning, not by mere observation. If we confine ourselves to the senses, we are prone to error, and progress requires us to free ourselves—our rational souls—from the distractions and errors of the senses. I normally regard my rational, considered judgements as *my* judgements, assuming that I am to be identified with the reflective, temporally extended process, rather than with the momentary impression of the senses.[26]

Plato draws the same contrast in a practical context. We attribute to the body both our sensory impressions and the sensual desires that result from its own physical states and from its interactions with other physical objects; and Plato claims that we find these bodily desires a distraction to *ourselves*, to our rational intellects. Perhaps I know it would be best to avoid drinking the water, because it is poisoned, but I am so thirsty that I want to drink it anyway; or perhaps I know I should take my injured neighbour to hospital, but I feel so tired that I am unwilling to leave home. In these cases, Plato assumes, one of these desires is really *mine*; the rational aim reflects *my* aims and values, and the non-rational opposition reflects the feelings and appetites that conflict with my real aims.[27]

These arguments from knowledge and action suggest that we identify ourselves with our rational rather than our non-rational aspects. But Plato's conclusion about immortality implies that we are identical to our rational capacities, to the *exclusion* of all the others. To accept this view we must agree that I would be the same person if my purely rational capacities were separated from all my other mental or physical states. We have no reason so far to accept this conception of ourselves. We might identify ourselves with the reason that organizes sensory impressions and impulses, but it does not follow that we are identical to reason without any impressions or impulses to organize.

Plato does not seem to have shown, then, that the immortality of Socrates' reason ensures the immortality of Socrates. If this pure reason lacks Socrates' sense-perceptions, emotions, desires, experiences, and memories, we may wonder how it differs from some limb or organ of his that happens to survive without the rest of the capacities that make a person. Moreover, if Socrates' pure reason and Napoleon's pure reason are both freed from the body, what will distinguish them? When each pure reason is freed from the experiences, desires, and aims of the life before death, it seems to be indistinguishable from all the others. Perhaps Plato can meet these objections. But at least they show some difficulties in his claim that the very same thing can be the focus of personal identity, the primary object of moral concern, and also immortal and separable from any body.[28]

xii. *The problem of justice*

Socrates' views on inquiry, knowledge and reality, soul and body, are all meant to give reasons for being virtuous and living a just life. In the *Republic* Plato examines the most difficult unresolved problems for Socratic moral theory; and he shows how his doctrines about knowledge and reality might support his answers to the ethical questions. The *Republic* takes up questions in moral and political theory, epistemology, metaphysics, psychology, and the philosophy of education and of art; but its argument as a whole is an elaborate effort to explain what justice is and why we should be just rather than unjust.

This case for injustice is urged by Thrasymachus in Book i, and by Glaucon and Adeimantus defending him in Book ii. They suggest that justice is 'another's good', and that rules of justice exist to maintain the established regime. I have good reason to want other people to obey the rules, in so far as I benefit from living under a stable regime; but since I will be even better off if most other people obey the rules and I get away with injustice, that is the option I will rationally prefer.

The Socratic dialogues make it clear that Socrates rejects this view of the point and benefits of justice. But he does not say what justice is, or how it benefits the just person:

And so, don't merely show us by argument that justice is better than injustice. Show us also what each of them does, itself because of itself, to the person who has it—whether or not it is noticed by gods or men— in such a way that justice is good and injustice bad.

We are to consider a just person who is badly off in every way except in being just, and an unjust person who is well off in every way except in being unjust. Plato claims that the just person is still better off than the unjust.[29]

Has Plato asked the right question? We might think that a genuinely just person will do the right action even when it is against his interest; if we are just for the right reasons, should we not avoid Plato's appeal to self-interest? Plato replies that the apparent conflict between morality and self-interest is really only a conflict between morality and a false conception of self-interest, based in turn on a false conception of the self.

xiii. *Reason and desire*

Plato agrees with Socrates that a defence of justice should show how it benefits the just person's soul. His main argument, therefore, rests on an account of the soul, and especially of desires.[30]

He examines the conflicts of motive that he appealed to in the *Phaedo.* If I am thirsty and want to drink, but also refuse to satisfy my desire to drink, because I think it would be unhealthy and hence bad for me to drink, my desire not to drink rests on my belief about what is good for me on the whole. If I decide, on reflexion, that after all it would be good for me to drink, then my desire not to drink will go away, and will be replaced by a desire to drink. Since this desire responds to reasoning about my good, we may call it a rational desire. On the other hand, my present desire to drink may not go away after rational reflexion; even if I realize that more whisky will make driving dangerous, I may still want it. This desire does not respond to reasoning about my good; it is a non-rational desire. On this principle Plato distinguishes rational from non-rational desires, assigning them to different 'parts' of the soul.[31]

The rational part considers the value of a present object of desire (e.g. to drink) against my other present desires (e.g. to be healthy) and against desires I will have in the future (e.g. tomorrow's desire not to be suffering from a hangover). Each non-rational desire, however, considers only itself, and so considers only a part or phase of me. My initial visual impressions (e.g.

that the stick in the water is bent) cannot be trusted without rational consideration of the other available information (showing, perhaps, that the stick is really straight). Similarly, the initial tendency of my desires, before I evaluate them by reason, cannot be trusted to discover my real interests. The rational part considers my other parts and phases, and is fair to them all. If I am really *self*-interested, I must be guided by the rational part.[32]

xiv. *The defence of justice*

This account of desires shows how three of the major virtues—courage, temperance, and wisdom—are easy to recognize as different aspects of a well-ordered soul. The true judgements in the rational part make a person wise, and the subordination of non-rational to rational desires makes him temperate and brave. These three virtues, then, clearly belong to the rationally prudent person.

To show that such a person is also just, Plato considers the structure of the best city. This city is composed of three parts—the ruling class, the military class, and the producing class. Such a city, Plato assumes (for reasons to be considered later), is organized for the common good of the whole and of each part; and this organization, to which each part contributes by performing its own function, is justice in the city. Since the soul also has parts that need to be organized for their good and the good of the whole, this organization, in which each part performs its own function, is justice in the soul. It would not be worth living without this justice, any more than it would be worth living without some reasonable degree of health, because without it we could not pursue our own interest.[33]

Plato has argued that this 'psychic justice', the right relation between the parts of the soul, benefits us. But has he answered the original question about *justice*? Glaucon and Adeimantus asked about the justice that is 'another's good', since it seems to be essentially directed to the benefit of others—call this 'ordinary justice'. Could I not have psychic justice without ordinary justice?

Could I not act firmly on my rational plans, unshaken by non-rational impulses, but still form rational plans that require me to cheat other people in my own interest?[34]

To answer this objection, Plato should show that psychic justice causes us to do actions plausibly regarded as just, and to avoid actions that seem clearly unjust. The injustices that seem to benefit me offer me unjust gains at other people's expense. But unjust gains appeal to me only if I have overdeveloped irrational impulses: I want lavish and expensive foods, or the unrestricted sexual pleasures that are gained by flattery, force, and deception, or I want to be admired for my wealth and I feel ashamed if I am despised for my poverty. I have these strong desires and act on them because my irrational parts are out of control. If they are rationally controlled, I no longer have these unreasonably demanding desires. Plato shifts the onus of proof back to the opponents, and focuses on the central question—what are the rational person's real interests?[35]

xv. *Virtue and philosophy*

So far Plato's argument has not appealed to his Theory of Forms. The argument of *Republic* ii–iv does not assume that just people are philosophers, or that they accept Plato's conception of knowledge and reality. In Book v, however, he assumes that the just person will become a philosopher, will come to know the Forms of justice and the other virtues, and will come to love them. Plato argues that once we understand love of persons correctly, we see how non-personal objects display the same beauty and the same admirable qualities that we find in persons.

In Plato's account, our initial and superficial love of persons is love for their physical beauty; deeper knowledge makes us love them (either the same or different people) for the admirable qualities of their mind and character. But we find these same admirable qualities in ways of life, social orders, social and political causes. When we speak of a 'passionate crusader for justice', or a 'lover of freedom', Plato thinks this is no mere metaphor or exaggeration; we are referring to the same love of what is beautiful and admirable that we express in love of persons. The supreme object of this love is the Form of beauty; this is perfectly and completely admirable, and the source of what is admirable in anything else.[36]

Plato supposes that if our love and aspiration are fully developed, we will come to love the Form of beauty and the other Forms, in so far as they display an admirable rational order:

He will go on, and not grow dull, nor will his love slacken, until he grasps the nature of each reality [the Forms] with the part of the soul naturally suited and akin to it. And when he draws near, has intercourse with reality, and begets understanding and truth, then he truly lives and grows; and then, and only then, his birth-pangs are over.

Having seen this order, we want to 'propagate' beauty in the ways we affect the world. Plato thinks this propagation of beauty is also propagation of ourselves, significantly similar to literal propagation. I propagate myself in so far as I embody aspects of my character and personality in others; and I propagate myself in propagating beauty, in so far as I embody in others the characteristics that I value and admire. Such propagation of ourselves is, in Plato's view, the best substitute for the immortality that is denied us. Since we cannot permanently embody our conception of beauty and value in ourselves, we want to propagate it in other people, works of art, institutions, and whole societies.[37]

Since philosophers have the correct values, they want to produce justice and the other virtues in their own lives and in other people's:

Then if he finds some necessity to practise the implanting of what he sees there [in looking at the Forms] in human characters, in private and public, and not to mould only himself, do you think he will be a bad craftsman of temperance, justice, and all the virtues of a people?

This 'necessity' moves the philosopher to undertake government in the ideal state.

What sort of necessity is it? Plato suggests that, once they come to know the Forms, the philosophers will think they are in the 'isles of the blessed', enjoying supreme happiness, and will be reluctant to return to human society. They will approach government as something 'necessary', not as a prize to be grabbed. Still, everything considered, the philosopher thinks it is in his own interest to govern, because the activity of government is the best way, in the appropriate circumstances, to express his love of the Forms in other human beings. He would prefer to avoid the burdensome tasks of government, if he could make other people just without it; but in the world as it is, government is necessary for the propagation of justice.[38]

Plato's theory of love explains why philosophers have reason to be just. We expect just people to benefit others, not merely themselves; and philosophers meet this expectation. For they want the state to be organized for everyone's benefit, as a state should be, and they see that the greatest benefit for anyone is to be psychically just; hence they want to propagate psychic justice in others. Since this is the greatest benefit anyone can confer, the philosophers will satisfy a condition for ordinary justice.

The philosopher's desires are unselfish, since they extend beyond states of himself, and seek the good of others for its own sake, as the right order expressing the order of the Forms. But his desires are still self-regarding rather than selfless; he wants to create, because he wants to reproduce the character of his own soul in the product of his creative work. Contrary to Thrasymachus' suggestion, his justice is both good for others and good for himself; his moral obligations do not involve a sacrifice of self-interest.

Plato's Theory of Forms contributes, therefore, to his solution of the main problem in the *Republic*. But the solution appealing to the love of the Forms applies only to philosophers. For other people he must rely on the arguments to show that a rationally prudent person will never find that ordinary injustice benefits him.

xvi. *Knowledge, morals, and politics*

To fulfil the main task of describing justice in the individual person, the *Republic* also describes justice in a state, and sketches an ideal state embodying justice. In doing this Plato answers some questions raised by Socrates. Though Socrates was suspected of disloyalty to the Athenian democracy, he says he prefers its laws to the less democratic laws of Sparta, Boeotia, and Megara. On the other hand, he attacks the democratic system for its conscious indifference to moral and political knowledge. He denounces democracy as a system that both flatters and moulds the impressionable and irrational impulses of the public, with no concern for people's real interests.

Socrates does not argue for one form of government over another. He does not formulate the ethical criteria for judging a government or a political system. Though he lived through civil war and constitutional change, he does not try to explain them, or to show how they can be avoided. Plato takes up these questions. The *Republic* argues that the right sort of state cannot exist unless philosophers rule it. Plato's argument for this intentionally paradoxical view exposes his main moral and political assumptions.[39]

He assumes that the properly ordered state promotes the good of all its members, and that actual states are defective to the extent that they fall short of this aim. They all fall short of it because, as Thucydides shows, the pursuit of security, wealth, honour, and power produces conflict. When groups and classes in a city regard their interests as antagonistic, they really no longer constitute one city. In Plato's view, 'Every city, of whatever size, is really two cities at war with each other—the city of the poor and the city of the rich.' For Plato, this class struggle is the source of the political conflict between partisans of oligarchy and of democracy.

Some political moderates might suggest that the current aims of the rich and the poor are reconcilable; but Plato rejects this attempt to dissolve class conflicts. People think their good consists in the achievement of fame, honour, wealth, and power; for these are the 'contested' goods that people fight over. In Plato's view, if the opposing sides are right about what their interest consists in, then their interests are irreconcilable. In that case, as Thrasymachus says, principles of justice simply express the advantage of the politically dominant class, and the disadvantage of the others. Democracy satisfies the appetites of the masses, and its leaders have to gratify the popular tastes and desires. Government becomes mere flattery or pandering, resting on techniques of persuasion and manipulation. The technique Plato attacks is rhetoric; but had he known the techniques of advertising, promotion, and public relations practised in modern political propaganda, he would have found his charges confirmed beyond his worst fears. And if democracy is bad, other forms of government are no better; they gratify the equally mistaken desires of fewer people.[40]

The *Republic* argues that a person's good requires justice and the other virtues. These are not contested goods, since we can pursue them as much as we want to without conflict; and in so far as we need the other goods, just people can distribute them without insoluble conflicts. To avoid class conflicts, therefore, a city must be ruled in the common interest by people who know how to achieve it. Since most people do not know what their own interest is, or what will promote the common good, they should not be rulers. The people with the necessary knowledge are the philosophers who know the Forms; hence they must rule the ideal state.

Since the rulers must use their knowledge correctly, for the common good, Plato strains to make them morally incorruptible. They have no private property or nuclear families to divert them from the common interest. Their early education encourages concern for the common interest. Their philosophical education cultivates love of the Forms, and a resulting desire to embody them in the institutions and practices of the state. To be qualified to rule, the people with the right natural abilities need many years of education, for which they are selected in childhood (most, but not all, from the children of the ruling class). Since Plato thinks the relevant natural abilities are found in women as well as men, he expects to recruit women as philosopher-rulers as well. Women rulers are an outrageously paradoxical result—as it would seem to most Greeks—of Plato's single-minded concern for the formation of a suitably qualified ruling class.[41]

The 'lower' classes, of soldiers and productive workers, are educated far enough to appreciate the benefits they gain from the rule of the philosophers, without wanting to interfere with them. Since they do not know their own real interests, they cannot be ruled by their own reason; but they will come closest to psychic justice if they are entirely subject to the reason of the philosophers.[42]

Plato regards other constitutions as the products of mistaken conceptions of the good, and of disordered relations between the parts of the soul, resulting in disordered relations between parts of the state. His criticisms do not imply that he ever wanted or planned to overthrow the Athenian democracy. Even if, in the right conditions, the rule of philosophers is preferable, still democracy might be the best in imperfect conditions and for imperfect people. If there are no philosopher-rulers available, or if most people are unwilling to accept the rule of philosophers, it might be better to accept a democracy than to overthrow it. Plato does not commit himself to the view that a less democratic regime is always preferable to a more democratic. Though he is a severe critic of democracy, he is not necessarily a supporter of oligarchy.

xvii. *Knowledge and freedom*

Plato rejects democracy because he believes in an objective human good; and his reasons apply no less to modern than to Greek democratic regimes, despite the great differences between a Greek democracy and every modern state. Some defenders of democracy agree that if some people could know about everyone's objective interests, then their views would, as Plato says, have to be authoritative. If there is no prospect of such knowledge, Plato's case against democracy fails. Hence these defenders of democracy deny the possibility of knowledge about objective interests.

If we deny objective interests, we seem to have equally good reason to reject objective moral and political values in general. And in fact some defenders of liberty and democracy argue that since (1) there are no objective values, and (2) all values are just expressions of taste and preference, it follows that (3) we should tolerate and respect other people's values.

This argument is open to grave objections. Once we accept (1) and (2), it follows that (3) is itself simply an expression of taste and preference. If so, why should we accept (3) rather than concluding that (4) if we feel like tolerating other people, we ought to, and if we feel like coercing them, we ought to? If we accept (4), then we admit that we have no argument against those who happen to prefer less liberal policies. A similar criticism will show what is wrong with a defence of democracy that relies on rejection of objective values.[43]

We need not choose between the self-defeating defence of democracy and Plato's anti-democratic outlook. His argument assumes that democratic participation in government has only instrumental value, determined by its efficiency in promoting interests that are quite distinct from it. Against Plato, however, we might value control over what happens to us, and shared responsibility for it, even at some cost in efficiency. Each of us values himself as an agent who to some extent plans his life; and each of us shows respect for others as agents of the same sort, in so far as we decide collectively about our lives. We need not claim that the values of responsibility and control always justify an enormous cost in efficiency. To cast doubt on Plato's argument, we need claim only that there is a potential conflict between efficiency and these other values, and that Plato overlooks the conflict, because he has not attended to the other values.

Plato's attitude to democracy began a tradition of philosophical hostility or indifference (to which Aristotle is only a partial exception). Socrates, Plato, and Aristotle profited from Athenian democracy; they might have found it hard to interest people in philosophical discussion if Athenians had not already grown used to hearing and evaluating purportedly rational arguments on moral and political questions. Their hostile attitude seems to betray failure to appreciate all the effects of democracy.

Greek democracy declined; eventually, though not immediately, the argumentative habits favourable to philosophy declined also. Rhetoric and public speaking turned from argument and (moderately) rational persuasion, to flattery, panegyric, and display.[44] Still later, philosophy lost its argumentative character also. It would be too simple to see a straightforward relation of cause and effect in this sequence, and wrong to put all the blame on Plato. But it is not unfair to suppose that the philosophers and their pupils, and especially Plato, bear some responsibility.

At a more general level, however, our criticism of Plato actually supports his approach to moral and political questions. He believes these are areas that allow rationally justified claims to knowledge of objective truths. By appealing against Plato to the value of control and responsibility we commit ourselves to finding some justification for these claims. If we agree that a conventionalist defence of democracy is self-defeating, and if we support democracy by appeal to objective values that Plato overlooks, then we admit that Plato is right in taking moral and political questions to be a proper area in which to seek objective truths. He wants to replace the dominance of force, manipulation, propaganda, and ignorance, with the results of rational and objective inquiry. But to agree with him about this is not to admire his ideal state.

xviii. *The cosmos*

Plato appeals to the Form of the Good, not simply to explain the moral virtues, but to provide a teleological account of reality as a whole, and to show how natural processes are related to each other in promoting some single good. The best explanation of the natural order should interpret the world as the product of intelligent design, and thereby (since intelligent design aims at what is best) should show how it is best that the world is as it is.

Any attempt to explain human action in purely material terms, without reference to its purpose, misses its real nature:

Suppose someone undertook to explain the causes of each thing I do, and said first that I am sitting here now because my body is composed of bones and sinews, and the bones are hard, and divided by joints, while the sinews are flexible . . . Surely it is utterly absurd to call such things causes. If someone said that without these . . . I would not be able to do what I have decided on, he would be right. But to say that these things, and not my choice of what is best, are the cause of my doing what I do when I act intelligently—that would be a long and idle story to tell.

To miss the role of design and purpose in human action is to neglect the cause in favour of the necessary conditions (the bones, sinews, etc.); and Plato suggests that the naturalists make the same mistake about the universe as a whole. He rejects Atomist attempts to eliminate cosmic justice. In Plato's view, appeals to justice suggest correctly that the world is the product of intelligence.[45]

In the *Republic* Plato claims that the Form of the Good explains the nature of the other Forms, which are as they are because that is the best way for them to be. The Good also explains the nature of the sensible world, which is as it is because it shares in the goal-directed order of the Forms.

The *Timaeus* describes how the natural world comes to display its goal-directed order. It undergoes change, and lacks the stability of a Form, and hence must have come into being. But it cannot result from random or purposeless processes, since it displays the sort of order that we find in an artifact. Plato suggests that the world is indeed an artifact, produced by a 'craftsman' (Greek *dêmiourgos*, hence 'Demiurge'), who referred to the Forms. Just as a carpenter refers to a Form to define the ideal and norm of the bed or table that he aims at in production, so also the Demiurge is guided by the Forms.

The world displays a goal-directed order in the behaviour of plants and animals, and in their adaptation to their environment. All this is hard to understand within an Atomist account of the universe: in a Democritean universe it has to be a mere coincidence, with no further explanation. It becomes easy to understand, however, if a rational, designing mind causes it; and hence Plato insists that mind is a cause (though not the only cause).[46]

To explain why the Demiurge produces the world Plato turns to his psychological and moral theory. The Demiurge is a god, and hence, in Plato's view, must be entirely good and free from envy and malice. Plato rejects the Homeric conception of gods with human limitations and vices; he takes these defects to be inconsistent with the proper nature of a god as designer of the world order. Like the philosopher, the Demiurge sees the harmony and goal-directed structure of the Forms, and wants to propagate it in the world, thereby reproducing in it the order of his own soul. His motive is the same as the motive of Plato's philosopher, whose love for the Forms makes him want to extend justice and order by taking part in government.

The philosopher cannot always expect complete success in his creative work, since the natural tendencies of human beings make them less than perfectly suitable for his work. The Demiurge faces the same imperfection in the natural material that he must form into an ordered world, and hence the order he creates is imperfect. As well as the divine cause—mind ordering things for the best results—we must recognize a secondary, 'wandering' or 'aberrant' cause explaining those processes, even some regular and uniform processes, that cannot be explained teleologically.[47] In admitting this second cause Plato concedes a point to the Atomists, agreeing that not every process has a teleological explanation. But he believes the Atomists, and indeed other naturalists, were wrong in trying to eliminate purpose from the universe altogether.

xix. *Misunderstandings of Plato*

Plato's philosophy consists of a series of sharply presented questions, and of bold, speculative, and incomplete answers to them. He admits the limitations of his knowledge, and before he has worked out his answers in any detail, he moves on to new questions. The Platonic dialogues do not constitute or contain a philosophical system, and in that way they differ from the works of such philosophers as Aristotle, the Stoics, Kant, and Hegel. It is not surprising that Plato has influenced thinkers and movements with different, even opposed, outlooks.

This was already true in later Greek philosophy, when both sceptics and dogmatists traced their origins to Plato. Plato's philosophical school, the Academy, under its heads from Speusippus (*c.*407–339) to Polemon (died 270), developed the speculative metaphysics that might be derived from (among other sources) parts of the *Republic* and the *Timaeus*. But in the mid-third century Arcesilaus (316–242) became head of the Academy, and made it a home of 'Academic' Scepticism; he developed the questioning, apparently negative tendencies of some of Plato's Socratic dialogues, and especially of the long and inconclusive discussion of knowledge in the *Theaetetus*. Arcesilaus claimed to preserve the Socratic aspects of Plato—the destructive cross-examination, deflation of pretensions to knowledge, and extreme caution about making claims to knowledge. It is easy to see how a rather selective reader of some Socratic dialogues might suppose that Plato presents conflicting appearances, exposing the flaws in arguments for each side, and encouraging the suspension of judgement.

In the first century BC Antiochus (? *c.*130–*c.*68) revolted from
the Sceptical Academy to found the 'Old Academy', reviving
the dogmatic movement in Platonism begun by Speusippus. A
prominent successor of this Platonist movement was Plotinus (AD
205–70). For Plotinus the task of philosophy is to turn the human
mind from concern with the senses and the physical world, and
to reveal to it the non-physical reality that we can come to know
when we abandon the senses.[48]

A picture of Plato would be incomplete if it did not show how
someone might find support in the dialogues for both scepticism
and other-worldly dogmatism. Still, neither of these is a fair view
of Plato; and the errors in both views result from misunderstanding of his Socratic method. The Socratic cross-
examination is Plato's method for self-examination and the
reform of common-sense beliefs, not for their wholesale abandonment. He denies that the rational conclusion to draw from
Socratic examination is scepticism. Nor does he believe, as Plotinus believes under Plato's inspiration, that other-worldly mysticism is the only alternative to scepticism. Though many of
Plato's conclusions are paradoxical, he argues both from and to
the beliefs of Socrates' interlocutors. If we focus on the Socratic
and dialectical character of Plato's arguments, we can see what is
wrong or over-simplified in some apparently plausible objections
to him.

Sometimes Plato is contrasted unfavourably with some of the
naturalists, on the ground that he turns attention away from
empirical study of the natural world to the fruitless pursuit of
a priori truths about Forms. He shows evident interest in mathematics, and values it so highly that it occupies a large part of the
education of his philosopher-rulers. He regards it as a way of
turning the mind from the senses to non-sensible reality. He shows
no similar enthusiasm for natural science; and it is easy to infer
that he disdains study of the physical world because he thinks it
is inferior in degree of reality to the Forms.

This complaint rests on a misunderstanding. Plato's respect for
mathematics is strictly limited; he does not regard it as the ideal
for philosophical knowledge, or as a substitute for study of the

physical world. Though he thinks it important to recognize non-sensible Forms as well as ordinary sensible objects, he does not infer that the physical world is illusory or unintelligible. Attention to the Forms should not lead us to disregard or devalue the physical world revealed by the senses. On the contrary, as the *Timaeus* shows, it should lead us to see what is good and rational in the physical world.[49]

On these points Plato is the reverse of other-worldly. His claims about the inadequacy of the senses do not imply that the senses are worthless. The cosmological claims of the *Timaeus* could be confirmed only by detailed empirical study, to confirm or undermine Plato's suggestion that natural processes show a goal-directed order. In fact Plato's suggestion stimulates Aristotle to undertake the necessary empirical research; and while there is no evidence to suggest that Plato actually encouraged such research, there is equally little reason to suppose that he discouraged it, or that his philosophical views must have made him hostile to it.

It is equally unfair, and for similar reasons, to suppose that Plato's dualism about body and soul implies an other-worldly attitude to ethics. The immortal soul has a body committed to its charge; and when it is aware of the Forms, it will want to reproduce their order in itself, in its life in the body, and in other people. Since the world already partly embodies the Forms, the immortal soul is encouraged to try to reproduce them more fully in the world.

This desire to reproduce the character of the Forms is a motive of Plato's philosopher-rulers; their knowledge of the Forms and of their own immortality makes them more, not less, concerned with the world. Plato may fairly be called other-worldly, in so far as he is concerned with more than the physical world and what we do in it. But he is not other-worldly to the extent of renouncing concern for this world; he retains a lively concern to understand the physical world and to change human lives and human societies. On this last point his position contrasts sharply with the conclusions that Plotinus later claims to derive from Platonic premises. The *Republic* does not advise rejection of the world; on the contrary, it explains why the just pursuit of moral and political aims is worth while.

XX. *The significance of Plato*

To see what is most important about Plato, apart from his particular doctrines or the issues that he raises, we have to make up our minds about the character of philosophy. We might claim (rather superficially) that the naturalists' achievement is their degree of success in developing scientific methods of research and inquiry. But Socrates and Plato consciously articulate philosophy as a discipline distinct from empirical science, and their degree of success in doing this is their major achievement.

Hostility to these claims of philosophy to be a distinct discipline results in Bentham's (1748-1832) verdict on Socrates and Plato:

While Xenophon was writing history, and Euclid giving instruction in geometry, Socrates and Plato were talking nonsense under pretence of teaching morality and wisdom. This morality of theirs consisted in words. This wisdom of theirs, in so far as it had a meaning, consisted in denying the existence of matters made known to every body by experience [and] in asserting the existence of a variety of matters the nonexistence of which was made known to every body by experience. Exactly in proportion as they and their notions thus differed from the general mass of mankind, exactly in that same proportion were they below the level of it.[50]

If we see no point in the Socratic method, we see no point in Platonic philosophy, and we must agree with Bentham.

The naturalists' questions included some that were answerable by empirical inquiry, and some that were not. Plato clarifies the issue by distinguishing some of the philosophical questions from the more empirical questions, and by arguing that philosophical argument is neither purely empirical nor inevitably inconclusive.

To make progress in empirical inquiry, empirical scientists normally lay aside the basic questions about the nature of knowledge and reality. We may think they should do this because the questions are really unanswerable, or because our answers must rest on taste and sentiment, not on rational argument. We will be especially prone to these views if the result of our epistemological inquiries is nihilism or scepticism or Protagorean conventionalism. In each case there is no room for philosophy as a rational and constructive discipline.

Plato wants to show that the Socratic method of cross-examination is the basis of philosophy as a rational discipline. It would be foolish to use the Socratic method to settle questions in chemistry or carpentry. But when we ask basic questions, such as those discussed in the *Republic*, the accumulation of empirical information will not answer them for us. Plato argues that the Socratic method need not be arbitrary or hopelessly subjective; carefully practised, it is a source of justified claims to knowledge on fundamental questions.

7
Aristotle

i. *Aristotle and his predecessors*

We owe to Aristotle the view of Greek philosophy that sees a
sharp break between the Presocratic naturalists and the new
movement started by Socrates and continued by Plato. Socrates
turned away from the study of nature to ethics, and Plato went
on to metaphysics; both of them practised dialectic with a higher
degree of self-consciousness than their predecessors had reached.
Aristotle draws this contrast between the naturalist and the dialectical outlooks partly because he intends his own philosophical
work to reconcile the two. Aristotle advocates the study of nature,
arguing that it deserves no less attention than some people devote
to more abstract studies such as mathematics; and perhaps he
intends these remarks as a reply to Platonist enthusiasm for mathematics. But he studies nature in the light of dialectical concepts
and arguments partly derived from Plato.[1]

Aristotle was born in Macedon, in northern Greece, in 384. He
came to Athens in 367, and was a student in Plato's Academy
until Plato's death in 347. He was away from Athens from 347 to
335, first in the eastern Aegean, and then in Macedon, where he
taught Alexander (the Great), the heir to the Macedonian throne.
After his return to Athens in 335 he gave lectures in the Lyceum
(a gymnasium, and so a meeting place for Athenian men), and
formed a philosophical school there (perhaps not formally constituted until after his death). The death of Alexander in 323
encouraged anti-Macedonian feeling, and Aristotle left again; he
died in 322.

It is tempting, but misguided, to try to connect phases of
Aristotle's life with phases of his philosophical development.
We have no good reason, for instance, to suppose that his leaving
Athens after Plato's death was a sign of disaffection with the

Academy or with its new head Speusippus; it is at least as likely
that Aristotle left because of anti-Macedonian tendencies in Athens (as in 323). Nor should we suppose that his interest in biology
began after his period in the Academy. We could infer this only
if we could fairly assume that Plato and the Academy would not
have encouraged the study of biology. We have no right to assume
this, however. Plato may well have encouraged biological research; and even if he did not, members of the Academy seem to
have taken quite independent lines.² Plato does not seem to have
encouraged his pupils to become his disciples. Three of his most
distinguished pupils—Speusippus, Xenocrates (the next two
heads of the Academy), and Aristotle—disagreed vigorously both
with each other and with Plato. Throughout his career, as far as
we know, Aristotle formed his own views partly by critical reflexion on Plato.³

ii. *Observation and experience*

Aristotle seeks to revive the study of nature, and to release it from
scepticism, by closer attention to observation. Previous naturalist
theories offered a rather confusing variety of very general hypotheses and speculative theories uncontrolled by detailed acquaintance with the empirical facts. Without the necessary
empirical evidence it might well prove hard to decide between
theories; such circumstances readily encourage the view that there
is no way to decide between theories and that scepticism is the
only proper reaction. Aristotle argues, however, that the situation
is not so bad; empirical investigation should help us to decide
between theories.

Inadequate empirical investigation, in his view, makes us unable to form a comprehensive and plausible theory:

Lack of experience diminishes our power of taking a comprehensive view
of the admitted facts. Hence those who are more closely acquainted with
natural things are more able to lay down principles of a sort that cohere
over a wide area; while those who because of their practice of arguments
[*logos*] have not studied the facts are more prone to state a view on the
basis of a few observations.

Aristotle rejects (for these purposes) the study and practice of argument in abstraction from observation. Plato's Socrates turned from the observation of nature to the study of arguments (*logos*), but Aristotle advocates the reverse process.[4] To prevent premature theorizing, he urges us to study the relevant 'appearances' (*phainomena*), the apparent observations, before we form theories, since otherwise we will not know what we want our theories to explain. Once we have formed our theory we should test it by looking for further appearances; for a good theory will cover the widest range of appearances we can find.

Aristotle proves his interest in appearances by his large and detailed plan of empirical research. His longest work is the *History of Animals* (Greek *historia*, 'inquiry'), better described as the 'Inquiry into Animals', a large compilation of observations about animals, which is to be the basis of his theoretical speculations in biology.[5] He conducts empirical inquiry with the attention to detail that is found in some of the medical case histories (Aristotle's own father was in fact a doctor). He also pursues empirical inquiry into human history and society; he compiled (perhaps with his pupils) accounts of 158 Greek constitutions (only one of which, the *Constitution of Athens*, largely survives). This detailed research lies behind Aristotle's political theory.[6]

Aristotle therefore claims to have studied the appearances better than his predecessors did; and he often likes to correct previous writers:

In hairy-coated animals the sperm is sticky, but in other animals it is not so. It is white in all cases, and Herodotus is under a misapprehension when he states that the Ethiopians eject black semen.

Herodotus, he says, was a spinner of tales (*muthologos*), too ready to believe tall stories.

Not surprisingly, Aristotle makes some mistakes of his own in reporting alleged observations. More important, he tends to exaggerate the decisiveness of observations in settling disputes between theories. He speaks as though it is a matter of observation that the four basic elements naturally tend towards different places in the universe, and he is apt to assume that observation can decide quite briskly against the claims of Atomist theories.

Still, Aristotle is right to advise students of nature to test their theories against a wider range of observations than they normally consider:

Such appears to be the truth about the reproduction of bees, judging from argument [*logos*] and from what are believed to be the facts about them. The facts, however, have not been sufficiently grasped. If they are grasped, then credence must be given to perceptions more than to arguments, and to arguments if what they affirm agrees with the appearances.

The Greek naturalists could not have made much progress if they had listened to Aristotle's advice from the beginning; but the advice is reasonable for a discipline that has passed its initial stages.[7]

iii. *Philosophical argument*

Aristotle owes his conception of philosophical method to Plato. Philosophy, like empirical inquiry, relies on 'appearances', but on appearances of a different sort from those we have described so far. The appearances relevant to it are not empirical observations, but common beliefs, assumptions widely shared by 'the many and the wise'; and the critical and constructive study of these common beliefs is 'dialectic'. Aristotle uses the term Plato uses for the Socratic cross-examination, and his method is basically Socratic. He raises puzzles in the common beliefs, looking for an account that will do them justice as a whole. He describes his method in the discussion of weakness of will:

We must, as in the other cases, set out the appearances, and then first raise the puzzles < about them >. In this way we must prove, ideally, all the common beliefs, and if not all of them, at least most of them, and the most important. For if the difficulties are dissolved, and the common beliefs are left standing, that will be a sufficient proof.

A theory that does not do justice to the common beliefs, but rejects them wholesale, or a theory that raises more puzzles than it solves, must be rejected. Aristotle believes that both Platonist and Atomist theories must be rejected, as they stand, for both of these reasons; but he thinks each theory offers some help in finding a better solution of the puzzles.

Aristotle thinks dialectic is the right method for finding the 'first principles of the sciences'. For our approach to the observed appearances is controlled by our attitude to the dialectical appearances; unexamined assumptions cause us to misinterpret observations in ways that lead us into insoluble puzzles. On the other hand, a better grasp of the dialectical appearances allows us to approach empirical questions with the right assumptions and presuppositions.[8]

iv. *Nature and change*

Aristotle's *Physics* is a dialectical examination of nature, *phusis*, the subject of Presocratic inquiries. Like the naturalists, Aristotle wants to find the laws and regularities that make natural change intelligible; and he argues that to find the right laws, we must recognize both form and matter.

In *Physics* i Aristotle analyses natural change:

(*a*) All change involves some subject that undergoes it; and the subject undergoes the change by losing one of a pair of contrary properties and acquiring the other.

(*b*) The general pattern in (*a*) applies both when (*b*1) the same subject persists and no new subject comes into being (a 'qualified' coming into being), and when (*b*2) a new subject comes into being (an 'unqualified' coming into being).

If, for instance, Socrates is first thin and then fat, he satisfies (*b*1). The same subject, Socrates, exists all the time, and no new subject comes into being; but he loses one contrary, thinness, and gains another, fatness. If, by contrast, a statue comes into being from a lump of bronze, it satisfies (*b*2). The lump of bronze acquires the shape of the statue, and loses the shapelessness it had, and so changes between contraries. But though the lump remains in existence, a new subject, the statue, has come into being.[9]

This example introduces some of the basic items that should be recognized in an account of change:

1. A particular subject of change (Socrates or the lump of bronze) is a 'first substance' (or 'first being'; the Greek *ousia* is

the abstract noun from the verb 'to be'). A first substance remains in existence when it exchanges one contrary for another, and Socrates does this in changing from being thin to being fat.

2. A second substance is a universal (e.g. man or horse). It is the sort of property that a first substance must possess if it is to remain in existence. Socrates, we may say, is essentially a man; if he ceases to be a man, he ceases to exist.[10] As Aristotle says, the second substance shows us what a first substance is. In applying a second-substance term to a first substance (as in 'Socrates is a man'), we place the first substance in the kind it belongs to; in predicating a non-substance term (as in 'Socrates is pale'), we simply describe the first substance, and do not place it in its kind.

3. The non-substantial particulars and universals belong to the categories of quality, quantity, relative, and so on. These are the properties that a first substance can gain or lose without itself ceasing to exist; they are its non-essential ('coincidental') properties.[11]

These three elements underlie Aristotle's account of qualified becoming (type *b*1).

The division between second substances and non-substances explains a feature of common beliefs that deserves the dialectician's attention because it might raise puzzles. If Socrates gets fat, why should we not say that Socrates has perished, and that he has been replaced by a new thing, fat-Socrates? This conception of change makes every ostensible qualified becoming into an unqualified becoming. Aristotle replies that not every loss of a property implies that the subject perishes; any reasonable conception of a subject requires a distinction between its essential and its non-essential properties, and this distinction underlies the division between the two types of becoming.

In recognizing universals (both substantial—e.g. horse, animal—and non-substantial—e.g. white, colour) as well as particulars, Aristotle seeks to explain how it is that many particulars of the same kind all have something in common. Just as Socrates in Plato's *Euthyphro* looks for the one pious besides the many piouses, Aristotle looks for the 'one over many' that is the same in all the relevant particulars. He agrees with Plato's belief in universals; but in so far as this belief led Plato to his Theory of Forms, Aristotle thinks Plato misunderstood the problem of universals.

To expose Plato's misunderstanding, Aristotle focuses on two aspects of Platonic Forms (as he conceives them): their separation from sensible particulars (beauty exists even if no beautiful sensible particular exists), and their self-predication (beauty is beautiful, the Form of man is a man, and so on). Both aspects of the Forms, in Aristotle's view, could belong only to particulars. Plato takes the Form of *F* to be the 'one over many'—the universal, or single property, that the many *F*s have in common; but acceptance of separation and self-predication shows, if Aristotle is right, that Plato has not succeeded in doing what he sets out to do. Though he takes the Forms to be universals, Plato treats universals, not as something different from particulars, but as rather unusual particulars.

Aristotle believes that Plato's conception of Forms not only fails to distinguish universals from particulars, but leads to intolerable consequences resulting from this failure. Self-predication and separation imply that what particular men have in common is not the Platonic Form of man, but the universal property that they share with the Platonic Form (assumed to be another particular man). Plato, then, has still not described the property he was trying to describe; if this is a Form it must be a second Form besides the initial Form of man (hence it is a 'third man', besides a given particular man and the Form); but the very same argument requires yet another Form, and so on in an infinite regress.

Aristotle refers to this as the 'Third Man' regress, and thinks it is the result of Plato's misconception of universals as particulars:

[That no universal is a first substance] is evident from the fact that nothing predicated in common signifies a this [i.e. a particular]. Otherwise many <difficulties> arise, including the Third Man.

Plato's Theory of Forms therefore fails to solve the initial puzzles in the appearances, and raises worse puzzles of its own; Aristotle argues that it simply reduplicates particulars without explaining anything about them. In Aristotle's view, Plato offers a pseudo-solution, because he does not correctly grasp the problem; but a fuller study of the appearances and the puzzles leads to a clearer grasp of the problem. The correctness of Aristotle's criticism of Plato is open to dispute; but his objections at least expose serious obscurities and difficulties in Plato's views. In rejecting Plato's views, he expresses his own belief in the reality of universals, and formulates, more clearly than Plato ever does, the differences between universals and particulars.[12]

v. *Form and matter*

When Aristotle turns to discussion of unqualified becoming (type *b2*), he introduces two further elements besides the three we have discussed:

4. Matter is the particular subject that underlies, since it existed previously, and remains in existence when a first substance comes into being from it—the lump of bronze, for example, is the matter of the statue.[13]

5. Form is what the matter acquires when a first substance comes into being. The lump of bronze acquires a form by acquiring the shape and representational features of the statue, and the wood in a tree has a form in so far as it has the right sort of order and structure for a tree.

We say what the sculptor has made by mentioning its form ('a statue representing Pericles') rather than its matter. Though the statue is *made of* bronze, *what* it is is a statue; it cannot simply be the bronze, since the statue may cease to exist (by being melted down) while the bronze still exists.[14]

Aristotle believes that formal things (e.g. statues and horses) as well as purely material things (e.g. lumps of bronze) are first substances. In making this claim he challenges an argument of Heracleitus. As we saw, Heracleitus accepts a compositional principle of identity, assuming that something remains the same thing only if it is composed of just the same stuff; this principle explains why we (allegedly) cannot step into the same river twice, and in general explains why there turn out to be many fewer persisting things than we supposed there were. Aristotle rejects the compositional principle; he argues that if the form remains stable, even though the composition changes, the same thing remains in existence, so that we can, contrary to Heracleitus, step into the same river twice.[15]

In this case Aristotle appeals to form to argue that there are fewer unqualified becomings than Heracleitus supposed. He also appeals to form to argue that there are more unqualified becomings than the Atomists supposed. From an Atomist point of view, the unqualified coming to be of a tree or a horse is simply a rearrangement of the underlying matter; why not say it is just a qualified becoming in the matter, and that no new substance comes into being at all? This argument led Anaxagoras to conclude that the Greek language was mistaken in speaking of unqualified becoming, and should have spoken simply of mixture and separation of elements.

Aristotle sees the possibility of such an argument to show that matter is the only substance:

Some identify the nature or substance of a natural object with the primary constituent of it, which is unordered in itself, e.g. the wood is the nature of the bed, and the bronze the nature of the statue ... But if each of these has itself the same relation to something else, say bronze (or gold) to water, bones (or wood) to earth, and so on, *that* (they say) would be their nature and substance.

In reply Aristotle argues that the unqualified becoming happens when a form comes into being in a bit of matter. Socrates survives a change of size because his form precedes and survives the change (i.e. the man still exists); but his coming into being and his perishing are not merely qualified becomings in his matter, because in these cases his form either does not precede the change or does not survive it.[16]

Unlike Heracleitus and the Atomists, Aristotle stays quite close to common sense. His scheme of substance, form, and matter captures common beliefs about when things come into existence or cease to exist, and when they simply change. But why should we prefer to follow common sense? Is it an arbitrary or unjustified preference?

vi. *Causes*

To show why form is important, Aristotle relies on his views about causes. He recognizes four types of cause, capturing four

ways we can answer the question 'Why does this event happen?',
or 'Why is this object as it is?' We can answer these why-questions
about a statue (e.g.), by saying:

1. It is made of bronze (the material cause, mentioning the
matter).

2. It represents Pericles (the formal cause, stating the definition
that says what the thing is).

3. A sculptor made it (the efficient cause, mentioning the origin
of the process that brought the statue into being).

4. It is intended to represent Pericles (the 'final' cause, mentioning the goal or end for which it was made).[17]

Each of these four is *an* answer to the why-question, and states a
cause; a complete answer states as many of the four causes as are
appropriate for a given type of event.

If something has a final cause, its final and formal causes will
be very closely connected; for the definition requires reference to
the goal and the intended function—a particular hammer remains
in being as long as this particular thing with this function of
hammering remains in being. Aristotle argues that we must admit
formal and final causes, not only the material causes recognized
by previous naturalists. A hammer's form and essence is a capacity to hammer nails into wood. The hammer was designed to
have this capacity for performing this function; and if this had
not been its function, it would not have been made in the way it
was, to have the properties it has. Since the design partly caused
the hammer to come into being with the properties it has, we
must mention the form to explain why the hammer has these
properties.

The explanatory role of form shows why Aristotle is right to
appeal to form in order to distinguish unqualified from qualified
becoming. If a hammer retains its function, even though it is
painted or gets dirty, the same properties explain its characteristics, and it is reasonable to say that the same thing survives.
The belief that the hammer's getting dirty is a qualified becoming,
but its breaking is an unqualified becoming (a perishing), turns
out to be well founded. Materialists may want to agree with the
common-sense judgements about when a hammer merely

changes, and when it perishes; but they are not entitled to agree
with them unless they recognize the reality of form. Aristotle
points out that simple and apparently uncontroversial judgements
about change and becoming presuppose the general views that he
sums up in his claims about form.

vii. *Nature and form*

Aristotle also insists on the reality of form in natural organisms.
For he argues that, contrary to the Presocratic view, plants and
animals have final causes, and therefore that their essence, no less
than the essence of artifacts, is to be found in their form, not in
their matter. He notices that the parts of a natural organism seem
to perform functions that benefit the whole: hearts pump blood,
the senses convey useful information, camouflage helps animals
to avoid predators, and so on. Aristotle claims that such parts as
hearts and teeth have final causes, that they exist in order to
produce the benefit they actually produce. 'In order to' may suggest to us that he believes natural organisms and their parts are
designed for a purpose; and Plato certainly believes this in the
Phaedo and the *Timaeus*. But Aristotle does not agree that every
final cause must involve a designer.[18]

Design is one case in which the character of the result of a
process explains the character and occurrence of the process (e.g.
the fact that the hammer drives nails into wood explains why it
was made as it was). But the result may explain the process even
in cases where there is no design. Social and economic institutions
and practices may become and remain dominant because they
serve the interests of the dominant class in a society, even if no
one intends them to have that effect (Marxists do not necessarily
believe in conspiracies). Similarly, a theory of evolution may show
that these animals have this colour because it camouflages them,
even if no design is involved. The ancestors of these animals may
have acquired the colour as a result of random mutation, and not
because it benefited them; but if the benefit of this colour to past
generations has promoted the survival and reproduction of this
species, then it is correct to say that the later generations have
this colour because it camouflages them, and hence benefits them.

When Aristotle claims that natural organisms and processes exist because they promote some good for organisms, his claim remains plausible, as it is in this example, even without any appeal to design.

To claim *that* form and function explain something, then, is not to say *how*—by what process—they produce a result. Plato's hypothesis of design is one possible account of how they do it. A theory of evolution is another. Aristotle in fact believes neither of these accounts.[19] His belief in final causes is not exactly a scientific hypothesis, but a claim about the type of scientific hypothesis we should accept. When he claims there are formal and final causes, he does not endorse design or evolution, or any other particular theory, as the right hypothesis about the relevant processes; he simply claims that the right sort of hypothesis must show how form and function explain the properties and behaviour of natural organisms.

Aristotle is right to suppose that final causes are important. We normally believe that animals' hearts have the structure they have because they are for pumping blood, and that teacups have the shape they have because they are for holding tea. These explanations lead us to expect some analogies and similarities between different hearts or teacups. We expect a teacup to be strong enough to hold tea, not liable to dissolve when hot liquid touches it, concave enough for tea to stay inside, open enough for the tea to run out fairly easily. If we did not think of the functional explanation, we would find it hard even to identity the class of teacups; for they differ in size, shape, colour, and material constitution. Any attempt at a purely material, non-functional account of teacups will display the compresence of opposites that Plato noticed in other defective attempts at definition.[20] If we cannot identify the class, we will not be able to identify the most important property that teacups have in common.

The same sort of argument shows what we lose if we give up thinking of organs or organisms in functional terms. In so far as laws about organs and organisms, as such, explain their structure and behaviour, we cannot ignore their functions and their goal-directed structures in trying to understand them. The materialists who appeal only to material processes cannot explain all we want explained. To this extent Aristotle argues that common sense is right in recognizing essentially formal things (artifacts, organisms) as substances, and in resisting the claim that matter is the only substance.

viii. *Soul and body*

In Aristotle's view, disputes about soul and body are simply a special case of the more general disputes about form and matter. Once again he contrasts the errors of the Presocratics and of Plato, and claims that a true conception of form and matter allows us to capture what is true in the conflicting views. Here as elsewhere, the good dialectician should show us how to understand the received views, why people arrive at them and find them plausible, and how we can avoid their difficulties while we retain their insights.

Atomist views about the soul expose the main tendency of naturalist materialism:

Democritus . . . uses language like that of the comic dramatist Philippus, who says Daedalus made his wooden Aphrodite move by pouring quicksilver into it. Similarly, Democritus says that the spherical atoms owing to their own ceaseless movements draw the whole body after them, and so cause it to move . . . In general it is not in this way that the soul appears to cause animals to move, but through some sort of decision or thought.

Aristotle's comment suggests that he thinks a purely material explanation is wrong in principle; it fails to recognize how a living organism differs from a wooden statue moved by purely material processes, with no goal of its own. The preference for 'decision or thought' recalls Plato's preference for rational explanation over mere reference to mechanical processes.[21]

Aristotle argues that soul is substance because it is the form of a natural body, and that the body is the matter informed by the soul. But he rejects Plato's further claim that it is independent of the body. He compares three relations that he takes to be instances of matter and form: the iron and the cutting in an axe; the flesh and the seeing in an eye; and body and soul. He claims that, like the cutting and the seeing, the soul is inseparable from matter. The form is something beyond the matter, just as the word 'cat' is something beyond its constituent letters (since the letters have to be arranged in the right order before they constitute this word rather than the word 'act' or the non-word 'tca'). But we should not regard the form as some further immaterial element or constituent that must be added to the material constituents:

> Hence we need not ask whether the soul and the body are one, any more than we need ask whether the wax and the shape are one, or in general whether something's matter and the thing that has the matter are one.

A mere collection of flesh and bones is not necessarily a living creature, and the collection that is left when Socrates dies is no more Socrates than a glass eye is really an eye. But it does not follow that the soul is independent of a material body.[22]

If the soul is the form of the body, reference to the soul should state the formal and final cause of a creature's behaviour. We say, for instance, that the dog leaped up to get the plate of meat because he saw it and wanted it. Here we mention the final cause or goal ('to get the plate of meat'), and show why this goal explains the action ('because he saw it and wanted it'). When we mention the states of a creature's soul—perception, belief, thought, desire, pleasure, or pain—we explain its behaviour in formal, functional terms. Aristotle therefore takes states of the soul to be formal, functional states of a living creature.

ix. *Dualism and materialism*

Aristotle does not claim that materialism cannot possibly be true—if materialism claims simply that persons, and other things with souls, have material constituents and no others. Aristotle neither accepts nor rejects this view, and he wants to show that it is consistent with the existence of souls that are substances distinct from matter.[23] When he protests against Democritus' account of how the soul moves the body, he does not mean that decision and thought require non-material events or processes. He means that Democritus is wrong to think he has an adequate account of psychological states.

The reasons that support functional explanation in general also support explanations referring to mental states. We claim confidently that if someone is hungry, sees food, likes it, and does not think it is rotten, poisoned, someone else's, etc., it is fairly probable that he will try to eat it. It is hard to state this rough, but useful, psychological law without psychological terms. The physiological states corresponding to hunger in different people, or in the same person at different times, may be quite different. If so, and if we avoid psychological terms, we will not be able to identify the right states to provide the explanations we want. The materialist attempt to eliminate reference to mental states removes the prospect of finding the laws and explanations that are available if we recognize mental states.

We may think that if materialism is true, then there can be no important difference between human beings and other collections of matter; though we think we act on reasons, and on free and responsible choices, must we not be wrong, if we are collections of matter governed by the same laws that govern other collections of matter? Democritus seems to be forced to this conclusion, not because he thinks everything is composed of atoms and of no immaterial components (constitutive atomism), but because he thinks only the atoms are real, and that the appearances are deceptive and misleading about the nature of reality (eliminative atomism). The appearances that Democritus explicitly rejects are those that involve colour and other perceptible properties; but acceptance of his argument equally commits us to rejection of our belief in mental states, as one of the illusions of common sense.[24]

Aristotle argues, however, that Democritean materialism should be rejected, and that forms, and therefore souls, not only matter, are parts of reality. If he is right, then we need not follow Democritean materialism in revising and rejecting our basic assumptions about minds and human beings. We are free to reject dualism, and still to maintain our views about the distinctiveness of human beings. Aristotle does not convince all his successors on this issue; but he suggests a reasonable third position besides those of Democritus and Plato.[25]

x. *The human good*

Common beliefs about morality contain the puzzles and apparent
conflicts that demand dialectical examination; for we tend to
believe that I have good reason to do what is in my own interest,
that I have good reason to accept justice and morality, and that
justice and morality are often not in my interest. Aristotle expects
a clearer account of a person's good to show us that justice is
good for us. Most people, he thinks, are wrong about the nature
of self-love or concern for one's own interest:

Those who use the term as one of reproach ascribe self-love to people
who assign to themselves the greater share of wealth, honours, and
bodily pleasures; for these are what most people desire and busy themselves about as though they were the best of all things, which is also the
reason why these things become objects of competition.

Aristotle thinks this is the wrong view of self-love, and that it
rests on the wrong view of one's own good.[26]

He has good reason, then, for beginning his *Ethics* with an
examination of the human good, which he identifies with *eudaimonia*. 'Happiness' is the commonest and best English rendering of '*eudaimonia*'; but it may suggest something more precise
and less plausible than what Socrates, Plato, and Aristotle (and
their audiences) initially have in mind. '*Eudaimonia*' refers to
well-being or welfare in general, with no presumption that this
must consist in pleasure, enjoyment, contentment, or indeed in
any particular sort of feeling.[27]

In describing the human good, Aristotle wants to find the ultimate goal for rational human action. Rational action is goal-
directed: a carpenter making a chair is guided by his conception
of the chair that is his goal, and a golfer playing a stroke is aiming
to move his ball nearer the hole. Each of these 'obvious' goals is
in turn a means to some further end: the carpenter perhaps wants
to make chairs to earn money, again for some further end, and
the golfer wants to win the game, perhaps for some further end.
In looking for the ultimate end, Aristotle looks for the end of *all*
rational action, the one end that is not itself a means to some
further end.

But why should there be any such thing? We might reply to Aristotle that each of us has many ultimate ends: we might want to have interesting careers, to be good athletes, to enjoy the pleasures of eating and drinking, to play musical instruments, and so on. We might say that each of these is *an* ultimate end, chosen for its own sake, and not merely as a means to some further end. Why, then, does Aristotle insist that there is some end more ultimate than these?

He claims that happiness is the compound of ends like these, rationally ordered so as to achieve the complete good. Rational order is needed because, even if I pursue these activities for their own sake, I will not get the total result I want if I pursue them in the wrong proportion or the wrong sequence. I may realistically want to be both a painter and a weightlifter. But if weight-lifting makes my hands shake too much for painting, I will be wise not to lift weights too often, and not to lift them just before I paint. To achieve the total result I want, I will have to combine, on some rational principles, the different activities I have reason to pursue. This rational combination is the sort of ultimate end that Aristotle calls 'happiness' or 'the human good'.

Aristotle appeals to the widely shared common belief that happiness is complete, including all that a rational being can reasonably want. If we think some good G is to be identified with happiness, but then find that we can add some further good H to G, so that the total of $G + H$ is a greater good than G alone, then G cannot be identified with happiness. If we agree that this is a reasonable assumption about happiness, then we challenge two conceptions of happiness that are popular among Aristotle's predecessors and successors.

First, we cast doubt on Socrates' claim that virtue is sufficient for happiness. For, however virtuous someone may be, we can imagine some further good being added that is not guaranteed by his virtue; if, for instance, the virtuous person is persecuted and tortured, he lacks some goods, and would be better off if he had them. Aristotle protests that if we say a virtuous person being tortured and abused is happy, our position is manifestly untenable—we will maintain it only if we are desperate to defend our position at all costs, and refuse to revise our beliefs according to normal dialectical principles advocated by Socrates himself. We should not agree, then, that virtue is sufficient for happiness.

Second, Aristotle thinks a similar appeal to the completeness of happiness defeats those who identify pleasure with happiness. He thinks I could be immensely pleased, not at all dissatisfied with my life, and entirely convinced I was getting everything I wanted, and still fail to achieve happiness:

> No one would choose to live with the intellect of a child throughout his life, even if he got the greatest possible pleasure from the things that please children, nor to enjoy doing some most shameful action, even if he were never going to feel any pain.

If I had a brain operation or an accident that reduced me to the condition of a contented child, I would have become worse off, not better off. Further goods can be added to contentment or pleasure to make the person who has them better off; since happiness is complete, and pleasure is not, pleasure cannot be happiness.[28]

Having rejected these two conceptions of happiness, Aristotle offers his own account. He claims that the good for a human being must be the exercise of the human 'function' (or 'characteristic activity', *ergon*). To find a person's function he appeals to his views on the form and essence of a human being. The general view of form implies that a creature's form is the goal, the pattern of activity for which the creature's different states and capacities are organized. The relevant pattern of activity specifying the form or function of a human being is life guided by reason; hence the good for a human being must be a good life guided by reason. A life that is not guided by reason might be good for some other sort of creature, but not for a human being.[29]

This sketch of the human good can claim support from the common beliefs that undermined the other two conceptions of happiness. The argument against pleasure suggested that I would be worse off if I sank to the condition of a fool or a child or a victim of severe brain-damage, and no longer realized the capacities of a rational human agent. Mere contentment or pleasure at a low level of rational activity does not seem to be the best condition for a human being; and to that extent we agree with

Aristotle in believing that a human being's good must involve some expression of his essentially (though not exclusively) rational nature. Moreover, we reject the Socratic claim, in so far as a virtuous person in unfavourable conditions loses opportunities for rational activity.

But even if Aristotle's sketch is plausible as far as it goes, is it too general and too vague? Does it really help to answer any interesting questions about morality?

xi. *Happiness and virtue*

In *Republic* iv Plato argues that not all our desires are rational; and he claims that domination by non-rational desires is a source of psychic damage and harm. Aristotle's account of happiness as a life guided by reason explains why Plato's claim is correct; for the more we are dominated by non-rational desires, the less rational activity is present in our lives. A person whose outlook and character express the right view of happiness will have his non-rational desires controlled and organized by rational desires. This is the virtuous person; and in describing the virtues Aristotle shows how different states of character should be formed and co-ordinated for the virtuous person's benefit.

Control and organization should not result in the suppression of non-rational desires, or in a permanent struggle and conflict. The completeness of happiness implies that the satisfaction of non-rational desires—for example, the desires for food, drink, and sex, or for honour and reputation—has a legitimate place in a human being's life. A life to which these satisfactions are added is, to that extent, better than one that lacks them; and since happiness is a complete life, it should include these goods. The virtuous person, then, allows the proper place to these non-rational desires, and keeps them in harmony, not in conflict, with his rational plans. When Aristotle says that virtue should aim at a 'mean' (or 'intermediate state') of feelings and appetites, between total suppression and total indulgence, this is the sort of harmony and moderation that he has in mind.[30]

This 'doctrine of the mean' provides a general outline of the virtues; now we need to know which states of character satisfy the outline. Aristotle's selection of virtues will determine the particular moral conclusions to be drawn from his general theory; and his theory will be informative, rather than uselessly empty, if it justifies the selection of some states of character rather than others.

Courage and temperance, two of Plato's four cardinal virtues, support Aristotle's claims. A brave person is not distracted from pursuit of his rational plans by excessive fears; nor, however, is he so recklessly over-confident that he fears nothing, or so indifferent to his own life that he does not care if he loses it. Similarly, a temperate person is not distracted from his rational plans by excessive attachment to particular appetites and enjoyments; but he is not so unaware of these appetites that he is indifferent to the pleasure of satisfying them in the right circumstances. In each case, a rational person benefits from the harmony of his rational and non-rational desires.

The further cardinal virtue of wisdom aims directly at the rational pursuit of happiness. The wise person is the one who can deliberate about the proper combination of different goods that will result in the best life as a whole; and this virtue of wisdom will also be essential to the happy life, as Aristotle conceives it.[31]

xii. *Virtue and the good of others*

Apparently I might agree with all that Aristotle has said about courage, temperance, and wisdom, and still reject justice. The self-regarding virtues, I might say, are good for me, but justice is concerned with the good of others, not with my good. If Aristotle is right to include justice among the virtues, he ought to show that my justice promotes my happiness.

To show this he relies on his claim that a human being's happiness depends on human nature:

The complete good is thought to be self-sufficient. Now by self-sufficient we do not mean that which is sufficient for a man all by himself, for one who lives a solitary life, but also for parents, children, wife, and in general for friends and fellow-citizens, since a human being is by nature a political < animal >.

A human being, he claims, is a political animal in so far as human capacities and aims are completely fulfilled only in a community; the individual's happiness must involve the good of fellow-members of a community.[32] Aristotle does not mean that everyone always desires the good of others as well as his own good. He means that someone lacks a complete life, fulfilling human nature, without some concern for the good of other people. If we are indifferent to the good of others, we deny ourselves the relations of co-operation and mutual concern and trust that are necessary for the fulfilment of human capacities.

Aristotle defends this claim in his discussion of friendship. Friendship of the best type requires concern for another person for his own sake; and when we act on this concern, we are capable of concerns, achievements, and co-operative activities that would otherwise be denied to us. I will not derive much enjoyment from playing in a team, or in an orchestra, or working on some collaborative project, if I care only about my own success. If I care about the success of others too, I can take pleasure in their success, and in collective successes, not simply in my own.[33] By expanding the range of my concerns, co-operative altruism expands the range of my possible activities, and thereby allows me to achieve my good more completely. Since happiness requires a complete and self-sufficient life, and since a solitary person with aims confined to himself cannot achieve such a life, the happy life requires friendship.

Aristotle therefore answers the attack on justice, not by urging us to sacrifice our own good to the claims of justice, but by showing that we sacrifice our own good if we ignore the claims of justice. Thrasymachus argues against justice by arguing that it sometimes requires me to sacrifice my good for the good of the community. Aristotle agrees that justice sometimes requires the sacrifice of some goods; but he argues that it actually advances my good. His general strategy is similar to Plato's; but his account of the benefits of friendship and community supports his own characteristic defence of justice.

xiii. Ethics and society

Aristotle, like Plato, wants to show how his ethical conclusions imply further consequences about the proper aims of a political community, and about its appropriate form of government.

He criticizes Plato for wanting the ideal state to be more unified than a state should be; Plato models the unity of the state on the unity of a single organism, and Aristotle thinks this is entirely the wrong model. He rejects Plato's abolition of private property, complaining that Plato removes the sort of discretion and freedom that is necessary for friendship and generosity: how can I benefit my friends, or be generous to the right causes, if I have no resources at my disposal? Plato makes an equally grave mistake when he concentrates power and political initiative in a small class of philosopher-rulers; Aristotle answers that all the citizens should share in political initiative.[34]

These criticisms reflect a more general ethical demand on political life, arising from Aristotle's claims about friendship. In his view, co-operative activity is a part of a person's own good, not a disagreeable obligation that he must undertake to avoid unwelcome consequences. The state is therefore not just a necessity or a convenience; it is also an area for active co-operation. Even a proof that philosopher-rulers would be more efficient than any other regime would not, in Aristotle's view, show that philosophers should rule and other citizens should have no share in ruling; for to deprive them of a share in government is to deprive them of part of their good.[35]

Aristotle, therefore, is much friendlier than Plato is to democracy, in both the Greek and the modern sense. He holds other views, however, that are strongly anti-democratic, in so far as they deny any share in political activity to people without a fairly high level of wealth and property. None of the citizens of his ideal state should be manual labourers, or engaged in trade or finance; these tasks should be assigned to non-citizens, and the most menial of them to slaves. Aristotle admits that slavery is unjust if it is the result of conquest; but he thinks there are 'natural slaves', who lack the developed rational capacities of a normal human being; and for a natural slave, he holds, slavery is not only excusable, but even beneficial to the slave himself. Unlike Plato,

Aristotle assumes that women must in principle be excluded from a share in political activity, because of presumed natural differences. In general, he believes that the natural differences between human beings are sharp enough to make the restriction of political activity both expedient and just.[36]

These anti-democratic views are consistent with the pro-democratic criticisms of Plato; indeed, they rest on the very same ethical principles. Aristotle believes that the state should promote the good of its citizens, and that political activity is a part of their good. He infers that people who are incapable of political activity should not be citizens, and that the happiness of citizens requires the labour of others to produce the necessities of life, leaving the citizens free for political activity.

To prove Aristotle wrong we must either deny that political activity is a part of a person's good or deny that menial labour (manual, industrial, commercial) precludes the right sort of political activity. He argues quite plausibly that people's predominant occupation in life is liable to affect their moral and political outlook; but we may well doubt whether the solution he adopts is the only reasonable inference to draw from these facts.

xiv. *Ethics and self-sufficiency*

We have seen how happiness requires justice and political activity. But Aristotle also *seems* to identify happiness exclusively with pure intellectual activity (or 'study', *theôria*)—the contemplation of scientific and philosophical truths, apart from any attempt to apply them to practice. Plato is sometimes attracted by this view of a person's good, and suggests that the philosopher will be wholly absorbed in the contemplation of Forms. Though Aristotle does not believe in Platonic Forms, he seems to share Plato's contemplative ideal.

Two features of contemplation seem to give Aristotle his reasons for thinking it is a plausible candidate for happiness. First, it is the highest fulfilment of our nature as rational beings; it is the sort of rational activity that we share with the gods, who are rational beings with no need to apply reason to practice. Second, it is the most self-contained activity, since, unlike other alleged components of happiness, it is not vulnerable to the sorts of external misfortune that might deprive a virtuous person of the opportunity to exercise his virtues.

Aristotle does not believe, however, that these features of contemplation justify us in identifying it with happiness. He agrees that if we were pure intellects with no other desires and no bodies, contemplation would be the whole of our good (as it is for an immortal soul, as Plato conceives it in the *Phaedo*). Still, we are not in fact merely intellects; and so Aristotle recognizes that the good must be the good of the whole human being. In his considered view, contemplation is the highest and best part of our good, but not the whole of it.

The same points apply to claims about self-sufficiency. We have good reason to prefer, other things being equal, a good that is invulnerable to external circumstances over one that is vulnerable to them. But in this case other things do not seem to be equal. Aristotle has argued that happiness must be complete, and for this reason he argues that neither virtue alone nor pleasure alone can be happiness. He should not, then, agree that contemplation is happiness just because it is invulnerable and self-contained. For contemplation is not the complete good; we can think of other goods (e.g. virtue and honour) that could be added to it to make a better good than contemplation alone.[37]

This dispute about happiness raises a question about self-sufficiency. Aristotle defines a self-sufficient good as one that 'all by itself makes life choiceworthy and lacking in nothing'; and since he assumes that a life lacks nothing only if it has a complete range of rational activities, he infers that a self-sufficient life includes the good of a community. On the other hand, if we think a life lacks nothing as soon as it has everything we want in it, then self-sufficiency requires much less. We might decide that the rational person should prefer a more self-contained life, more independent of external circumstances; and in that case the contemplative life seems a better candidate for happiness.[38]

The prominence of contemplation in some of Aristotle's remarks about happiness shows that the other-directed, social conception of happiness is not the only one that might seem attractive. If we emphasize rational activity and independence of externals, we reach the non-social, other-worldly conception of happiness that sometimes appeals to both Plato and Aristotle. It becomes important to decide whether Aristotle has assigned the right relative weight to completeness on the one hand, and to rationality and independence on the other, in his account of happiness.

xv. *The significance of Aristotle*

A popular contrast opposes the visionary, other-worldly Plato to the hard-headed but rather boring Aristotle. As Yeats says:

> Plato thought nature but a spume that plays
> Upon a ghostly paradigm of things.
> Solider Aristotle played the taws
>   Upon the bottom of a king of kings.

This contrast began among the Platonists of later antiquity; while some fused Platonic and Aristotelian views, others reacted by opposing mundane Aristotelianism to high-minded Platonism.[39]

We have seen reasons to challenge the other-worldly view of Plato; and there are equally good reasons to challenge the contrast between Plato and Aristotle. While Aristotle is partly a naturalist and partly a Platonist, he is primarily a critical defender of Plato. He thinks Plato was right on major points on which the Presocratic naturalists were wrong, and that he made a permanent contribution to the understanding of nature and of the human good. Plato only half understood (in Aristotle's view) his advances over the naturalists; for he entangled some of his important advances with errors from which Aristotle seeks to free them. Aristotle tries to show that Plato was right to insist on the reality of form, on natural teleology, and on the harmony of justice and self-interest; and he tries to free these true Platonic claims from any dependence on the Theory of Forms, the immaterial soul, and the authoritarian ideal state.

Aristotle's acknowledged influence on his immediate successors, the Stoics and the Epicureans, is less than might be expected; doubts have even been expressed about whether they knew most of Aristotle's works. Though the doubts are probably

mistaken, the fact that they could be raised suggests that Aristotle
did not become a philosophical authority for philosophers of the
next few generations. In fact both Stoics and Epicureans rejected
Aristotelian metaphysics for more thoroughly materialist doctrines; and the later Platonists reasserted his defence of form in
thoroughly immaterialist, other-worldly terms, influenced by their
reading of Aristotle in the light of their interpretation of Plato.[40]

His influence on mediaeval philosophy contrasts sharply with
his position in later antiquity. After the rediscovery of Aristotle
in the early middle ages, he became the primary authority, 'the
Philosopher'; and not only philosophy, but also natural science
and theology, were conducted within assumptions taken to be
Aristotelian (though often partly influenced by later Platonism).

Aristotle's authority made him an irresistible target for early
modern philosophers attacking the mediaeval scholasticism derived from him. Descartes (1596-1650), Locke (1632-1704),
Hobbes (1588-1679), and Berkeley (1685-1753) could all appeal
to the success of modern science, which had freed itself from
the assumptions of Aristotelian cosmology and astronomy. They
supposed that Aristotle's general philosophical position should
be rejected together with the particular empirical assumptions
that had been superseded by modern science. His doctrine of
substantial forms seemed to involve strange non-empirical mech-
anisms that had been discredited by better scientific theories.
These attacks on Aristotle seemed to Hume to have succeeded
so completely that in 1748 he could write: 'The fame of Cicero
flourishes at present; but that of Aristotle is utterly decayed.'[41]

His critics in the seventeenth and eighteenth centuries were
not entirely wrong. When Aristotle relies on appearances and
common sense, he is in danger of treating error, prejudice, or
superficial assumptions as firm data to be accepted by every
reasonable theory. One bad effect of his over-confidence appears
in the attitude of the astronomer Ptolemy (*fl.* AD 127-48) to the
assumption that the earth tends towards the centre of the universe:

So I, for one, think it gratuitous for anyone to inquire into the causes of
the motion towards the centre once the fact that the earth occupies the
middle place in the universe, and that all weights move towards it, is
made so patent by the observed phenomena themselves.[42]

In this case the 'observed phenomena' make it unreasonable, in Ptolemy's view, even to consider challenging the view that the earth is the centre of the universe and that the sun moves around the earth. Sometimes, however, the right theory is found only if apparently clear observations are rejected or reinterpreted.

On the other hand, it would be wrong to suppose that Aristotle's philosophical position as a whole is undermined by this sort of criticism; and the revival of Aristotle's reputation in the nineteenth and twentieth centuries is partly the result of a more discriminating attitude to him. No one could now reasonably regard him as the supreme authority; but neither could anyone reasonably agree with Hume's estimate. The questions that he tries to answer, about matter, form, causation, teleology, body, soul, happiness, and morality, are philosophical questions that persist, with surprisingly little change, through changes in science, religion, and culture. Aristotle's answers to them are not obsolete. On the contrary, his claim to defend the reality and non-eliminability of forms and souls, and his account of the place of morality in the human good, present reasonable options that have sometimes been prematurely abandoned, and have not yet been adequately explored.

8

Epicureanism

i. *The Hellenistic world*[1]

The 'Hellenistic Age' (a term coined by modern historians, not
by the Greeks) begins with the death of Alexander the Great in
323, and ends with the end of the Roman Republic and the victory
of Octavian (later Augustus) in 31 BC. Alexander conquered the
empires of Persia and Egypt, and his successors ruled over them
until they were incorporated in the Roman Empire under
Augustus.

Alexander's conquests extended the Greek-speaking world.
Greek cities (Alexandria in Egypt being the most famous) were
founded throughout his empire; and they made the Greek language and culture familiar and dominant far beyond mainland
Greece and Ionia.[2] Though Greek culture spread over a wide
area, however, it did not penetrate very deeply; for the new Greek
cities remained sharply separated from the surrounding rural
areas, where native language, culture, and religion survived, and
Greek speakers were an alien elite.[3] Still, Greek became the primary language of the Eastern Roman Empire, and remained so
until AD 1453, when the last Byzantine emperor was deposed.
Because Greek was the dominant language, the Hebrew scriptures
were translated into Greek (the 'Septuagint', from the seventy-two
translators traditionally supposed to have produced it), and the
Christian scriptures were originally composed in Greek.[4]

Alexander succeeded his father Philip as king of Macedon; and
the Macedonians became the dominant power in Greece even
before their Asian conquests. From then on, the major Greek
states, including Athens (Sparta was now a minor power), no
longer enjoyed their previous degree of autonomy. The Athenian
orator Demosthenes (384–322) was one of those who regarded
the coming of the Macedonians as the end of Greek freedom;

and he urged resistance to Philip and Alexander.[5] Not everyone, however, thought the Macedonians were so dangerous to freedom. Two centuries later the historian Polybius (*c*.200–after 118 BC) vigorously defended the other side of the case, in his argument for the pro-Macedonians in the Peloponnese:

By inducing Philip into the Peloponnese, and by humiliating the Spartans, they allowed all the Peloponnesians to draw new breath, and to form the thought of freedom; further they [the Peloponnesians] recovered the territories and cities that the Spartans had, during their prosperity, taken from them . . . and undoubtedly strengthened their own states.

Nor did Macedonian domination completely transform the political life of Greek cities. When new Greek cities were founded across Alexander's empire, a similar pattern of political life was to some degree repeated.[6]

The condition of the Greek cities in the Hellenistic world helps to explain some new developments in Greek intellectual life. The foundation of the Museum and Library in Alexandria, as centres of study and research, helped to make that city the main focus of natural science, medicine, and literary studies. Athens remained the centre of philosophy. This division tended to encourage some separation of philosophical from scientific studies. This was not a sharp division. Theophrastus (*c*.370–*c*.287) and Straton (died 269), for instance, two of Aristotle's successors in his school the Lyceum, continued his strong interest in empirical scientific research and theory. But the Lyceum lost influence and vigour, and no other philosophical school arrested the tendencies to specialization—and these were in any case a natural result of the development and elaboration of philosophy.

In Athens distinct schools of philosophy formed, arguing with each other, and competing for the attention of students. Stoics, Epicureans, Sceptics, and Peripatetics (i.e. Aristotelians) formulated their own doctrines and strategies. This tendency was a predictable result of developments in philosophy; but the concentration of these schools in Athens (in contrast to the early fifth century) also reflected the place of that city in Greek culture and higher education. Both Athens and other cities began to require some philosophical instruction as part of the course of training (originally military) for young men of the upper classes. The Athenian philosophical schools therefore influenced some of the content of higher education for the ruling classes.[7]

Athens eventually became an international centre of philosophical study not just for the Greek world, but also for the whole Roman Empire; and it retained this position for at least six centuries. In 146 BC the Romans completed the conquest of Greece, with the sack and destruction of Corinth; but, as the Roman poet Horace (65 BC-AD 8) remarks, 'Greece took its brutish captor captive and introduced the arts into rustic Latium'. From then on the Roman ruling class cultivated Greek literary and philosophical studies, with increasing success.[8]

ii. *Epicurus: general aims*

For Epicurus (341-271), as for Socrates, philosophy is a way to reform our lives. We conduct our lives badly because we fear death; and we fear death because we fear punishment after death. Cephalus' remarks at the beginning of Plato's *Republic* illustrate the fears that Epicurus has in mind:

When a man begins to realize he is going to die, he is filled with apprehension and concern about matters that previously did not occur to him. <He remembers> the stories (*muthos*) that are told about Hades and how the men who have done injustice here must pay the just penalty there; and though he may have ridiculed them hitherto, they now begin to torture his soul with the fear that they may after all be true.

According to Cephalus, wealth is some protection against these fears, since it removes the temptation to cheat people, and allows us to make lavish offerings to the gods—two ways to avoid punishment after death. Hence the fear of death stimulates the desire to accumulate wealth.

Epicurus thinks that fear of death underlies all the acquisitive and competitive aspects of our lives; indeed, he thinks it explains our tendency to accept a Homeric outlook. Fearing death, we try to assure ourselves of security and protection against other people. The search for security leads us to pursue power, wealth, and honour, and makes us constantly afraid of losing them. We

seek posthumous fame and honour, as Achilles did, because we
refuse to admit to ourselves that we will not be present to enjoy
it; and our fear of death explains why we refuse to admit that we
will not be present. We occupy ourselves in constant activity and
competition, to conceal our fear of death from ourselves. We do
not realize that fear of death is our basic motive; each of us
'flees from himself'; we need occupations to divert us from the
oppressive awareness of ourselves and our fears, but we do not
know why we find the awareness of ourselves so oppressive.[9]

Epicurus' diagnosis of human fears and ambitions is his reason
for studying the nature of the universe. As Lucretius (? 94–55), a
Roman poet and Epicurean, says:

We must disperse this terror of the mind, this darkness, not by the sun's
rays and the day's gleaming shafts, but by nature's face and law.

Epicurus himself claims that this is the only reason that we need
to study nature:

If we had never been troubled by suspicions about the heavens, or
that death might be something to us, or by ignorance of the limits of
pains and appetites, we would have had no need to study nature (*phusiologia*).[10]

To remove our fears, both the known and the unacknowledged,
we need an account of the universe that gives us no reason to
fear death. We free ourselves from fear once we believe that the
universe is not controlled by gods who determine or modify natural processes for their own purposes, and that we do not survive
death. If we have reason to believe this, then (in Epicurus' view)
we have no reason to think death does any harm to us; hence we
have no reason to fear death; hence we will no longer fear death.

iii. *The challenge of Scepticism*

To find a theory of the universe that dissolves our fear of death
and the gods, Epicurus turns to the Atomism of Leucippus and
Democritus. Aristotle attacks Atomism in so far as he insists on
the reality of form and the truth of teleological explanations;
and Epicurus presents a defence of Atomism against Aristotle's
attacks.

On one important point, however, he is closer to Aristotle than to Democritus. In Democritus' view, the atomic theory depends on principles that are evident to reason, but contrary to the testimony of the senses; the world revealed by reason is quite different from anything that the senses show us. The conflict between sense and reason leads Democritus some way towards scepticism, and forces him to ask where he will find the evidence for his theory if he disregards the senses.[11] Not surprisingly, Aristotle criticizes Atomism for its conflicts with the appearances. Epicurus, however, starts from an epistemological position quite close to Aristotle's, and argues, against both Aristotle and Democritus, that this position actually supports Atomism.

Epicurus has good reason to reconsider Democritus' epistemological position, not only because of Aristotle's criticism, but also because of the revival of scepticism after Aristotle. A central Sceptical question concerns the problem of the 'criterion' (or 'standard'; Greek *kritêrion*, from *krinein*, 'judge' or 'discriminate') to be used in discriminating true appearances from false ones. The Sceptic argues that we have no reliable standard. Appearances conflict; different things appear true to different people; even if we confine ourselves to sensory appearances, these conflict; and hence we cannot rely on the senses as a criterion. How, in any case, do we know we have found a criterion? We can justifiably treat some principle or method P1 as a criterion only if we know that P1 gives us true answers; but apparently we cannot know that without appealing to some further principle P2 to serve as a criterion for deciding about P1; but we can ask the same question about P2, leading us to a further principle P3; and now we face an infinite regress, giving us no answer to our original question.[12]

The Sceptic facing arguments of apparently equal strength for conflicting conclusions finds no basis for choosing between the conclusions, suspends judgement about their truth, and thereby claims to achieve tranquillity (*ataraxia*)—freedom from fear and anxiety. This Sceptical claim suggests a further challenge to Epicurus. For he and the Sceptic seem to agree that tranquillity is the right goal; and the Sceptic seems to offer a short cut to it by suspension of judgement. Why should Epicurus pursue tranquillity by the more laborious route of a dogmatic theory about the world?

Epicurus rejects this Sceptical solution. If we are Sceptics, he thinks, we will be full of indecision and, therefore, of disturbance. If we cannot decide between two views, our indecision will leave us worried and agitated; we therefore need some basis for judgement and decision. The Sceptic admits that it is simply a matter of good luck that tranquillity follows suspension of judgement. Epicurus suggests that the Sceptic is foolishly optimistic in hoping for tranquillity rather than anxiety.[13]

iv. *The appeal to the senses*

In reply to Scepticism, Epicurus thinks we must trust the senses: 'If you fight with all your perceptions, you will have nothing to refer to in your judgement of whichever ones of them you say are false.' He relies on the argument that Democritus offers on behalf of the senses; we have no more confidence in anything than we have in the senses, and so if we lose confidence in them, we lose it in everything else as well. Trust in the senses is the only alternative to scepticism, since it is the only way out of complete suspension of judgement about everything.

This argument claims that we cannot *totally* reject the senses, and must accept *some* of their reports. But Epicurus accepts *all* their reports, and so claims that all perceptions are true. In developing a sceptical argument, Descartes argues that 'it is sometimes proved to me that these senses are deceptive, and it is wiser not to trust entirely to anything by which we have once been deceived'. Epicurus takes this sceptical doubt further, arguing that any doubt about any sensory report requires general doubt about all sensory reports, and hence total suspension of judgement.[14]

This total confidence in the senses appears to expose them to a different attack. For we might think that if we accept every report of the senses, we will have to accept conflicting reports (e.g. the stick appears bent when I see it in water, and straight when I pull it out); then we will have to admit conflicting appearances (the stick appears both bent and straight); since we are not allowed to choose between them, and both cannot be true of the same object, we cannot say how the object is. This argument drove Democritus to scepticism about the senses.

In reply Epicurus denies any conflict between the two appearances of the stick, and appeals to the Atomic theory. The appearance of the bent stick is true, in so far as it corresponds to a bent configuration of atoms thrown off by the stick and eventually hitting the eyes. The appearance of the straight stick is true, in so far as it corresponds to a straight configuration of atoms. We are usually wrong if we expect the bent-stick-in-water appearance to be followed by a bent-stick-out-of-water appearance. But the error lies with us and our hasty inferences and false beliefs, not in the senses themselves.

If Epicurus is right, then our appearance of a chair is an accurate presentation of a chair-shaped configuration of atoms. But this answer does not undermine sceptical doubts about our belief in such things as chairs. For chair-shaped configurations may be momentary and short-lived, and further beliefs are needed for the inference that the configuration belongs to the longerlasting configuration that is a chair. We avoid scepticism only if we can show that these inferences are warranted. Sometimes we explain our chair-shaped appearances as the products of dreams or hallucinations, even though, in Epicurus' view, they result from some external chair-shaped configuration. Why should this not always be so?[15]

Epicurus defends the senses by restricting our normal view of what they say, and hence rejecting our belief that sensory reports may conflict. But since sensory reports, as he construes them, tell us so little, his defence of their accuracy does not answer a Sceptical doubt about common beliefs that are based on the senses. Epicurus has not shown that he has good reason for believing in the ordinary external world of persisting objects. Though he defends the truth of the purely sensory appearances, he does not defend the appearances that matter most for the construction of a scientific theory.

v. *Sense and science*

In Democritus' view, the atomic theory is the product of reason
superseding the senses; the conflicting appearances of sense show
that reality cannot consist of things with colour, taste, and so on,
but must consist of indestructible atoms. Since Epicurus insists
on the senses as the criterion of truth, he cannot use Democritus'
argument. He must argue that the evidence of the senses themselves supports atomism. For this purpose we must allow that
Epicurus has answered sceptical threats to our belief in an objective world; and we must see whether he can argue from this
belief to the truth of the atomic theory.

Some examples suggest the strategy. Atomism tells us (a1) the
atoms are in constant motion, and (a2) they lack colour. The
senses, however, seem to tell us (b1) there are stable bodies not in
constant motion, and (b2) bodies are coloured. The evidence of
the senses, then, seems to conflict with atomism, because we cannot understand how (c1) apparently stable bodies are simply collections of moving constituents, or how (c2) apparently coloured
bodies are simply collections of colourless constituents.

Lucretius, however, argues that the senses provide us with examples of (c), and hence do not commit us to (b) against (a). He
describes two cases: (c1) We see a flock of sheep on a distant hill;
though from a distance they appear still, we see, when we come
closer, that they are moving. (c2) We tear a red rag into smaller
and smaller pieces, and gradually lose the colour. Attention to
these examples supports the claims in (c); and so trust in the
senses does not conflict with (a). When we think the evidence of
the senses requires the truth of (b), we are looking carelessly at
ill-chosen examples. In fact the evidence of the senses tells us to
accept the atomic theory, not to reject it.[16]

Epicurus concludes, against Democritus, that atomists need
not reject the senses; they need only attend carefully and without
prejudice to what the senses really tell us. Aristotle assumes that
judgements such as (b) are among the appearances that a theory
should vindicate; but Epicurus replies that these are common
beliefs, not genuine sensory appearances, and that the genuine
sensory appearances do not commit us to (b).

His attempted defence raises a general difficulty about all the numerous and elaborate arguments for the atomic theory. In Epicurus' view, some questions allow only one answer that is consistent with the evidence of the senses, whereas other questions allow several answers that are consistent with such evidence. Questions of the second type (e.g. about the size of the sun) arise because the relevant observations are not available. These cases allow many 'empirically equivalent' theories and explanations, all equally consistent with the evidence of the senses; an Epicurean does not choose between them.[17]

It is important for Epicurus to show that the atomic theory answers a question of the first type, so that he has reason to believe in it as opposed to rival theories. His arguments, however, seem to show only that it is consistent with observation; he hardly shows that it is the only theory of this sort. It seems easy to imagine a non-atomist account of the world that is consistent with the evidence of the senses. We argued, indeed, that the Homeric view could easily show itself to be consistent with any observations; that was why the naturalists could not hope to refute Homer by a simple appeal to the senses.[18] If this is true, then the atomic theory does not answer questions of the first type, since such questions do not seem decidable by the test of mere consistency with observations. The atomic theory seems to be only one of a number of empirically equivalent theories, and Epicurus' own principles forbid us to prefer it over rival theories that are equally consistent with observations.

This difficulty for Epicurus is parallel to one we raised at a more elementary level, in arguing that he fails to rule out the suggestion that our purported experience of an objective world is really a dream or hallucination. In each case the view that Epicurus chooses may well be the most reasonable; but his demand for mere consistency with the senses does not support his choice.

vi. *Atomism and the soul*

Epicurus wants to show that the soul is a collection of atoms, just as trees and chairs are, and therefore is just as certain to decay and dissolve into its constituents. If Epicurus is right about this, then Plato cannot be right to believe in an immaterial and immortal soul. If we do not believe in immortality, we will not believe that we can suffer harm after death, and therefore, Epicurus thinks, we have no reason to fear death and will not fear death.

Lucretius collects a series of twenty-nine Epicurean arguments for the mortality of the soul; but most of them show the characteristic weakness of Epicurean empiricism. Lucretius finds abundant evidence to show that the soul is affected by what happens to the body: a blow on the head causes me pain, my mind decays with my body, and so on. One possible explanation of these facts will say that the soul is material and destructible, and depends on the body for its existence. But that is only one possible explanation, and someone who agrees with Plato that the soul is immaterial and immortal can offer other explanations.[19]

To rule out these other explanations, a materialist might claim that only material bodies can be affected by material bodies. If this claim is true, the soul cannot be immaterial; but how do we know it is true? Epicurus will hardly convince us that no other view is consistent with the evidence of the senses; to justify his materialism he must rely on a claim that is not warranted by his empiricism. Since he believes that a claim about reality is illegitimate unless it is warranted by his empiricism, his argument faces grave objections, on purely Epicurean grounds.

Epicurus' treatment of the soul raises a broader question about the extent of his disagreement with Aristotle. He wants to show not only that the soul is mortal, but also that it is simply a collection of atoms. He therefore argues for eliminative atomism, rejecting the claims of form (and therefore of soul) to be anything distinct from the collection of atoms. He speaks of compounds of atoms, roughly corresponding to macroscopic objects as ordinarily conceived; but their status is obscure. He thinks every change in a compound implies its destruction, probably because he follows Heracleitus in accepting a compositional principle of identity; in that case he cannot recognize the persistent substances that Aristotle recognizes.[20] Though Epicurus' conception of the world leaves no room for Aristotelian substance and form, he hardly justifies their exclusion.

vii. *The gods*

Plato's *Laws* contains a discussion of different types of unsound views about the gods. After replying to a complete atheist, Plato turns to the person who believes in the gods but is so impressed by the apparent imperfections of the world that he concludes that the gods have no concern for it. This is Epicurus' view; and whereas Plato condemns it as a threat to religion and morality, Epicurus thinks we need it for a sound attitude to death, and therefore to our lives.

To show that the gods are not concerned with the world, Epicurus attacks a particular teleological doctrine. Plato and the Stoics argue that the order in individual organisms depends on the larger order that maintains them, and that this order is plausibly explained as the product of intelligent design. The order in the world supplies an argument for the existence of a designing god.

In reply Epicurus holds that the disorder in the world tells against the existence of any designing gods. Natural disasters and other apparent imperfections suggest that only non-purposive forces could control the processes in the world—unless the gods are remarkably stupid, malicious, or incompetent. The flaws in the observed character of the world confirm the atomic theory, and undermine belief in gods who care about the world.[21]

These arguments against design do not answer all of Aristotle's reasons for believing in teleology. Aristotle claims that organisms are to be understood and explained teleologically, without claiming that they must be products of design. Epicurus must reject this claim if he rejects the reality of form. But though his commitment to eliminative atomism requires rejection of form, he does not undermine Aristotle's case. His failure to answer Aristotle does not necessarily affect his specific arguments against design; but it may affect his reasons for believing the basic atomist principles.

Though Epicurus denies that the gods design or control the world order, he believes that empiricism requires him to accept gods. For in dreams and visions people claim to be aware of gods; and something external must correspond to their perceptions, since all perceptions are true; but the only external things that could correspond to our perceptions are immortal, intelligent, and blessedly happy beings looking like human beings with human bodies. The gods, like everything else with human or animal bodies, must be composed of atoms; but they are not destroyed in the way other collections of atoms are destroyed, since they live between the worlds that are subject to destruction, and so avoid the atomic forces that destroy other collections of atoms.[22]

This account of the gods maintains empiricism, and remains strikingly congenial to one element of traditional Greek religious thought. He agrees with Homer's description of the gods as blessedly happy, not vulnerable to the dangers that threaten human beings. By insisting on this aspect of the gods, Epicurus raises a serious question: why should an invulnerable and blessed being interest himself in the world or in us? Plato appeals to the Demiurge's desire to create something that embodies the Forms; but we may wonder how that desire is consistent with the gods' independence. Why should they want to create a world, if they are already completely happy and need nothing more?[23]

viii. *Necessity and freedom*

In accepting the atomic theory, Epicurus agrees with Democritus' naturalist determinism: all natural processes are the necessary results of atomic movements, with no external interference from gods, and no laws irreducible to laws about atomic movements. The same patterns are repeated in nature because the same atomic forces operate, and their operations necessarily produce the same results.

This belief in necessity, however, seems to conflict with our belief that human beings are free and responsible agents. We suppose that it is up to us how we act, and that we can fairly be praised or blamed for our actions. Moreover, the Epicurean message is addressed to us on the assumption that we have a real choice about how to live our lives. The Epicurean takes control of his life, and frees himself from the fears that preoccupy most people. But if atomist determinism is true, all our actions are nothing but the necessary result of atomic movements, all the way back to the infinitely distant past. How could our belief in responsibility be true, and how could it be up to us to take control of our lives?[24]

Aristotle seems to suggest that I am justly held responsible for my action if certain negative conditions are met—if I am not pushed or otherwise physically forced, and my action is not the result of ignorance. But Epicurus notices that even if Aristotle's conditions are met, my action might still be necessitated by past states of the world beyond my control. Epicurus thinks determination by the past excludes responsibility; indeed, he says it would be better to believe in interfering gods than to believe the philosophers who speak of fate and natural necessity.[25]

Epicurus might well argue that other remarks of Aristotle's support the *incompatibilist* view that responsibility is incompatible with determinism. Aristotle claims that if I am responsible for an action, the action is 'up to me'—I am free to do and not to do it; and 'the origin is in me'—I am the cause. Epicurus implicitly argues:

(1) If determinism is true, events in the distant past make my action inevitable.

(2) If so, then they are the cause, and I am not.

(3) If I am not the cause, it is not up to me, and I am not responsible for it.

(4) Hence, if determinism is true, I am not responsible for my actions.

Steps (1) and (2) spell out the apparent consequences of determinism; Aristotle accepts (3); and so we seem to have no escape from (4).[26]

Since Epicurus is an incompatibilist, but believes we are responsible for our actions, he rejects determinism, and modifies Democritean atomism. He claims that some atoms at some times undergo a random and imperceptible swerve from their normal course. This swerve introduces an uncaused motion; and in so far as our act of choice includes an atomic swerve, it is undetermined. This solution violates (so Epicurus claims) neither our experience of the world nor our firm belief in free will.[27]

The solution is not clearly convincing. If each choice we think is free really is free, then every such choice includes a swerve. If

Epicurus thinks the immediate evidence of sensation assures us that we are free, and therefore that there must have been an atomic swerve, he faces the usual difficulty for his empiricism: he does not rule out alternative explanations of the sensations of freedom.

But even if swerves happen on the right occasions, do they imply the sort of freedom that is needed for responsibility? If a choice involves a swerve, it is uncaused, and therefore cannot be caused by my past choices and my states of character. But actions that are unconnected to my past and my character are not the ones we think we are responsible for; indeed, we are more likely to regard them as aberrations allowing us to claim diminished responsibility. Epicurus' view implies, then, that I am no more responsible for any of my 'free' actions than I am for aberrations unconnected with my character; hence he seems to undermine claims of responsibility, not to defend them.

To answer this objection Epicurus needs to show that the inference from indeterminism to absence of causal connexion is unwarranted, or that responsibility does not require causal connexion between my action, my past choices, and my character. Other incompatibilists have taken up the tasks that he leaves unfinished; the issue has not yet been settled in their favour.

Epicurus is an incompatibilist about responsibility partly because he is an eliminative atomist. An alternative approach might say that claims about responsibility apply to Aristotelian souls and forms, not to their constituent matter, and that the eliminative, not the determinist, aspects of Democritus threaten responsibility. This approach is not open to Epicurus; but the Stoics exploit it.[28]

ix. *Pleasure, happiness, and virtue*

Epicurus' ethical theory rests on his hedonism—his belief that pleasure is the ultimate good, and other things are good only to the extent that they are means to pleasure. Aristotle accepts the common belief that pleasure is *a* good and must be a component of any credible account of *the* good. Epicurus claims that this belief about pleasure is no mere common belief (an 'appearance' in Aristotle's broad sense), but an immediate appearance of sensation, and therefore infallible; and he claims that the infallible appearance recognizes pleasure as *the* good. All animals immediately recognize that pleasure is good, and pursue it as their end; children pursue it spontaneously before they have acquired any other beliefs about what is good.[29]

Epicurus rejects the sensual pleasures that require expanded and demanding desires and abundant material resources. A life of such pleasures would, he concedes, be a happy life if it really maximized pleasure. But it cannot do this; the only way to maximize the balance of pleasure over pain is to eliminate anxiety, but sensual pleasures simply leave us prey to pains, fears, and needs. Dependence on external resources that are not in our control is a source of anxiety to be avoided. The Epicurean is to approach the independence and invulnerability of the gods, secure in his pleasures, and free from the external hazards causing fear and apprehension.[30]

This conception of the good is meant to explain why the Epicurean cultivates the virtues that Plato and Aristotle describe. The Epicurean wants to regulate his desires so that they do not make him dependent on external fortune; he therefore values the results of temperance. He does not fear the loss of worldly goods, since he does not need many; he is therefore not tempted to act like a coward. He finds mutual aid and pleasure in the society of friends, and so he cultivates friendships.[31]

The Epicurean is not greedy for power or domination over others. He finds it a source of severe anxiety and insecurity. Since he understands the benefits of mutual aid and physical security, he follows rules of justice, for the reasons given by Glaucon and Adeimantus in Plato's *Republic*. Since he values freedom from anxiety, he will want to avoid the risk of detection and punishment—a risk that is the inevitable penalty of injustice, even if it leads to no further penalty. The evolution of society is to be explained neither as a product of divine design, nor (following Aristotle) as the expression of the inherently social nature of human beings, but simply as the product of particular responses to insecurity and danger. The needs that cause the formation of the state also give the Epicurean hedonist reason to conform to justice.[32]

In all these ways Epicurus defends the Aristotelian virtues, as he conceives them, by means of quite un-Aristotelian premisses. He argues that the pursuit of pleasure, properly understood, actually requires the cultivation of the moral virtues.

x. *Questions about Epicurean ethics*

Doubts about Epicurus' argument may arise even if we accept hedonism. He argues for a version of hedonism that values freedom and independence from externals; he avoids the excitements of gross sensual pleasures, and of the more subtle pleasures that depend heavily on external resources, because these pleasures are sources of anxiety. But can this preference for independence and security be defended on hedonistic grounds? Epicurus claims that the anxiety, fear, and insecurity resulting from self-indulgence and intemperance are too severe to be tolerated; but it is hard to justify this claim on purely hedonistic grounds, and any non-hedonistic argument is, for Epicurus, quite worthless.

Hedonism in general faces wider questions about the relation of pleasure to happiness and the human good. Aristotle insists that no one would want to return to the condition of a child, even if he could maximize the sorts of pleasures that a child enjoys.[33] He implies that objective features of my situation—including the nature of the activities I enjoy—make a difference to my well-being and happiness. On Aristotle's view, my subjective attitude to my situation does not by itself determine whether or not I am happy or well off. This objection applies to Epicurus no less than to other hedonists. We could be content and free from anxiety even if we were crippled, our friends and family were being tortured, and we were sold into slavery, as long as we were deceived about these things or did not care about them. But if we apply Aristotle's test for the complete good, we see that we would be better off if all these things were going better. Epicurus does not seem to answer this objection to hedonism in general.

The objection is important if we want to evaluate a central assumption of the whole Epicurean outlook. Epicurus tries to relieve us from the fear of death:

Get used to thinking that death is nothing to us, since every good and evil is in sensation, and death is deprivation of sensation. Hence correct knowledge that death is nothing to us makes the mortal aspect of life enjoyable, not by adding unlimited time, but by having removed the longing for immortality.[34]

He assumes that being dead would harm us only if it were painful after death. His whole method of removing the fear of death assumes a hedonist conception of a person's good.

Once we challenge hedonism, however, the fear of death may be harder to remove. If we say that a young person who dies before he has fulfilled his striking promise has suffered some harm, we do not mean that he felt or is feeling anything painful; we mean that he would have gained some great benefit if he had lived and that he has lost it because he has died. If death can do us this sort of harm, then we seem to have good reason (in some circumstances) to fear it. In this case Epicurus' theory of the good seems to leave out those goods that underlie some of our reasonable fears of death; for they are goods distinct from pleasure.

His hedonism also seems to threaten his defence of the virtues. He claims that they are simply instrumental to pleasure. Though an Epicurean is free of some temptations to act like a coward, that does not seem to make him brave. For a brave person is normally concerned about some important interest of himself or of other people he cares about; but the Epicurean's indifference to external conditions will apparently make him indifferent to these sorts of interests as well. Though he will not be tempted to shirk danger for the sake of his life, health, or material goods, he seems to have no particular reason to face danger either; when so few things matter to him, he seems to have no positive incentive to be brave.[35]

For similar reasons, we may doubt the Epicurean's commitment to justice and friendship. Even if the threat of punishment deters him from all or most unjust actions, he seems to have no positive reason to care about the good of others for its own sake; for to care about it for its own sake would be to regard it as a good in itself, not simply a means to some other good, whereas a hedonist cannot allow this status to any good except pleasure. If the Epicurean is indifferent to the interest of others as a good in itself, he seems to have no reason for doing any good to them, except when it is instrumental to some further benefit to himself, and ultimately instrumental to his own pleasure.[36]

We may reasonably be unconvinced, then, by Epicurus' efforts to reconcile his hedonism with the commonly recognized virtues that are defended by Plato and Aristotle. The failure of these efforts does not refute his hedonism; it may simply show the falsity of common views about the virtues. If Epicurus has to choose between the common views ('appearances' in the broad sense) and his hedonism (allegedly resting on immediate appearances of sensation), his empiricism requires him to choose hedonism. But is the truth of hedonism so clear that we are right to maintain it against so many of our fairly confident and considered judgements about goods and virtues? If the truth of hedonism is so obvious to sensation, should we perhaps doubt the truth of sensation? If we do that, we challenge the whole basis of Epicurus' system.

xi. *The coherence of the system*

Epicurus tries to construct a system of simple, coherent, and plausible principles. He is a hedonist who regards the fear of death as the most dangerous source of fear, insecurity, and unhappiness. To avoid insecurity we must trust the senses, since otherwise we will be filled with doubts and anxieties; and the senses assure us of the truth of atomism and hedonism. Each principle seems attractively simple, and they seem to combine into an attractive system. But in fact each is open to doubt, and they are hard to combine satisfactorily.

Epicurus' defence of atomism has often appealed to those who suppose that they take empirical science seriously. It often seems natural to suppose that science is justified by experience and observation. Epicurus takes the empiricist view to extreme lengths, refusing to reject the evidence of the senses on any occasion for any reason. In doing this, however, he prevents himself from justifying any reasonable scientific theory at all.

Epicurus believes we cannot choose between empirically equivalent explanations; and in believing this, he undermines his own empiricist defence of a scientific theory. For sense-perception (as he construes it) cannot rule out the possibility that our perceptions are a consistent hallucination, not matching any external objects; nor can it rule out rivals to the atomic theory. Epicurus' narrow view of sense-perception, and his exclusive trust in consistency with sense-perception as a test of a theory, undermine his argument from empiricism to atomism.

Hedonism in moral philosophy seems to be parallel to empiricism in the theory of knowledge—an intuitively appealing and superficially clear general principle that offers a method of understanding and criticizing other principles. Epicurus claims that it is not merely parallel to empiricism, but actually justified by empiricism, since he thinks we can see the truth of hedonism by appeal to immediate sensation. Like empiricism, hedonism seems easier and more plausible than its more complicated rivals; but once we examine its implications, we see it is neither clear nor plausible.

In antiquity Epicureanism was often brusquely dismissed. Its anti-religious tendencies (real and supposed) aroused suspicion; and its hedonism was sometimes misinterpreted as advocacy of immoral self-indulgence.[37] These dismissals did not rest on any careful criticism of the basic Epicurean principles; and so they did not undermine the appeal of the principles themselves. Brusque dismissal of Epicurus is unwarranted and self-defeating, failing to expose the real difficulties in his position. Exposure of the difficulties, however, has a useful result: it shows us why principles that initially seem simple and attractive are neither simple nor attractive after all.

9
Stoicism

i. *The Stoic system*

Stoic philosophy began in the generation after the death of Aristotle. For at least two centuries Stoics competed with Epicureans for the support of educated Greeks and Romans; and we can grasp the Stoic position more easily by comparison both with Epicurus and with Aristotle.[1]

Epicurus defends Atomism by appeal to the appearances, and to this extent uses Aristotelian method to reach un-Aristotelian conclusions. We have seen, though, that he construes appearances more narrowly than Aristotle normally does, and that he thinks the appearances, as he construes them, support him against Aristotle. While Aristotle believes in formal and final, as well as material, causes, Epicurus denies the fundamental reality of formal and final causes. While Plato and Aristotle regard pleasure as only one sort of good, Epicurus insists that it is *the* good, and that other goods are merely instrumental to it.

The Stoics defend much more of the Aristotelian outlook. While they rely on the senses, they do not appeal to the senses alone. While they are materialists, they think they can also justify belief in formal and final causes. Whereas Epicurus rejects any belief in gods controlling the world, the Stoics argue for complete and pervasive divine control. They appeal, as Epicurus does, to nature as the basis of ethics; but their conception of human nature is more Aristotelian than Epicurean. They differ from both Epicurus and Aristotle in the moral conclusions they draw. For they think the appeal to nature justifies the rejection of hedonism and the acceptance of virtue as the only constituent of happiness.

ii. *The problem of the criterion*

The first main division of Stoic philosophy is 'logic', the theory of *logos*.[2] Its subject matter reflects the related senses of *logos*,

including the theory of reasoning and valid inference ('logic' in
the modern sense), philosophy of language (since *logos* includes
uttered speech and the thought it expresses), and epistemology
(the types of reasoning that support justified claims to
knowledge).

Stoic epistemology faces the problem of the criterion of truth;
indeed, Stoic claims about the criterion are partly the cause and
partly the effect of Sceptical criticisms.[3] Epicurus tries to answer
the Sceptics by treating the senses as the criterion of truth, but
the Stoics try a more complex reply, including a broader attack
on the Sceptical presuppositions.

They insist that a sensory appearance derived from an external
object is not enough for a belief about the object; though I may
have an appearance of, say, a red wall, I will not believe I see a
red wall if I have other reasons for believing that the wall is white
and a red light is shining on it. To believe that the wall is red, I
must also 'assent' to the appearance; and this assent is an act of
thought and reason, not merely a product of sense. For the Stoic,
then, the problem of the criterion is the question: 'What sorts of
appearances justify us in assenting to them?' They answer that the
criterion of truth is the 'grasping' or 'apprehending' (*kataléptiké*)
appearance, the one that grasps reality. This is the sort of appearance that presents a real object as it is, could not have come
from an unreal object, and compels our assent.[4]

It is easy to see how such an appearance is reliable. But the
Sceptic will ask, quite fairly, how we can tell which appearances
grasp reality and so deserve our assent. The Stoics cannot say
that if just anyone feels compelled to assent to an appearance,
that appearance grasps reality; for many people mistakenly feel
compelled to assent to an appearance that turns out to be false.
The person who, in the Stoic view, reliably identifies the appearances that grasp reality is the 'sage' (*sophos*)—the exper-
ienced, fully informed Stoic who has complete knowledge of the
world.

But if we must turn to the sage for a reliable source of appearances that grasp reality, the Stoic answer to the problem of
the criterion seems to be open to further Sceptical objections
about an infinite regress. Since the sage is the one with reliably

true beliefs on the questions at issue, we can identify him only if we can identify the true beliefs. But did we not begin looking for a criterion in order to identify the true beliefs? If we must first identify them in order to find a criterion, the criterion seems to be undiscoverable.[5]

This Sceptical objection assumes that we want a wholly self-sufficient criterion; the criterion, on this view, should allow us, all by itself and without any further information or inference, to see that a given belief is true, and should therefore supply a self-evident foundation for claims to knowledge. The Stoics certainly fail to supply such a criterion.

But should they try to supply it? The Sceptical demand for a self-sufficient criterion does not itself seem self-evidently correct; and it is not clear what further argument should persuade us to accept it. If we think we should not look for a self-sufficient criterion, then the Stoic appeal to the appearance that grasps reality, and to the sage as the reliable source of such appearances, seems more reasonable. The Stoics assume that in deciding whether to accept or reject the appearances given by the senses, we can legitimately appeal to our other beliefs.

The senses, on this view, do not provide the self-evident foundation that Epicurus expects from them. We must begin with some confidence in some beliefs, and we cannot throw all our beliefs into doubt at once. For the Stoics, the senses are one important foundation for the outlook of common sense and natural science (and indeed, as we will see, for ethics). But they are not self-sufficient; they do not interpret themselves, and for interpretation and understanding we must rely on the rest of the theory that seeks to explain appearances as a whole.

In rejecting the Sceptic's doubts, and therefore denying that the senses are a wholly self-evident and self-sufficient foundation for claims to knowledge, the Stoics are on quite strong ground. They often insist on the systematic character of their philosophical outlook; and they are right to use it against the Sceptical conception of the problem of the criterion.[6] They suggest, usefully, that we should not simply take for granted the legitimacy of the terms in which the Sceptic raises the problem.

iii. *Nature, form, and matter*

The Stoics' general view of natural bodies results from their combination of Aristotelian and materialist principles. In their view, Aristotle is right, against the Atomists, to believe in the reality of form as well as matter; but the Atomists are right to be materialists, since everything that is real is a material body. While Aristotle neither accepts nor rejects materialism, the Stoics endorse it.

They believe that there are stable, unified, coherent bodies whose properties and behaviour are explained by their natures as wholes, not by mere reference to the stuff that constitutes them. Pools of water, rocks, blocks of wood all have some degree of unity and stability; and the Stoics analyse all these into form and matter. Bodies that have a form are kept in some 'condition' (or 'holding', *hexis*), by having their matter in the right sort of 'tension' or 'balance' (*tonos*, hence 'tone'). Even the most elementary bodies can be analysed into unqualified matter and the form that gives the matter its qualities. The Stoics reject the eliminative atomism that denies any fundamental explanatory role to the properties of complexes and wholes, and so they accept Aristotle's reasons for recognizing the reality of form. Aristotelian substances—artifacts and organisms—turn out to be a subset of the essentially formal things that the Stoics recognize.

Being materialists, however, the Stoics argue that since form is real, and only bodies are real, form must be a body. The Stoics identify it with breath (or wind; *pneuma*), a very fine and subtle body, whose movements in different directions keep the matter in the right unity and tension. This *pneuma* explains the cohesion of the particles in a rock, and, at a more complex level, the growth of a plant, the behaviour of an animal, and the rational action of a human being; soul and reason are simply particular manifestations of *pneuma*.[7]

The Stoics believe that form must be a sort of body because they accept this argument:

(1) Something is real if and only if it can act or be acted on.

(2) Something can act or be acted on if and only if it is a body.

(3) Therefore something is real if and only if it is a body.[8]

The first premiss is widely accepted; but non-materialists are free to accept it and to challenge the second premiss, if, for instance, they believe that non-material minds cause movements in material bodies. Perhaps such a belief is false; but we need to be convinced that it is false before we have reason to accept (2), and (2) is hardly a strong argument against it.[9]

Doubts about the general argument for materialism do not refute the identification of form with *pneuma*; but Aristotle seems to challenge it. He argues that the form cannot be a bodily element; we cannot say, for instance, that we make letters into a syllable by adding a further letter to them, since we can still ask what unifies this collection of the old letters plus the new letter.[10] If the form is one of the elements that constitute the unified whole, then apparently it cannot explain the unity of the whole. If Aristotle is right in this argument, then the Stoics seem to conceive the form as the wrong sort of thing; they cannot account for its role as the principle of unity in a body.

To reject Stoic materialism about form is not necessarily to believe that the form is an immaterial component of anything. As we saw, Aristotle does not conceive the soul as an immaterial component, added to the material body, to make the complex of soul and body that is a human being. He does not deny that living organisms and their forms are wholly constituted by their matter, in the way the house is composed of bricks and a seal is composed of wax. The Stoics' search for a more rigorous materialism seems to obscure some plausible aspects of Aristotle's view of form.[11]

iv. *Nature and the world order*

Aristotle finds formal and final causes in particular organisms. The Stoics, following the suggestion of Plato's *Timaeus*, extend Aristotle's argument to nature as a whole—the natural environment with which particular organisms interact in the goal-directed activities that benefit them and their species.

They begin by appealing to the nature of a particular rational animal. Such an animal displays a characteristic level of complex organization in its bodily parts and their relations (different animals reaching different levels of complexity); and it guides its actions intelligently for the good of the whole and the parts. The Stoics argue that the world as a whole displays the same sort of order, and hence that it is also an intelligent animal with its own rational soul. They follow Aristotle in identifying soul with form; and they also identify form with *pneuma*; they therefore argue that the world's formal aspect is its rational soul, and that this is the cosmic *pneuma*. *Pneuma* is dispersed throughout all the individual bodies and organisms, maintaining each in its proper state and its proper relation to its environment.[12]

By claiming that the world as a whole is a rational animal, the Stoics find an explanation and defence of Aristotle's views on teleology. Aristotle claims that individual organisms embody final causation, but he does not say much to explain why it is present in them. The Stoics, like Plato and unlike Aristotle, believe that teleology in individual organisms is best explained as the result of intelligent and purposive design. Unlike Plato, however, they do not derive the design of the world from an intelligent designer outside it—the Demiurge in the *Timaeus*. They derive cosmic design from the *pneuma* immanent in the universe; this is the intelligent element forming and maintaining the universe, and it is present in the whole and in every single one of the parts.

The Stoics' belief in cosmic reason and intelligent design allows them to defend some aspects of traditional beliefs in the gods. The Stoic Cleanthes (331-232) wrote a 'Hymn to Zeus', combining the expressions of traditional piety with the doctrines of Stoic natural philosophy.[13] The difference from Epicurus' treatment of traditional beliefs is quite striking. Epicurus preserves some central elements of the Homeric tradition about the gods, giving them anthropomorphic characters and making them ideals of the happy life; but he thinks that in ascribing these features to the gods, he must deprive them of their traditional role as designers, removing them from any concern with the world and its imperfections. The Stoics follow the *Timaeus* in stressing the gods' role in the world; and in describing that role more fully, they deny anthropomorphic personality to the gods. They cannot go too far, however, in denying divine personality. For, though the divine element in the world is simply the *pneuma* diffused throughout the world, this divine element must also have sufficient personality to count as an intelligent and benevolent designer.

Epicurus attacks the Stoics for claiming to find evidence of intelligent design in the world; and his attack is renewed and elaborated much later, in Hume's examination of natural religion.[14] The Stoics argue that the existence of a designer makes the best sense of the actual state of the world and the interactions of different creatures with each other and with their environment. But the critic asks what sort of designer we are entitled to assume; the Stoics, like other theists, claim that the designer is both competent and benevolent, but the apparent imperfections in the world seem to suggest a different conclusion. If we must assume imperfections in a designer to match the imperfections of the world, then it is not clear that the assumption of a designer explains much; might we not just as well put it down to the workings of some non-intelligent causes?

The Stoics challenge the alleged evidence for imperfection. They agree that in our uninstructed view some features of the actual world may seem to be evils; but we do not fully understand the divine intelligence, and if we did, we would realize that these apparent imperfections are really necessary for the goodness of the whole.[15]

The Stoics are right to suggest that our uninstructed judgements about imperfections in the world may be unreliable; but in that case can we trust the original judgements about goodness that led us to believe in design? The initial argument for design, and the initial appeal to apparent evils, both seem intuitive and attractive; but to reach a consistent conclusion we must reject or explain away one or other of them. It is easy, then, to find some criticism of the Stoic view, but much harder to find a conclusive criticism.

v. *Determinism and freedom*

The Stoics recognize a single, teleologically organized, cosmic order. It is an order rather than a mere series of events, because it follows unchanging laws in regular and predictable ways. Rivers flow downwards rather than upwards, apples rather than bullets grow on apple trees; present events are determined by past events

according to laws, and completely random exceptions to these
laws do not happen.

This belief in law and regularity leads the Stoics, with other
naturalists, to the determinist view that every event is caused by
a previous event according to laws necessitating the later event. To
this extent they accept and reinterpret one aspect of the traditional
Greek belief in fate (just as they reinterpret other aspects of
traditional religion), and they refer to Zeus and fate with no
obvious distinction.[16] Since they believe in a designing intelligence
immanent in the universe, they believe that in some way the
sequence of causes and effects is the expression of destiny and
intelligent providence.

The Stoics believe that their determinist doctrine is compatible
with our responsibility for (some of) our actions. Against them
Epicurus argues that since events in the distant past make my
action inevitable, it follows that these events, rather than my
choice and decision, cause my action, and that therefore I am not
responsible for it. The Stoics see that this incompatibilist argument deserves an answer.

In their view, the incompatibilist argument rests on an equi-
vocation. To say that A makes B inevitable might mean (i) that
A all by itself ensures B, no matter what else happens (complete
inevitability), or (ii) that A is part of a sequence each of whose
members is necessitated by a previous one, and which results in
B (causal inevitability). The importance of distinguishing (i) from
(ii) is illustrated by the 'Lazy Argument':

(1) Either it is now inevitable that I will pass the examination
tomorrow or it is inevitable that I will fail it.

(2) If it is now inevitable that I will pass (fail), then I will pass
(fail) whether I study or not.

(3) Hence there is no point in my studying, since it will make
no difference whether I study or not.

The first premiss is true only if it refers to causal inevitability;
and the second is true only if it refers to complete inevitability.
But the conclusion requires both premisses to involve complete
inevitability. No interpretation of the premisses yields a sound
argument.

Similarly, in the Stoic view, my action has a series of causes, each of which is made inevitable by its cause, and which together make the action causally inevitable. But sometimes my choice contributes to the result; and my choice depends on appearance and assent. The appearance may not be up to me: whether I have an appearance of a tomato or not may depend on whether there is a tomato-like object in the environment. But whether or not I assent to the appearance, and judge that there is a tomato, depends on me and on my rational estimate of the appearance. Since the action is caused by the assent, the action is up to me; I am fairly held responsible for it, and praise and blame are fairly applied to me, since they influence my assent and rational judgement, and these determine my action.[17]

When the Stoics say my action is up to me, and in particular that it depends on my assent and rational judgement, they do not mean that my assent is the only cause, or that the assent itself is uncaused. On the contrary, if determinism is true, the assent itself must be causally inevitable, given the previous events and the laws of nature. For the Stoics, as opposed to Epicurus, the cause is in me, the action is up to me, and I am responsible for it, even if determinism is true. The Stoics do not accept eliminative materialism. Since they recognize the reality of form and soul, they also recognize choices and beliefs as causes in their own right. The existence of these causes justifies claims about responsibility; but it does not presuppose any special sort of event, corresponding to an Epicurean swerve, at the basic material level.

The Stoics believe that this defence of compatibilism is equally a defence of the appropriateness of praise and blame for actions. If our rational assent makes a crucial causal difference to our actions, and if praise and blame are appropriate ways of affecting our rational assent, then praise and blame seem appropriate for the actions resulting from assent. And if praise and blame are appropriate for these actions, we have some reason to think we are responsible for them.[18]

This Stoic defence of compatibilism has not always seemed convincing. Incompatibilists have argued that the Stoic distinction between types of inevitability does not face the real difficulty in reconciling responsibility with determination by the past. But their compatibilist strategy has not been discredited; it shows that incompatibilist doubts need to be carefully examined, to see whether they are both reasonable and untouched by the Stoic argument.

vi. *Nature, happiness, and virtue*

If someone takes a 'stoical' attitude to pain, failure, or disappointment, he is untroubled by it and detached from it. This use of 'stoical' represents Stoic ethics less inaccurately than 'epicure' represents Epicurean ethics.[19] But it does not capture the basis of Stoic ethics, which is strikingly Aristotelian.

The Stoics assume that the good life for a human being is life according to nature.[20] To find what accords with nature, they attend to the development of a human being, and to the expanding exercise of his capacities. A human being's aims are not like an animal's, an unselfconscious and uncoordinated series of appetites. Instead, the agent soon learns to organize and arrange the satisfaction of his desires by reason; soon reason modifies his desires, once he sees that the satisfaction of some of them conflicts with the satisfaction of others. Having used reason instrumentally, to satisfy his desires, he comes to value the exercise of reason for its own sake. If I am told I will not have to make rational plans for my life because everything I would achieve by planning will be provided for me without it, I will see that I am being deprived of something that matters to me—the possibility of controlling my life by the exercise of my own reason.[21]

This account of human development seems to support Aristotle's claim that the function and essence of a human being is a life in accord with reason, and hence his claim that a human being's good is the complete life fully realizing a rational agent's capacities. Against Epicurus, the Stoics argue that rational activity, not pleasure, is a human being's ultimate end; they take pleasure to be a mere by-product of the satisfaction of desire.

In their view, a rational agent takes control of his life as far as he can, and guides it by his rational choice and agency; he should therefore select aims and goals that are within his power to secure. If I aim at health, wealth, enjoyment of friendship, or political

power, my aims and rational plans may be frustrated by external
conditions that are beyond my rational control—financial disaster, sickness, an injury to my friends, or foreign invasion. Epicureans want to protect themselves from these hazards, in order
to avoid pain and anxiety. Stoics give a different reason, arguing
that exposure to external hazards conflicts with the demands of
rational planning. If I concentrate on taking the right sort of
attitude to my life, and expressing the right sort of character in
what I do, then it is within my power as a rational agent to fulfil
this aim, since I can fulfil it no matter what external disasters may
overtake me. I will want, then, to be a virtuous person; if I succeed
in this, I achieve my ultimate aim of happiness.

By insisting that happiness must be up to me, within my control
as a rational agent, the Stoics reach a position closer to Socrates
than to Plato or Aristotle. For they agree with Socrates' claim
that the good person cannot suffer any harm, against Aristotle's
apparently reasonable admission that external disasters can cause
the loss of a virtuous person's happiness. Cicero correctly remarks
that 'the views that the Stoics call paradoxes seem to me to be
Socratic to the highest degree'. The Stoics begin from Aristotelian
premisses, claiming that a person's good consists in rational activity, and infer that we achieve this good by maximizing the
extent of rational control over our lives. The choice presented in
Plato's *Republic*, between justice and all the external goods, is
easy, since these external 'goods' are not real components of
happiness, and not real goods at all; they offer no attractions to
compete with virtue.[22]

But if nothing else besides virtue is good at all, then we apparently have no reason to choose health over sickness, wealth
over poverty, for ourselves or for other people. If someone attacks
me, takes my money, and breaks my leg, the Stoic realizes that I
suffer no real harm. Why then should the Stoic want to help or
protect me? And if I cannot expect help from him in such a case,
does he have much of a claim to be a genuinely virtuous person?
If the Stoics claim that virtue is the only thing that matters, they
seem to leave themselves with no intelligible account of virtue.[23]

To avoid this conclusion, the Stoics draw a distinction among
the commonly recognized goods and evils. All of these are 'indifferents', in so far as they make no difference to happiness, and

are therefore neither good nor evil; but still some are 'preferred', some 'non-preferred', indifferents. Though health and security are not goods, they are legitimately preferred over their opposites, because they contribute to the life that accords with a human being's nature.

The Stoics argue, then, that happiness does not require the complete fulfilment of human nature, since virtue is both necessary and sufficient for happiness. But it is still preferable to fulfil the other aspects of human nature; and this is why we are right to prefer some indifferents over others. Though the preferred indifferents make no difference to happiness, they are not indifferent altogether; they make some difference to the character of the life we lead, bringing it closer to its natural fulfilment.[24]

The doctrine of preferred indifferents should explain why a Stoic shares reasonable non-moral concerns with other people. Critics (most prominently the Academic Sceptic Carneades (214-c.129)) object that the preferred indifferents are legitimate objects of concern if and only if they are parts of happiness; if the critics are right, the Stoic cannot find a position between Aristotle's view (that these recognized goods are parts of happiness), and the Socratic and Cynic view (that they do not matter at all).[25] The Stoics' distinctions will serve their purpose only if they show that these criticisms are unfair.

vii. *Self and society*

It is easiest to examine the Stoics' reply to their critics if we look more closely at some of their views on practical ethics.[26] They defend the basis of human society by appeal to human nature. Human beings naturally seek the society of others, forming families, friendships, and larger communities. Since these express natural desires and fulfil human nature, the Stoics are in favour of them. Since justice, honesty, and courage are needed to maintain a stable community resting on mutual trust, the Stoics will cultivate these virtues, and since a community needs to be governed, they will want to take part in government when the good of the community requires this of them. Early Stoic political theory is radical and utopian, in the tradition of Plato's *Republic* and its early

Cynic critics. But this is not the predominant later Stoic attitude.[27]

Believing as they do in the value of a human community, practical Stoics are reliable public servants. During the later Roman Republic and early Empire, the Stoics were recognized as upright, courageous, and resolute in public life. Such an attitude is consistent with commitment to radical political ideas; but in fact the adaptive side of Stoicism tended to overshadow its critical political theory. During the reign of the emperor Augustus (27 BC–AD 14) this aspect of Stoicism made it to some extent the preferred official philosophy. The early poems of Virgil (70–19 BC) and Horace (65 BC–AD 8), written before they came under Augustus' influence, show Epicurean tendencies. But some of Horace's later Odes are celebrations of the Stoic virtues; and Aeneas, the hero of Virgil's *Aeneid*, learns (with some difficulty and backsliding) the Stoic virtues of courage, loyalty, resolution, justice, and piety.[28] These poems reflect some of the esteem that Stoicism won from the Roman ruling class; and in the second century AD the emperor Marcus Aurelius (AD 121–80) was both a Stoic philosopher and a strenuously devoted public servant.

The Stoics regard human society and its advantages as no more than preferred indifferents. Though they prefer them to their opposites, they do not regard them as necessary for their happiness or for anyone else's. They therefore do not regard failure in these areas as any genuine harm or loss of goods. Epictetus (AD $c.55$–$c.135$) was a Stoic moralist who had been a slave, used to adversity, and was later freed. For him slavery and freedom are indifferents, though freedom is preferable. He advises us to love our family, but not to regard their death as a real loss; we should not think it is any worse harm to us than the breaking of a cup would be, since both are indifferent to our happiness. In giving this advice, Epictetus takes to extremes the Socratic doctrine that the good person cannot be harmed.[29]

This Stoic independence of external fortune made some Stoic senators (members of the traditional governing class) adopt a highly independent attitude to some of the Roman emperors. Their opposition did not rest primarily on any alternative political theory, but on their refusal to accept the loss of individual dignity resulting from the monarchical tendencies in the Empire. In an attempt to undermine the status and independence of the old ruling class, the emperors tried to make its individual members more dependent on imperial favours, more like officials, servants, and functionaries, and less like independent partners in ruling. Stoics prized their dignity and independence, and could not reasonably care enough about the rewards of servility, or the penalties of independence, to accept any compromise inconsistent with virtue and integrity. When their independence became intolerable to the emperors, they did not wait to be punished, but committed suicide first.[30]

The Stoics' acceptance of suicide expresses the apparently paradoxical results of several of their doctrines. At the very moment when the sage commits suicide, he is virtuous, and therefore happy, and if he remained alive, he would still be virtuous and happy; hence his suicide cuts off a happy life. In the Stoic view, however, it is justified because of the loss of preferred indifferents that the sage would suffer if he remained alive; imprisonment, hunger, sickness, indignity, humiliation, all give him good reason for thinking the price of staying alive is too high. A virtuous person's life does not become happier or more virtuous simply by being prolonged; once I have reached the summit, I have not reached it any the more by staying there longer; and so I gain no further happiness by staying alive. Hence the Stoic believes that in some conditions suicide is, as he puts it, the 'rational departure' from life; and under the Roman Empire some leading Roman Stoics acted on this conviction.[31]

viii. *Stoic detachment*

Is the Stoic attitude to indifferents consistent, and is it morally attractive? Stoics try to avoid Epicurean withdrawal from the world; they are not concerned exclusively with their own happiness, and their concern for other people is not purely instrumental. They claim, with some justification, to be genuinely and unselfishly committed to the welfare of other people; and their commitment is all the more unselfish to the extent that their

178 Stoicism

success or failure in it does not affect their own happiness one way or the other.

We might object that a Stoic who claims to prefer one condition over another, and yet does not regret the loss of the preferable condition, cannot have an ordinary emotional life. The Stoic entirely agrees; but he denies that he therefore becomes inhuman or insensitive in any objectionable sense. For, in the Stoic view, ordinary people's attitudes to their circumstances are irrational and diseased; our feelings cause us to exaggerate the value of indifferents. We are elated by their possession and depressed by their loss; but both the elation and the depression blind us to the real value of these indifferents, and paralyse our capacity for rational judgement about them. The Stoic sage avoids this paralysis. He is concerned for his family, friends, and community; he works for their benefit, and attends to their needs for preferred indifferents. Like the rest of us, he must face the unwelcome possibility of losing them; but such a loss does not deceive him into exaggerated and irrational laments for himself.[32]

Still, we may wonder how the Stoic can be genuinely committed to a particular aim if failure in it does not cause him pain or regret, or any other damage to his happiness. We might agree that the Stoic sage will be a benevolent and energetic spouse, or parent, or friend, or ally. But can he be a sympathetic one, if his own happiness and his own feelings are unaffected by the circumstances of the people whose welfare he tries to promote? The Stoics are accused of abolishing sympathy, and so of increasing vices in the attempt to cure them. Their claim to be exempt from irrational emotions may well appear, as it does to Milton, an expression of self-deceiving pride:

> The Stoic last in Philosophic pride,
> By him call'd virtue; and his virtuous man,
> Wise, perfect in himself, and all possessing
> Equal to God, oft shames not to prefer,
> As fearing God nor man, contemning all
> Wealth, pleasure, pain or torment, death and life,
> Which when he lists, he leaves, or boasts he can,
> For all his tedious talk is but vain boast,
> Or subtle shifts, conviction to evade.[33]

The 'philosophic pride' that claims exemption from ordinary human weaknesses may appear to exclude a Stoic from genuine human virtue.

The Stoics need not admit this charge. They might argue that they display 'Stoic sympathy'—the concern and attention that results from taking other people's loss of preferred indifferents seriously, and being able to think of oneself in their position. They cannot show 'pathological sympathy'—the sort of feeling that requires the belief that a similar loss to oneself would be a loss of happiness. It is quite possible that we—as non-Stoics who have not learnt that virtue is identical to happiness—demand pathological sympathy from others. We think our happiness is affected by external conditions, and so we want a friend to share our mistaken distress when we think we are harmed. But, in the Stoic view, this outlook of ours simply betrays how far we are from being proper Stoics. In a community of Stoics no one will demand pathological sympathy, and no one will blame the Stoic sage for not offering it. Everyone will realize that they are better off without pathological sympathy, and will value the expression of Stoic sympathy.

Would we be better off if (assuming that it is psychologically possible) we gave up pathological for Stoic sympathy? The Stoic argues that once we allow ourselves ordinary emotional reactions, we concede that preferred indifferents are parts of our good, and that in that case we cannot take virtue seriously enough. We may well doubt whether the Stoics need to go to such lengths to defend the appropriate sort of primacy for virtue and reason.

ix. *The self and the cosmos*

Stoic ethics begins from nature, and tries to describe the life in agreement with nature. So far we have understood 'nature' as the human nature to be realized in an individual person; and this is certainly part of what the Stoics intend. But they also intend 'nature' in another way, to refer to universal nature as a whole. As we saw, they regard the world as an ordered whole, guided by the *pneuma* immanent in it. They require the virtuous person to live 'in accordance with experience of what happens by nature'.

The Stoic does not think of himself and his actions simply in relation to his own interest, or to the interest of people around him, but also thinks of his place in the world order as a whole. He plays his part well and steadfastly in the cosmic drama.[34]

Even though we will conform to the world order whether we want to or not, and even if we try to act against it, still it is in our power to understand and accept it for ourselves. The fates 'lead us if we are willing and drag us if we are not'; and playing our part well is not playing or failing to play our causally determined part, but doing it with the right aims, which are up to us (even though it is causally determined whether we have them or not). The apparent difficulties in the Stoic position are supposed to disappear once we apply the Stoic doctrines of fate, assent, and responsibility.[35]

The Stoics ascribe some of the traditional properties of the gods to their cosmic reason; they approve of Homer's claim that 'the will of Zeus was fulfilled' in the events of history, and they attribute some intelligible purpose to the cosmic reason. They must attribute some plan to it, if their understanding of cosmic reason is to guide their moral choices.[36]

Still, it is not very clear what the cosmic reason prescribes, in the Stoic view, or how we find this out. The Stoics reject any cosmic dualism which recognizes both a good and an evil intelligence; but we might wonder how they have ruled out such a dualist explanation of the observed characteristics of the world. Some aspects of the world seem to damage human welfare; the Stoics do not infer that the sage should also try to damage human welfare, but they do not explain why not. They need some reason for being selective in following the natural course of the world in making moral choices.

x. *Conclusion*

Stoicism was the most durably attractive philosophical system in the Classical world, both to philosophers and to the educated upper classes in general. Some of the reasons for the success of Stoicism were no doubt distinct from its philosophical merits. It could absorb much traditional morality and religion in an apparently rational framework. It could therefore offer comfort and reassurance to conservative and patriotic people who found it hard to take traditional Greek and Roman morality and religion at face value, but still found it difficult and dangerous to reject them entirely.[37] The results of Stoicism may in fact have been less conservative than the results of Epicurean withdrawal; but the appearance was far less revolutionary. While the Epicureans enjoyed some notoriety among the more unsettled educated classes of the late Roman Republic (for whom Lucretius wrote), Stoicism suited the rather more earnest, staid, and conservative temper of the Empire. Both the Epicurean Cassius and the Stoic Brutus were moved by political and philosophical ideals to assassinate Julius Caesar; but under the Empire Epicureans lost any collective political concerns. While the Stoics were not mere conformists, they eventually adapted themselves to the outlook of the Roman upper class.[38]

Stoicism did not endorse or depend on a particular social or political structure, in the way that Aristotle both supports the city-state and relies on it for the application to social life of his ethical principles. Nor was the Stoic identified with a particular place within any social structure. Stoicism could appeal to Africans, Italians, and Syrians, to emperors, bureaucrats, generals, and slaves (though not to those without access to the education typically reserved for the upper classes and some of their more privileged dependents). In these ways the Stoic message was well adapted for its potential customers in the Hellenistic world and the Roman Empire.

But these features of Stoicism do not entirely explain its success, which cannot be entirely separated from its philosophical merits. Unlike Epicureanism, which quickly froze into a fixed dogma, Stoicism developed, and became more complex, comprehensive, and plausible. It forms a system of interconnected doctrines confirming and supporting each other. Plato, Aristotle, and Epicurus never managed as much; and the Stoics' successors in the history of philosophy have produced nothing more comprehensive and systematic.

The Stoics faced some acute critics, and, to their credit, took criticism seriously. We can therefore form some idea of the main difficulties and apparent weaknesses in the system:

1. The Stoics' attempt to be complete materialists raises difficulties for their treatment of form.

2. Stoic ethics seems to be an unstable combination of self-sufficiency and concern for others.

3. By identifying the divine with the natural the Stoics raise at least as many puzzles as they solve. If the god is nothing more than the order of nature, how can the god be a moral ideal or a source of guidance? And if the god is simply nature, are the Stoics reducing the divine to the natural, and so proving themselves to be atheists?

The Stoics tried to answer objections on these points. Philosophers who were unsatisfied with their answers developed new philosophical positions partly by trying to do better than the Stoics had done. Neoplatonism and Christianity, the main philosophical successors of Stoicism, tried to correct what they took to be Stoic errors. In doing so, however, they paid one considerable, indeed exaggerated, compliment to Stoicism. For they took the Stoic and Aristotelian systems to be the best that scientific reason and argument could provide; and they concluded that if these systems were inadequate, something more than scientific reason must be needed.

In the Neoplatonist view, expressed by Plotinus, scientific, argumentative, discursive reason, of the sort that is applied to the study of nature, is only an inferior expression of reason, and can therefore grasp only superficial and misleading impressions of ultimate reality. To reach an adequate grasp of ultimate reality, reason must transcend these limits imposed by argument and inference, and turn to immediate and non-argumentative intuition. The Stoics built an impressive structure of scientific argument; and Plotinus, examining what they built, believes that scientific argument necessarily falls short of the complete truth.

The Christian response goes still further. In Neoplatonism reason transcends the ordinary level of scientific argument, but still relies on some rational process and insight to reach a grasp of ultimate reality. Christian critics of philosophical reason decided that reason, in its Stoic or its Plotinian embodiment, could not grasp ultimate reality at all. While the Stoics could express some plausible thoughts about God, they could not separate these from the errors about God that resulted from identifying him with the order of nature. Christians looked outside reason for revelation; God had to reveal the truth about himself, and human reason could not discover this truth from its own resources. Though Christian theology tries to answer many of the questions that also concern Stoic natural theology, its answers do not belong to natural theology, since they do not depend wholly on philosophical arguments derived from the study of nature.

Philosophers, then, tended to suppose that in turning away from Stoicism they had to turn away from the scientific reason that would get them no further than Stoicism. In return, Stoicism, or some modification of it, has tended to appeal to those who could neither accept the claims of a dogmatic religion nor dismiss a religious attitude altogether. This attitude to Stoicism survived the Classical world, and was revived with the rediscovery of Stoicism in the sixteenth century. Since the Renaissance Stoic ethics and some aspects of the Stoic view of nature have attracted those who have found it impossible either to accept Christianity or to lapse into complete atheism. The Stoic sage's sense of duty, his concern for others, his constancy, his independence of external conditions, his freedom from irrational impulses, have offered a secular moral ideal that has influenced philosophers as different as Spinoza, Hume, and Kant.

Still, though Stoicism has appeared to be an alternative to Christianity, it has also influenced the development of Christian doctrine. Christian thinkers wanted to show that natural reason laid a foundation for faith; and to show this they turned naturally to the Stoic view of the cosmos as an ordered whole, guided by an immanent law, and manifesting a divine intelligence. Saint Paul argues on Stoic grounds that the Gentiles had some access to the nature of God. For the Stoic, as for the Jew and the Christian, it was true both that 'the heavens declare the glory of God', and that 'the law of the Lord is perfect'. Much of Stoic natural religion, therefore, was incorporated into Christian defences of faith, addressed to non-believers.[39]

Similarly, Stoic ethics showed how someone might live his life with integrity and concern for others, without devoting himself to worldly success or rewards from society. In Stoic ethics Christians could see how to be unworldly, without being indifferent to the state of the world or to the practices and institutions needed to maintain a human community. For these reasons Stoic ethics came to be included in expositions of Christian ethics. Through these influences on Christianity, Stoic ideas came to guide some of the thoughts and actions of people who would have been wholly untouched by a purely philosophical movement.[40]

10

Plotinus

i. *The revival of Platonism*

In 80 BC Antiochus revived dogmatic Platonism, by founding the 'Old Academy'. In the mid-first century BC Andronicus' new edition of the works of Aristotle was both a symptom and a cause of reviving interest in Aristotle.[1] In the first two centuries AD the 'Middle Platonists' continued the movement begun by Antiochus. In the same period Aspasius (AD *c.*100–50) and Alexander (AD *c.*200) began the series of commentaries on Aristotle that both deepened understanding of the philosopher and included further philosophical reflexion on Aristotelian questions in their relation to later schools of philosophy.[2]

The philosophy of Plotinus (205–70) is the product of these Platonic and Aristotelian revivals. The influence of Plato is obvious; and as Plotinus' biographer Porphyry writes: 'Stoic and Peripatetic doctrines are mixed inconspicuously in his writings.' He normally began his lectures by commenting on some passage from a Platonist writer or a commentator on Aristotle. 'But he said nothing straight out of these books, but had a distinctive view of his own.' The results of his reflexion are concentrated in the treatises divided by Porphyry into six groups of nine, and hence called 'Enneads' (Greek *ennea*, 'nine'). These are more like meditations than systematic treatises; but together they present Plotinus' view of the conclusions that ought to be drawn from Plato.[3]

ii. *Plotinus' universe*

Plotinus recognizes three primary realities or 'hypostases': the One (also called the Good), Intellect, and Soul. These are the primary realities because all the realities, or things with any degree of reality, in the universe, are manifestations of them. Much of Plotinus' argument tries to explain the nature of the three hypostases, to show how other things manifest them, and to demonstrate that we need not recognize any other hypostases.[4]

To see if Plotinus is right, we need to examine the three hypostases in two different roles, derived from the 'upward' and 'downward' paths distinguished in Plato's *Republic*. The upward path turns the inquirer's mind 'from becoming to being', leading him from his exclusive preoccupation with the sensible world to the discovery of the Good (which Plotinus identifies with the One). Once we have discovered the Good, we follow the downward path, and understand how the other realities depend on the Good. In Plotinus' view we follow the upward path by recognizing Soul, then Intellect, then the One, advancing to steadily higher realities. When we follow the downward path, we begin with the One, and see first how Intellect emerges from it, and then how Soul emerges from Intellect. The upward path gradually reveals to us the realities there are; the downward path shows how their existence explains the world of our experience.[5]

Two puzzles about the three hypostases will focus some of our questions. First, why are there three rather than one? Plotinus' task is to 'turn them [his hearers] round to the opposite and primary things, and lead them back to what is supreme, one, and primary'. He advises us to 'lead back the god in you to the divine in the universe [literally, the all]'. In this discovery the inquirer recognizes his own unity with the One, and also recognizes that in some way the One is all there is. If that is so, and if the other two supposed realities really just correspond to inadequate ways of conceiving the One, should Plotinus not recognize just one reality rather than three?[6] Second, why are there only three hypostases? Even if we allow that the universe we know includes intellects and souls, we are also inclined to think it contains material bodies; we may even believe that souls and intellects are reducible to features of material bodies. Plotinus' three hypostases seem to leave out the most basic reality of all.

Plotinus maintains none the less that there are exactly three hypostases, neither more nor fewer. To show that he has left nothing out, he reverses the order of a materialist argument.

Whereas the materialist seeks to understand soul and intellect as features of body, Plotinus seeks to interpret matter by reference to soul and intellect. If we examine our beliefs about matter, we should see that it cannot be an independent reality, and that our conception of it is incoherent.[7] These rather startling claims about matter and the physical world give us the best opportunity to understand Plotinus' arguments.

iii. *Form and matter*

Plotinus begins with the common conception of matter as 'some sort of subject and receptacle of forms'. Following Aristotle, he argues that unqualified change requires matter as its subject; since the most basic stuffs, the four elements (earth, air, fire, and water), can change, these changes also require a material subject, which must be without positive qualities of its own altogether. Matter must therefore be completely indeterminate, and we can think of it only indeterminately. Indeed, this is why matter is necessary for bodies, since a mere combination of perceptible properties would not result in a body. We must assume matter as the basis for all the changes in bodies, even though it cannot itself be acted on.[8]

This argument to show that change requires bare matter is open to objection. Plotinus argues correctly, following Aristotle, that if it is possible for one and the same subject x to change from being F to being G, then neither F nor G can be essential to x. It still might be true, however, that x is essentially either-F-or-G (even though a surface is neither essentially red nor essentially green nor . . . (etc.), it still essentially has some colour or other); moreover it might be x's being F that makes x capable of changing to being G (in order to become white, a surface must be not-white to begin with). Plotinus seems to argue that if x is neither essentially F nor essentially G, x is essentially neither F nor G, so that the ultimate subject of change must be unqualified. Since this argument is unsound, he does not show that change requires unqualified matter; he seems to misunderstand the relation of a subject to its properties.[9]

Though the argument from change fails, Plotinus also argues from the deficiencies of the senses. We might naively suppose that the senses assure us that matter has perceptible properties in its own right. But in fact the senses do not tell us anything about matter in its own right. For we know from experience of illusions and perceptual errors that we could be aware of these perceptible properties even if nothing external is correlated with them. Hence the perceptible properties are simply appearances, not properties of the external matter in its own right. 'What is known through sense is an image of the thing, and sense does not grasp the thing itself, since it [the thing itself] remains external.' The external thing is matter, which in itself has none of the properties that we attribute to it in perception.[10]

Plotinus is too confident in his use of the argument from perceptual errors. For it supports, at most, the sceptical conclusion that we cannot know whether matter has perceptible properties; but Plotinus too readily reaches the much more definite conclusion that we know that matter cannot have perceptible properties. He might, however, following Democritus, supply some further argument for this conclusion.[11]

If we accept Plotinus' conclusion, however, we might still object that unqualified matter, with no positive qualities, scarcely counts as a being. Plotinus quite agrees; for he calls matter complete privation and not-being. The basis of what we took to be physical reality turns out to be unreality.[12]

Plotinus approaches this contrast between form and matter not only from our ordinary experience of the external world, but also from our awareness of beauty. He begins from Plato's account of our gradual advance through different types of beauty to the Form of beauty; but he adapts Plato's account to fit his own metaphysical views. He argues that the object of aesthetic awareness—the beauty in the object that produces our characteristic response—is not matter, or any of the properties of a material object as such, but form. The beauty of the Parthenon does not consist in its colour or size, since we could find ugly things with the same colour and size; but the beauty would be destroyed if we dismantled the building, and arranged the same pieces in a different order. Hence the beauty of the Parthenon remains in so far as the same structure and order remains in these materials. Our experience of beauty confirms the result of our analysis of matter and form, in so far as it reveals the superiority of form.[13]

iv. *Soul*

So far, reflexion on common sense has revealed the reality of form and the unreality of matter. Plotinus now follows Aristotle's suggestion beyond Aristotle's own intention, and identifies form with soul; and so he infers that by proving the reality of form and the unreality of matter, he has equally proved the reality of soul and the unreality of body. He infers that the only reality is mind-dependent, essentially an object of awareness for some soul.[14]

Though we might at first suppose that there are many souls— Socrates', yours, mine, and so on—Plotinus rejects this common-sense view, and believes there is only one Soul. He argues that the common belief in many souls depends on belief in matter; for we distinguish different souls by the different bodies they belong to, and if we admit the unreality of bodies, we cannot recognize distinct material bodies. To this extent Plotinus is more of a materialist than Plato; for he challenges Plato's assumption that Socrates remains a particular soul even without a body.[15]

We might still find it hard to abandon belief in a plurality of souls; your experiences are not accessible to me in the way that mine are, and their inaccessibility to me might seem to imply that you and I have two different souls. Plotinus denies any such implication. We ordinarily believe that there is one soul in one body, but we do not expect that each part of the body will be aware of every other part, or that the soul will be aware of every disturbance in the body. Similarly, if we come to believe that there is just one soul in the two (alleged) bodies that are yours and mine, we can still explain the apparent differences in our experiences by ascribing them to different states of one soul. Reflexion on the complex relations between the states of one soul (as commonly conceived) should undermine our confidence in a plurality of souls. We need not, therefore, hesitate to accept the consequence of the unreality of matter, and hence to recognize a single Soul (the Plotinian hypostasis). This is not to say that the appearance of many souls is a mere illusion; for their apparent plurality reflects some genuine plurality in the Soul itself. It is wrong to call individual souls parts of the Soul; but each of them expresses partially what is fully expressed by the Soul as a whole.[16]

Soul, however, is not the highest level of reality; even when we recognize it, our conception of reality is still defective. For the Soul's mode of being is temporal; we cannot conceive conscious life except as a temporal sequence. Time is 'the life of the soul in change that moves from one way of life to another'; and since time is unreal, the soul cannot be part of reality either.

Though time depends on soul, it also requires a world of change for the soul to be aware of. To this extent Plotinus agrees with Plato in making time depend on the orderly changes in the universe. The reality of time depends on the reality of the material universe, and, conversely, the unreality of matter implies the unreality of time. Our belief in the temporality of our own experience—indeed, our inability to think of our experience in non-temporal terms—simply reflects our deep attachment to the false belief in matter.[17]

We begin by thinking of ourselves as distinct souls with temporal sequences of experiences, each soul attached to some bit of matter. But gradually we come to see that we have no ground for this view of ourselves. As we free ourselves from our false beliefs, we no longer regard ourselves as essentially temporal sequences of conscious states. We conceive ourselves no longer as Soul, but as Intellect.

v. *Intellect*

Rejection of the material universe and of time requires rejection of all claims to knowledge of spatio-temporal and perceptible objects, properties, and events. All we can know without reference to time, sense, and matter are the non-sensible, immaterial, unchanging Platonic Forms. Plotinus regards these as the objects of knowledge for Intellect.

In Plato's view, the Forms are extra-mental; they exist independently of any mind that knows them, and are discovered, not invented, by the knower. But this claim about independence and externality raises the questions that also arise for the claim that one mind is external to another. In both cases Plotinus believes that since any clear notion of externality applies to spatio-temporal, sensible, material things, and not to other things, non-spatial Forms cannot be outside anything; and since we know about external objects by perceiving them, we could not know about non-sensible Forms if they were external to us. Forms must therefore be within Intellect and part of it. Though Plotinus (as usual) does not explicitly criticize Plato, he implicitly criticizes him for making the Forms too much like ordinary sensible objects.[18]

On the other hand, he agrees with Plato that Forms are not the arbitrary creation of intellect. Just as there are no objects of knowledge without Intellect, so also Intellect would not be what it is without the Forms. Plato's doctrine of recollection, as Plotinus interprets it, describes the intellect's discovery of its own nature and structure, not of something outside it.[19]

We might suppose that intellect argues from premisses to conclusions, or that it formulates definitions and traces their consequences. But this inferential conception of intellect is essentially temporal, and therefore, in Plotinus' view, quite inadequate. But it is hard to avoid; for Intellect knows itself and the different objects that are parts of itself, and we conceive our awareness of such plurality as inferential and temporal awareness.[20]

We have therefore not yet reached an adequate conception of reality. Just as Soul involved the temporal being that seemed to depend on matter, so Intellect seems to involve the discursive reasoning that seems to depend on time, and hence ultimately on matter. If we cannot conceive reality without appealing to concepts that we have already rejected, we cannot have found the right conception of reality. Hence we cannot conceive either Soul or Intellect as parts of ultimate reality.

vi. *The One*

To show how we can go beyond our conception of Intellect, Plotinus appeals to Plato's alleged contrast between inferential and intuitive knowledge. Intuitive knowledge does not require reasoning, or any temporally extended process of surveying different aspects of a situation. It is the mode of cognition appropriate to eternity, the non-temporal mode of being in which 'the whole is always present to it, not this at one time, and that at another, but all things together'. The normal way of gaining knowledge in a temporal mode is to survey parts of an object at different times; but in a non-temporal mode knowledge requires the presence of the object all together, to be taken in (we might roughly say) at a glance. Since intuitive knowledge takes everything in at a glance, it does not require inference; and since it does not distinguish different aspects of the object, it does not apply concepts to the object in the ordinary way.[21]

If intuitive Intellect recognizes no plurality, its object must be absolutely simple; hence Plotinus calls it the One. But 'One' is to be understood strictly negatively, as involving simply the denial of plurality; Plotinus does not mean that it is just one object, or that it has just one property. For he agrees with Plato that to be one is to be one of something—one tree, one dog, one Form of beauty, and so on; hence if the One is one of something, at least two concepts must apply to it, and we introduce plurality. Similarly, we cannot say that the One is a being, since nothing can be without being something or other. Following Plato (as he supposes) Plotinus identifies the One with the Good; for it is 'beyond being', an absolutely simple object of intuitive knowledge underlying our discursive knowledge of the Forms. It is not a being, but the source of what we regard as beings; and it is not a good, except in so far as it is the cause of other goods.[22]

This account of the ultimate object of knowledge still fails to eliminate plurality. For in so far as Intellect distinguishes itself from its object, it still recognizes plurality and applies concepts to the object it is aware of (it still thinks of the subject as 'I', in contrast to 'the object I am aware of', and so must use the necessary concepts to draw this distinction). It must recognize that it is not allowed this distinction, and so must cease to distinguish itself from its object. Moreover, Plotinus argues that we cannot know any object that we grasp only through some mediating thought or image. We do not know external perceptible objects, since we do not know them directly, but depend on sensory impressions for our access to them. Similarly, if Intellect had to receive impressions of its objects, and were not itself identical to them, it could not claim knowledge of them.²³

Plotinus' conception of beauty gives still another reason for rejecting any distinction between the knower and the object known. We initially found beauty in form rather than matter; and our desire for beauty leads us to seek knowledge of the purely formal and immaterial objects of Intellect, freeing ourselves from the illusions and distractions of the senses. Since our aspiration for intelligible reality leads us to the One, the One is also the ultimate source of beauty and the primary object of love. Plotinus follows Plato in regarding our attitude to beauty, not as some disinterested contemplation or intellectual pleasure, but as passionate desire. The lover discovers his identity with the object of love when he discovers that the highest object of love is the Good, which is the One; for we cannot discover the One without discovering that we are identical to it. As Berkeley says:

The supreme Being, saith Plotinus, as he excludes all diversity, is ever alike present, and we are then present to him, when, recollected and abstracted from the world and sensible objects, we are most free and disengaged from all variety.²⁴

In our identification of ourselves with the One we have reached the limit of our progress from common sense and the perceptible world. Plotinus has tried to show us that each stage of the progress is forced on us by some conflict or inadequacy in our present conception of reality—as material, temporal, or plural. But we may wonder if the results are worth the effort. For if we are identified with a One that can have no predicate—not even 'one' or 'being'—truly applied to it, this result seems rather similar to being left with nothing at all.

Plotinus does not agree that he has left us with nothing. Though the One transcends all the properties we attribute to it, we reach a less inaccurate account if we attribute to it the properties of all the Platonic Forms rather than none or only some of them. The negative conclusions about the One should not lead us to think we have found out nothing about it.

vii. *Emanation from the One*

The positive side of Plotinus' views about the One appears more clearly in the 'downward path', the derivation of the lower hypostases from the higher. This path is not a temporal process of derivation; Plotinus insists that it indicates only relations of priority and dependence. He describes it as 'emanation' or 'radiation' from the higher reality, involving no change or diminution in the higher reality.[25]

The One's completeness and perfection inevitably and timelessly result in its producing something; and Plotinus sometimes suggests that Intellect is simply the One's way of understanding itself. Though we do not completely or correctly grasp the One if we take it to be expressed in Intellect, this is the best we can do to grasp it. Similarly, Soul adds change and temporality to the reality that is recognized by Intellect. Though these cannot strictly apply to the world of the Forms, we need them to understand what it is like; hence discursive reason is the necessary offspring of Intellect. We cannot say what the One is like without articulating it into Forms; and similarly we cannot say what the Forms are like without inferential thought and reasoning, which we must conceive as temporal processes.[26]

Since Plotinus thinks matter is not-being and illusion, he refuses it a place among the realities. None the less, he recognizes something like a further stage of emanation; he has to explain why we think we are in a material world, and why we do not at once accept his view of reality. He refers to the soul's 'audacity', and desire to 'belong to itself'. Wanting to affirm its individuality, it attaches itself to different bodies, and so divides itself into individual souls.[27]

Sometimes Plotinus seems to regret the soul's self-assertion, and to treat it as an original act of rebellion, similar to the Fall in Genesis. But he seems equally to suggest that self-assertion is inevitable and beneficial. If we are to grasp the Forms, we need conceptual discursive thought; we cannot grasp this except as a process in a single consciousness; and in grasping such a process the soul asserts and individualizes itself. It individualizes itself in different souls connected to different bits of matter, since Plotinus believes that this is the only way to distinguish different individual souls.[28]

This account of Plotinus' view suggests that matter is a pre-existent reality that the soul somehow connects with itself; and some of his other remarks also suggest this. Matter is the source of evil, and (as Plato says in the *Phaedo*) of the soul's forgetfulness and error. If it has this effect on the soul, it seems to have real causal influence. If, however, the soul's self-assertion is the origin of evil, and if matter is an illusion, a figment of a deceived and self-assertive soul, its role in evil seems very slight.[29]

A soul's connexion with a particular body may lead it to identify itself exclusively with this embodied individual, and so may make it forget its identity with Soul as a whole, and hence with Intellect and the One. But matter itself need not be responsible for this error; for belief in the reality of matter may simply be the result of a soul's taking its own individuality too seriously, and once the false belief is removed, a soul's association with matter need not harm it.[30]

viii. *Matter and evil*

Plotinus' harsh remarks about matter might suggest that he will reject the whole material universe as evil. His apparently other-worldly attitude seems to encourage the sort of cosmological dualism that treats the material world as the product of the evil in conflict with the good in the universe. He allows that the visible universe, being material, displays the conflict and discord that are absent from the higher reality. We might infer that the bad aspects of the world result from the recalcitrance of matter, and the good aspects from the presence of reason. But this conclusion would accord to matter a degree of independent reality that Plotinus denies it. He argues that the evils are necessary for the good of the whole; without them goodness would not be active in the material world, since good is the avoidance of evil.[31]

Plotinus uses two analogies to explain away the presence of evil—the organism and the drama. An organism has different parts with superior and inferior functions, sometimes in apparent conflict, but really co-operating to serve the good of the whole.

In a drama, similarly, different actors play different parts, superior and inferior, but their parts are all designed for the perfection of the whole play. The objector who argues from the apparent evils in the material world to the denial of providence concentrates on unfairly selected parts, without attending to the character of the whole. Moreover, if we see the comparative unimportance of pain, death, and anything else that happens to the body, we will not overestimate the evils.[32]

But if all of an evil person's actions promote the greater good, and if he is simply playing a part he is required to play in the cosmic drama, how is his action evil, and how can he properly be blamed for it? Plotinus faces the question about responsibility that also arises for the Stoics. In any case, how can he maintain that matter or the soul's self-assertion explains evil, if there is no evil for it to explain?[33]

At this point we must look more closely at Plotinus' conception of the individual person. Several problems in his doctrine converge here, and it is hard to find a clear or consistent view.

ix. *The Soul and the self*

Plotinus regards a particular embodied person as a compound of body and soul, resulting from the soul's descent into matter and individuality. But the descent is not complete; not all of the soul that belongs to each of us has descended into body, and part of it remains associated with the world of Intellect, even though we do not realize this.[34]

Plotinus calls the embodied person a 'compound' or 'animal', as Aristotle does; but this compound includes both a soul and a living body, and the living body has a further soul or 'shadow of soul'. The second soul, not the first, is the cause of ordinary physical life. Plotinus rejects Aristotle's conception of the soul as the realization of the body—the substantial, but inseparable, form of the living body. He agrees that soul is substance, but insists that it is separable; it cannot be in a body, in any ordinary sense of 'in', because it is immaterial and therefore cannot be in any place.[35]

Since he believes in an immaterial soul, Plotinus has to explain the soul's apparent tendency to be affected by changes in the body or the external world. Sense-perception and emotion seem to be mental effects of bodily or external stimuli, and we might wonder how such stimuli could affect an immaterial soul. In Plotinus' view, however, only the body is affected, and the soul simply notices what happens to the body, without being itself affected. He believes 'we' are really identical to the reasoning soul, and that other aspects of us (as we normally think of ourselves) are 'ours', but not parts of 'us'. We are not strictly affected by the body; but we are concerned for it as a close dependent.[36]

Plotinus wants to explain vice as the result of the soul's attachment to the body, without conceding that the body affects the soul. Hence he claims that the vicious soul attaches itself to the body, by its own free choice, by being too concerned with the body's desires; and once again the body seems to provide the opportunity for evil rather than its cause. Training in the virtues is needed to cure this excessive attachment to the body. Some virtues require the training of the 'compound', the living animal belonging to each of us; but the higher virtues are purifications of the soul from concern with the body.[37]

The good pursued by these higher virtues is contemplation; for Plotinus agrees with one side of Aristotle's argument, and values contemplation far more highly than action. Aristotle cannot regard contemplation as the whole of our good without violating his own demand that the good should be complete; for pure contemplation seems to leave out the legitimate aims of the human being as a whole, which include action and the moral virtues. Plotinus need not admit this difficulty. Since, in his view, contemplative reason is proper to the reasoning soul that is really ourselves, it is the whole of *our* good, and the misfortunes and pains suffered by the body are not really ours. He therefore agrees with Socrates, Epicurus, and the Stoics, in their view that the virtuous person is happy even when he is being tortured. But he disagrees with them on a more basic issue, since he does not think the torture really happens to the virtuous person himself—it happens to the animal from which the rational soul detaches itself.[38]

Plotinus speaks as though contemplatives will practise the recognized moral virtues. But if we cultivate indifference to the
body, why should we not allow it to behave viciously? We might
think that a contemplative could detach himself from concern
with the body, and not take its desires too seriously; why then
should he not indulge them, without going to the trouble of
restraining them? Plotinus needs to explain why this sort of intemperance is incompatible with a life devoted to contemplation.
He replies that the professed detachment of intemperate people
conceals a persistent attraction for bodily satisfactions. But to
defend this reply, and hence to show that a life of intemperance
and injustice cannot also be a life of contemplation and detachment, he seems to be forced to assume a closer connexion between
body and soul than he is willing to admit.[39]

Plotinus affirms that we are responsible for our actions, and
rejects Stoic determinism because he takes it to be incompatible
with such responsibility. But he admits that our physical movements are, to a considerable degree, externally determined; and
sometimes he suggests that we act freely, on our own initiative,
only when we act on correct reason. Elsewhere he insists, in
Aristotelian terms, that our actions are up to us, and that we are
rightly held responsible for them. In a third context he simply
insists that the wicked should not be excused even if they are not
responsible for being wicked.[40]

These claims do not constitute a clearly consistent view. If we
agree with Plotinus in identifying ourselves only with our reason,
and in regarding the body as something outside ourselves, we
might want to argue that we have no reasonable concern with
what it does, and so are not legitimately blamed for what it does.
Plotinus rejects this line of argument, just as he rejects criticism
of the conventional virtues; but his own views do not seem to
leave him the sort of reply he needs.

Plotinus' identification of the self with the rational soul draws
our attention to the paradox in his own ethical ideal. In one way,
he describes the realization and fulfilment of ourselves; but it is
an unusual kind of fulfilment. If I conceive myself as a rational
soul, I still have not grasped the highest level of reality; and once
I reach the highest level, I cease to believe in any distinction

between myself and the One. The result of my detachment from the body is the eventual loss, if I face the truth about ultimate reality, of any sense of my own distinct reality. We may wonder if, in that case, it is good for us to face the truth. Plotinus never contemplates any such gap between theory and practice; but since his theory threatens us with our own destruction, he seems to force the question on us.

x. *The significance of Plotinus*

Plotinus pursues a tendency in Plato to assert the claims of the rational soul over those of the body and the senses. We noticed lines of thought in the *Phaedo* and the *Republic* that are sometimes uneasily balanced with Plato's other beliefs; and in Plotinus these lines of thought are fully developed. His views on body and soul, form and matter, perception and thought, all claim to reveal incoherences in common sense. His claim to find these incoherences is a serious challenge, even if we do not accept his alternative conception of reality.

Exposure of the incoherences in common sense leads Plotinus not to scepticism, but to a mystical conception of reality. He claims that the aims and aspirations of the knowing and desiring subject are fully satisfied only by union between the knower and the known, and between the lover and the beloved. Indeed, he argues that every conception below this one undermines itself, because it relies on untenable assumptions about matter, time, and individuality. He seeks to show how rigorous use of discursive, inferential reason eventually rejects itself, and forces us to conceive reality in ways that satisfy our rational aspirations more fully than reason itself can satisfy them.

In presenting his view of ultimate reality, Plotinus shows an unusual degree of self-consciousness about his own descriptive resources. He reminds us that he is trying to say and think the unsayable and unthinkable. Thinking and describing involve discursive reason, making distinctions, drawing conclusions—activities that essentially misrepresent the character of the reality being described.

He is more careful than many philosophers to avoid the literal application to ultimate, non-spatial, and non-temporal reality of terms that presuppose spatial and temporal conditions; and he sees how pervasive these presuppositions are. As we have seen, he is more thoroughly empiricist and materialist than either Plato or Aristotle. For he argues that we are often tempted to apply many concepts to non-spatio-temporal, immaterial things, when in fact these concepts apply, if at all, only to spatio-temporal, material things; that is why we cannot coherently think of an immaterial intellect recognizing a plurality of objects and distinguishing itself from them. To this extent Plotinus agrees with some forms of empiricism and materialism, in rejecting claims to give a coherent account of anything beyond the bounds of ordinary experience. On the other hand, he rejects empiricism and materialism, since he argues that these same concepts cannot be coherently applied to anything. This aspect of Plotinus' argument is more thoroughly destructive than most sceptical arguments have been.

Still, he argues that some inaccurate conceptions of the One are better than others; and his account of emanation is the closest he thinks we can come to describing the non-spatial and non-temporal realities that explain the appearance of a spatio-temporal world. Though the limitations of our conceptual scheme limit our capacity to describe ultimate reality, the demand for an explanation of our experience forces us to exploit our capacity beyond the limits of its accuracy.

Plotinus argues that this conflict between the limits of our resources and the demands we make of them is inevitable, but not intolerable; reason allows us both to know that there is an indescribable ultimate reality, and to find the right way to misdescribe it. This aspect of Plotinus, and of later Platonism in general, explains some of its appeal to Christian thinkers (following the lead of the Jewish philosopher Philo (*c*.20 BC–*c*. AD 50)).[41] For Christian theology, in contrast to both the Greek and the Hebrew religious traditions, it seemed necessary to conceive God as transcending the concepts and descriptions appropriate to other forms of reality. Christian thinkers, therefore, found that they shared Plotinus' concern to describe a transcendent reality, with proper awareness of the inadequacy of any description. The origins of Christianity make it surprising that it should draw on the most abstract of Greek philosophical systems; and we must see why Christian thought developed in this particular direction.

I I

Christianity and Greek Thought

i. *Introduction*

To move from Greek philosophy to the first four centuries of
Christian thought is to introduce a large new subject. But we
would leave a serious gap in an account of Greek philosophy if
we said nothing about Christianity. The formation of Christian
thought was influenced from the beginning by Greek philosophy.
Some of the Jewish scriptures, and especially some of the Apo-
cryphal works, are affected by Stoicism; and Philo's (*c.*20 BC–
c. AD 50) attempt to explain Jewish religion in Platonist terms
began a Christian tradition.[1]

It would not have been easy to predict the mutual influence of
Christian faith and Greek philosophy. Saint Paul is quite defiant:

For the Jews ask for a sign, and the Greeks inquire after wisdom, but
we proclaim Christ crucified, a cause of offence for Jews, and a piece of
foolishness to Gentiles, but for those who are called, both Jews and
Greeks, God's power and God's wisdom.

Many Greeks agreed with his account of their attitude; but he
suggests that their impression of Christianity is superficial. Similarly, Christ claims continuity with the ethical traditions familiar
to his audience: 'Do not suppose that I came to abolish the law
and the prophets; I did not come to abolish them, but to complete
them.' Christians eventually agreed that his claim to complete
human traditions was true not only of the Jewish law and prophets, but of Greek rational inquiry as well.[2]

In the three centuries after the writing of the New Testament
the Church was forced to decide between conflicting interpretations of the faith that Christ and the Apostles had taught;
and Christian theologians turned to Greek philosophy, especially
to later Platonism, to answer questions about God and Christ
that had been left without explicit answers in the Scriptures. Some

of the answers were embodied in the Creeds and the decisions of the oecumenical councils.

Though at first it was philosophy that influenced Christianity, the influence later ran in the other direction as well. Even when it used Greek philosophy as a means of self-expression, Christianity challenged some of its most widely shared assumptions. Both the topics of philosophical discussion and the range of answers to be taken seriously were affected by the claims of faith. There have always been some Christians deploring the alleged 'Hellenization' of Christianity. The protest of the heretic Tertullian (*c*.160–*c*.225) has also received orthodox support:

What indeed has Athens to do with Jerusalem? What has the Academy to do with the Church? What have heretics to do with Christians? . . . Away with all attempts to produce a Stoic, Platonic, and dialectical Christianity.

On the other hand, there have been philosophers distrusting the influence of dogmatic Christianity on philosophy, indeed on rational inquiry generally. The Christian apologist Origen (*c*.185–*c*.254) thinks it important to answer the attack of the pagan Celsus, who complains about Christians:

Such is the effect of the faith which has prejudiced their minds . . . They show that they want and are able to convince only the foolish, dishonourable, and stupid, and only slaves, women, and little children.

Origen regards this charge as a misrepresentation of Christianity, and his attitude became the orthodox view of Christian faith and Greek philosophy. But it never seemed obvious that the two outlooks could be reconciled.[3]

ii. *Early Christianity*

The earliest evidence for Christian teaching comes from Saint Paul's letters, written from the 50s up to 66 or so (when he probably died in the persecution by Nero). These letters show that some fairly definite beliefs about Christ's teaching were already taken for granted among Christian communities. Paul sharply distinguishes the teaching of Christ from his own inferences from it. He plainly expects members of the Church to

assume that Christ had taught definite doctrines, and to have firm
and undisputed views about what the doctrines were.[4] Paul's
letters, then, show Christian teaching (oral or written) in a fairly
developed state in the mid 60s. Other evidence of Christian teaching at this time may be found in the earlier versions of the two
written accounts of the life and teaching of Christ, by Saint Mark
and Saint Luke, if these versions were written (as they probably
were) before the death of Paul.[5]

Beyond this there is very little evidence to help us to date the
New Testament books, or to check the accuracy of their con-
tents.[6] We have good reasons to place the Gospels between
65 and 100, but no clear reason for preferring any more definite
dates. In particular, we have no historical reason for believing that
the fourth Gospel is much later than the first three ('Synoptic')
Gospels. Belief in its lateness rests on the argument that it is more
influenced by Greek philosophy than the Synoptic Gospels are,
and therefore must be later. Both the premises and the inference
in this line of argument are open to doubt.

After the New Testament, the 'Apostolic Fathers' come first in
the long sequence of early Christian writers. They show that in the
second century the Church had organized worship, sacraments,
orders of ministry, and doctrinal standards. In this period the
conflict between Christianity and the Roman authorities led to
persecution—sporadic and unsystematic, but sometimes severe.
The persecutions continued until the Edict of Milan, enjoining
toleration, was issued in 313 by Constantine, the first Christian
emperor. From then on the Church gradually acquired the status
of an established religion, using its relief from persecution to
persecute non-Christians and heretical or schismatic Christians.

While the Church expanded, and improved its position in society, it also formulated its doctrines. The Catholic doctrine
emerged from conflicts and heresies that eventually forced decisions on doctrinal questions. Though the doctrinal definitions
did not end dispute in the Church, they formed a body of orthodox teaching expressing the rational commitments of a Christian believer. The Councils of Nicaea (325) and Chalcedon (451)
more or less define the period of fundamental theological argument and definition.[7]

Here we will focus on the beginning and the end of these four centuries or so of Christian history. After describing some of the main points of New Testament Christianity, we will turn to Augustine's encounter with Christianity and its rivals three centuries later, to give some idea of the development of Christian thought in its relations with Greek philosophy.

iii. *Christian moral teaching*

Early Christian preachers claimed that Jesus was the Messiah expected by the Jews, crucified by the Romans, and raised from the dead; they demand repentance, and they promise forgiveness. The demand for repentance and reform is a traditional theme of the Hebrew prophets, often connected with a threat of punishment. The Jews looked forward to a Messiah, a king who would free them from foreign domination; but the prophets warned them that the coming of the Messiah would bring punishment rather than victory.[8]

The Hebrew prophets hold distinctive views about the sorts of offence that require repentance. Greek gods are characteristically offended by a breach of some ritual requirement, or by some slight to their status; and the Hebrew god Yahweh sometimes punishes for similar ritual errors. The prophets, however, often denounce violations of humanity and justice rather than of ritual law. They point out the social effects of injustice, showing that there are reasons to avoid it apart from its being prohibited by God.[9]

Similarly, Jesus denounces those who do not distinguish the ritual law from the moral law, or do not see that the moral law is prior and overriding. When he is asked a standard question, asking him to identify the 'great commandment', he picks out love of God and love of one's neighbour, in that order, as the two greatest commandments. If Jesus had simply insisted on the priority of the moral law, his views would have been controversial, but fairly familiar.[10]

His actual attitude is more complex. For he criticizes people who keep the moral laws, as commonly understood. A justified belief in one's own success in keeping the moral law actually makes it harder to accept Jesus' teaching. For this reason Paul claims to have been 'touching the righteousness which is in the law, blameless', but still counts himself a sinner. Indeed, he claims that 'all have sinned and come short of the glory of God'. This charge is reasonable only if the accepted standards are wrong.[11]

Jesus argues that the moral law requires us to be 'perfect' (or 'completely good'). He presents a series of contrasts between 'You have heard that it was said to you by the men of old . . . ' and 'But I say to you . . . '. The 'men of old' offer convenient and workable principles telling us not to commit murder, to love our neighbour and hate our enemy, and so on. For these convenient interpretations Jesus substitutes perfectionist demands—to love other people without distinction, and to avoid anger and resentment, not just its violent or murderous expression.[12]

He appeals to the point and underlying principle of each requirement of the law, and then explains and criticizes the convenient interpretation. The demand for love of one's neighbour expresses the fact that my neighbour is another human being with the same needs and rights as I have; and it is easy to recognize that the Good Samaritan behaved as a neighbour should to the injured person. The only reason we actually demand less than this is the fact that people are not likely to fulfil the complete demands of the law. But this is our fault, the result of 'the hardness of our hearts', not a restriction inherent in the law itself.[13]

The underlying principles are far more difficult to follow. Jesus tells the person who accepts and keeps the convenient rules that he must do more 'if you want to be perfect'. But he does not mean that perfection is a further goal beyond the requirements of the moral law; it is just what the law itself requires. If this is Jesus' conception of the demands of morality, his call for perfection and moral reform is rather disputable. He does not encourage confidence in our ability to meet his standards; but if we cannot meet them, what is the point of urging them on us at all?[14]

iv. *Human nature*

Saint Paul believes that 'law brings only the consciousness of sin'; but it brings this consciousness only if we think it demands a degree of perfection that we cannot achieve. Greek moralists agree that the standards followed by the virtuous person are too demanding for ordinary people; but, in their view, a person who acquires the appropriate knowledge and character becomes capable of following the most demanding moral standard that it is reasonable to accept. Christianity stands against this Greek philosophical tradition, in so far as it denies any ordinary human capacity for the sort of virtue that is demanded by the moral law.[15]

Paul's estimate of human capacity results partly from his view that the moral law necessarily encourages the very desires that reject it. Law gives sin its opportunity, because it is an external requirement imposed by authority; in rejecting it we assert ourselves and our independent will. According to Paul, human beings facing the demands of the law take the attitude that is most vividly expressed by Milton's Satan; they value the self-assertion and freedom that result from deliberate rejection of moral authority. Admittedly, Greek moralists recognize some apparent conflicts of motives. But from the Christian point of view, their accounts of the sources of conflict are rather superficial, since they do not recognize the reasonableness and inevitability of our self-assertion against morality.[16]

If morality only intensifies the conflict between the law and human self-assertion, the Christian attitude may seem intolerably pessimistic. Our pessimism will increase if we take the moral law to be as demanding as Jesus thinks it is. We might not rebel at a moderate degree of self-sacrifice; but when Jesus asks us to go the second mile, turn the other cheek, give to anyone who asks us, love our enemies, and so on, we may object that he goes far beyond any reasonable degree of self-sacrifice. If these are genuine moral ideals with some claim to our acceptance, we may well despair at our inability to follow them. But perhaps we should repudiate them completely, and deny that they are reasonable moral ideals at all.

Jesus argues that his demands express genuine moral ideals with some claim on our acceptance. Despair would be warranted if we had to rely completely on our own ordinary human resources in trying to meet these moral demands; but we are not left to our own resources.

v. *The work of Christ*

Paul claims that what the law could not do, and what we could not do by observing the moral law, God himself does for us: 'sending his son in the likeness of sinful flesh and to deal with sin, he has condemned sin in the flesh, so that the justification of the law might be fulfilled in us, walking not in conformity with the flesh, but in conformity with the spirit.' Human beings cannot achieve this result by their own efforts. The central Christian rituals of Baptism and the Eucharist express this conviction that the fulfilment of human moral aims and aspirations depends on God's action rather than on the actions of the moral agents themselves. The work of Christ is to 'redeem' or release human beings from their own sin by suffering on their behalf; human beings are acquitted 'as a free gift, by God's grace, through redemption in Christ Jesus, whom God predetermined to be an expiation through faith in his blood'.[17]

These metaphors—financial ('redeem'), legal ('justify'), and sacrificial ('expiation')—do not present a clear or morally attractive picture of the actions of Christ. If God offers Jesus to placate or deceive the Devil, or if Jesus offers himself as an innocent victim to placate or deceive God, it does not seem to reflect well on God's moral character, and it is not clear why it should be much help to human agents. Christian doctrine, however, seeks to make the crucifixion seem morally intelligible.

The death of Christ is supposed to be at least exemplary. It displays the integrity of a morally perfect person struggling with the evil in the world, but not corrupted by it: 'he was tested in every way similarly to us, without sinning', and 'in so far as he has undergone it himself, by being tested, he is able to come to the help of those who are being tested'. Christ shows that the ideal demands of morality are achievable; he observes them, no matter what the cost, and his integrity shows what we are capable of.[18]

But while such an example might inspire us to greater effort, Paul assures us that the effort will fail. The extreme of self-sacrifice represented by Christ may simply increase our own self-assertive tendencies, and encourage us to rebel more strongly against the demands of the law. Christ's action should also make us able to approach his perfection more closely. Paul claims that when someone is 'in Christ', there is a new creation, and that human beings are in Christ to the extent that Christ is also present in them, when they are born again of the Holy Spirit: 'you are not in the flesh, but in the Spirit, if the Spirit of God dwells in you'. God gives us the capacity as well as the desire to pursue perfection effectively. God acts within us, inspiring both the will and the action.[19]

Attempts to understand the effective side of the work of Christ have produced radically opposed conceptions of the Christian outlook. From one point of view, it seems to reject human initiative and autonomy. Paul claims that pride and boasting are excluded, because genuine human goodness is not really a human achievement. We are saved by the grace of God and justified by faith, not by any action or merit of our own. God himself gives us the will to accept his grace and to approach the perfection that we vainly sought to achieve for ourselves.

Such an attitude might seem to turn human agents into passive recipients, lucky enough to be favoured by the grace they have done nothing to deserve. Christianity seems to abolish rational agents' control over their own lives—the sort of control that the Greek philosophers unanimously welcome and advocate. Moreover, if God freely forgives sin, human agents seem to lose their reason to avoid sin and to seek moral perfection. Why should they not agree with Paul's claim that Christ has liberated us from the law, and then infer that he has liberated us from following the requirements of the moral law?[21]

This is not the interpretation that Paul intends. Christ demands perfection, and Paul aims at it. Once we understand what Christian perfection requires, we expect to fail. But failure need not produce despair, as it would for those who try to follow morality without Christ, the people who are 'without hope and without God'. Christians who realize that they are not left to their own

resources have better reasons to use their own resources fully—
just as in other cases the assurance of co-operation makes it reasonable to undertake tasks that would otherwise be unrealistic.
Paul takes the moral law to require complete love of one's neighbour, not simply respect for his interests. If a Christian had to
rely only on himself, he would be foolish to accept Paul's interpretation of the law; it is a reasonable aim only in so far as he
relies on God.[22]

Christian history shows that it is easy to think of salvation as a
free gift that produces psychological security in believers, but
makes no particular difference to what they do. Paul's moral
advice is sometimes very general and idealistic, prescribing un-
conditional love for one's neighbour, but sometimes very specific,
prescribing submission to the ruling authorities and to the prevailing institutions of marriage and slavery. His ideals might well
seem too general and too idealistic to perform any clear critical
function; and it is not surprising if Christian believers follow
Paul in assuming that they require conformity to prevailing
institutions.

In Paul's view, the objections to his position rest on a misunderstanding of it, and do not identify any real faults in it. He
argues that the Christian view of the work of Christ does not
remove moral initiative from human agents, and that it does not
support moral passivity. Christian moral demands, he agrees,
are severe; but he denies that they are unrealistically severe for
Christians who recognize that they are not left to their own resources. The ideals are rather general, but it does not follow that
they are empty; and if it is not always easy to say what they
require in practice, the same is true of many other reasonable
moral principles. If we accept this answer, we should not accept
uncritically Paul's claims about the practical implications of
Christian moral principles.

vi. *The person of Christ*

Christians formed themselves into local communities, for ritual
observances, including Baptism and the Eucharist, for teaching
and preaching, on the model of the Jewish synagogue, and for

mutual support and practical activities. But they also sought a rational, authoritative account of their faith; and Christian teachers, organized from the earliest times in the orders of bishops, priests, and deacons, claimed universal assent from the Church. Christian thinkers tried to work out a systematic view of the person of Christ and his relation to God that would explain all the New Testament claims about the work of Christ. The doctrinal formulas that were eventually accepted as Catholic teaching and as authentic interpretations of the Apostolic faith were certainly not accepted because they were clear, easy to understand, or immediately plausible. They were accepted, however, because clearer, more easily intelligible, and more immediately plausible solutions seemed not to capture the facts about Christ expressed in the New Testament accounts of him.

It has often been suggested that Christ himself did not claim to be anything more than human. The earliest Christian sources offer no support to this suggestion. Paul describes Christ as 'the image of the unseen God . . . in him all things were created . . . For in him all the fullness < of God > was pleased to dwell.' The fourth Gospel regards Christ as the incarnation of the 'word' (*logos*) of God, implying that an aspect of the nature of God was actually present in Christ. Moreover, the claims that Jesus makes about himself imply that he is more than the Messiah expected by the Jews. The New Testament implies that Jesus claimed divine status for himself; and there is no specific historical evidence on the other side.[23]

Orthodox Christian thinkers therefore claim to derive the divinity of Christ from the New Testament. If Christ had not been God, it would not have been true that 'God was in Christ, reconciling the world to himself'. Christ's death is effective because it is the action of God; and by having Christ within them believers have the presence of God with them. These claims would not correspond to any reality independent of the ideals and aspirations of the believer, unless Christ was more than an unusually striking human being. On the other hand, Christ must have really been human, not God merely appearing to be a human being. His life and death would have no exemplary function if it were not the life and death of a human being. Paul insists that though

Christ really was God, he genuinely 'emptied himself', and really acquired the limitations implied by becoming a human being. Jesus has emotions, appetites, limited knowledge—all properties that seem necessary for being human, but not clearly compatible with being divine.[24]

It is difficult to see, then, how Christ can be both 'one with the Father' to the degree that he claims and still fully human. To be fully human he must be really distinct from the Father (not just the Father under another name). Moreover, he would not be one person at all if he were really an alliance of two persons, one human and one divine; and so his divine and his human characteristics must not constitute two persons.

Christ promises the presence of the Holy Spirit to continue his own presence when he is no longer physically present. Unlike the Stoics, Christians do not simply identify God with the spirit (*pneuma*) immanent in the cosmos; they regard the Spirit as the immanent aspect of an essentially transcendent God. They must fit some conception of the Holy Spirit into their account of God and Christ.[25]

vii. *The doctrine of God*

A long series of reflexions, arguments, controversies, schisms, heresies, and persecutions resulted in some measure of agreement, eventually over most of the Christian world, on the doctrine of the Holy Trinity. The doctrine claims that the Father, the Son, and the Holy Spirit are three persons (*hupostasis*), not three Gods, but one substance (*ousia*). As the so-called Athanasian Creed (late fifth century?) puts it: 'And yet they are not three eternals, but one eternal; as also there are not three uncreateds, nor three infinites, but one uncreated and one infinite.'[26]

The Catholic position rejects two accounts of the persons and the substance:

1. If we regard *hupostasis* as Aristotle's first substance and *ousia* as second substance, we might think the persons are related as different individual human beings are related to other members of the human species. This view 'divides the substance', since the

three persons must have more than the specific unity of members of a species; and so it falls into the heresy of Tritheism.

2. If we regard *ousia* as first substance, we might suppose that the three persons are simply different aspects of the same individual, as the Prime Minister and the First Lord of the Treasury are the same person performing different roles. Such a view cannot account for the real differences between the persons; it was not God the Father who was crucified. This view 'confounds the persons', and so falls into the Sabellian heresy.

Some of the Greek Fathers try to reach a more satisfactory position by modifying the first view. The mere membership of a species implies no particular degree of unity of thought or will or action among its members; but different human beings related by mutual love and knowledge may acquire something closer to the unity of thought and will that is characteristic of one person. The persons of the Trinity have something like this sort of unity to an unimaginably greater degree, so that Augustine can compare them to the different faculties of an individual person. Two perfect mathematicians co-operating on the derivation of the same theorem might contribute individually to a single series of inferences, and for this purpose function as though they were a single system; they count as two minds because these periods of co-operation are episodic and intermittent. In the persons of the Trinity they are permanent and uninterrupted; and to this extent it is more reasonable to think of the distinct persons as constituting a single mind and will.[27]

The doctrine of the Trinity was formulated at the Council of Nicaea in 325; but it did not settle all the disputes. Only the Council of Chalcedon (451) formulated a view of the relation between the divine and the human nature of Christ. Against the view that he had a purely divine nature, or a purely human nature, or that he had two natures juxtaposed, or a single divine-and-human nature, the Council determined that Christ was 'one and the same Christ . . . acknowledged as of two natures, unconfusedly, unchangeably, indivisibly, inseparably'.[28]

We might suppose that a human soul cannot be a component of a single person whose other component is a divine soul, because the human outlook will be so different from the divine that the two souls will constitute two different people, not a single person. The doctrine of Christ's double nature must assume that this natural supposition rests on a false generalization from the human souls that set their wills against the divine will. The perfect human will of Christ, however, harmonizes so closely with the divine will that nothing prevents them from being parts or aspects of a single person. The human soul feels the pleasures, pains, and emotions that the divine soul cannot feel, and lacks the knowledge that the divine soul cannot lack; but these differences do not cause discord between the two souls. Though the human soul of Christ suffered and the divine soul did not, that is not sufficient reason for refusing to believe that they could constitute a single person.

It would be rather an understatement to say that the Nicene and Chalcedonian formulas have remained obscure; indeed, doctrines like these have provoked strong reactions, and given Christian theology a bad name among believers and unbelievers alike. To see that such reactions are unjustified, it is not necessary to prejudge questions about the truth or coherence of these Christian doctrines; it is enough if we see that they confront questions that ought to be confronted, and that the answers they suggest are not plainly incoherent. Those who take the religious or the ethical aspects of the New Testament seriously cannot reasonably avoid the attempt to see if they add up to a consistent or intelligible view of God.

viii. *Augustine and his environment*

The *Confessions* of Augustine (354-430) show us, more clearly than any other literary work of late antiquity, what it was like to approach Christianity through the outlook of Greek philosophy, and more generally from the literary and cultural background of the later Roman Empire.[29]

Augustine was born in an empire that officially accepted Christianity, but where traditional religion and non-Christian cults and philosophies retained much of their influence. The official Catholic Church, then as now, did not seem to have much to offer to an educated, curious, and intense person such as Augustine. Compared with the zealous Donatist schismatics (who disavowed

clergy who had shown weakness in persecutions) or the sophisticated Manichean elite (to be discussed shortly), the body of
Catholics seemed lazy and complacent. Ordinary Christians did
not understand Christian theology, and Augustine was later ap-
palled by the ignorant and superstitious views that he derived
from his Catholic upbringing. Many Catholics accepted their
Christianity rather nominally; they believed that once they received baptism they would have to give up sin, and to avoid such
a grave inconvenience they did their best to postpone baptism
until their deathbed. Augustine's parents and others of their social
class held their Christianity together with basically pagan, ultimately Homeric, ambitions for wealth, success, and honour; and
for Augustine, as for the young men who admired Gorgias, these
ambitions led naturally to a career in rhetoric and public speaking.

   To someone who had absorbed the normal literary education, the Christian Scriptures sounded primitive and uncouth.
Christian doctrines sounded naive and unpersuasive to anyone
acquainted with philosophy. It is surprising that Augustine eventually accepted Catholic Christianity. He wrote his *Confessions*
to explain how and why this happened. 'Confession' no doubt
includes confession of sins and errors, but it also includes the
acknowledgement and open statement of God's nature and actions (as in 'confession of faith').[30]

ix. *Manichean dualism*

When Augustine began to study law, he fell in with a group of
rowdy young men calling themselves the 'Wreckers', who apparently enjoyed flouting conventional morality. His reading of
Cicero encouraged him to study philosophy; and at about the
same time he joined the Manicheans. This sect held a basically
dualist conception of the universe as the result of a conflict between good and evil principles. The difficulties in Stoic explanations of the problem of evil suggest why dualism might seem
a reasonable solution. Since good and evil seem to conflict and to
interfere with each other, we might trace the conflict to an unresolved conflict between the cosmic principles themselves.[31]

This cosmological dualism offers to explain both the New and the Old Testament. It demonstrates the necessity of the death and resurrection of Christ, the son of the good God, who struggles with the evil God of the Old Testament. His followers are those who identify themselves with the good and the light, and who gradually purify themselves from the evil aspects of this world. This view allows Christians to dismiss the uncouth and bloodthirsty aspects of the Hebrew Scriptures as the record of the misdeeds of the evil God.

The Manicheans took very seriously Christ's claim to be the light overcoming the darkness, and they gave this claim their own particular interpretation. They accepted Stoic materialism, and conceived the light as a mass of material particles trapped in human beings and in other material bodies. The Manichean's task was to release the light in other things and to absorb it, by the appropriate dietary and ritual practices. Manichean cosmic dualism and materialism are easily comprehensible answers to evident problems in Jewish and Christian theology; and the rigorous but clear-cut demand for ritual purity promised a radical break from the difficulties and compromises of the ordinary moral life. It was not at all foolish of Augustine to find the Manichean way plausible and appealing.[32]

x. *Criticisms of the Manicheans*

Augustine became dissatisfied with the Manichean system, even before he had found another positive outlook to replace it:

Finally I despaired of getting any benefit from that false doctrine, and I began to hold more slackly and carelessly those very doctrines that I had resolved to be content with if I found nothing better.

Following Nebridius, he asks the Manicheans what the evil substance (the material substance that the Manicheans identified with the evil principle) would have done if the good substance had refused to fight it. Either the good would have suffered nothing (and so did not need to defend itself), and would have had no reason to fight, or it would have suffered something.

Augustine argues that if we conceive a vulnerable and corruptible being, that being is not God: in conceiving something incorruptible

> I was able to attain by my thought to something that would be better than my God, unless You were incorruptible . . . And what is the point of explaining at length why the substance that is God is not corruptible, since if it were corruptible it would not be God?

He assumes that we know that any vulnerable, corruptible being cannot be God. While this assumption might seem strange to Homer and to many Classical Greeks, it would not seem strange to Plato or to the prophets who tried to free the Hebrews from an excessively anthropomorphic conception of God.[33]

Augustine's assumption does not rule out cosmological dualism. It shows at most that the Manicheans ought to describe themselves as atheists. The question about God's vulnerability shows why the Christian conception of God could not fit into cosmological dualism.

xi. *Neoplatonism*

When Augustine was attracted by Manichean views, he did not see anything wrong with conceiving God as a material substance; and even when he rejected the Manichean position, he did not see what other sort of thing God might be. Cosmological dualism made the Catholic doctrine of the Incarnation difficult to accept: if flesh is evil, God's incarnation seems to imply his corruption. Manichean objections to Catholicism seem powerful if God has to be regarded as a material being. Neoplatonism, therefore, raises an important new possibility for Augustine, by suggesting how to conceive an immaterial reality. Augustine regards Plotinus as Plato come to life again; and he relies, within strict limits, on Neoplatonist doctrines to make some aspects of Christian theology more intelligible.[34]

The possibility of immaterial reality makes it easier for Augustine to conceive the relation between the three persons of the Trinity. Plotinus suggests that Intellect and Soul are in some way distinct realities—different things are true of them—and yet they are both expressions of the nature of the One, and the best way for us to form the least inadequate conception of the One that we can form. Augustine finds that the relation between the three Plotinian hypostases removes some objections to the Christian conception of the Trinity.[35]

The difficulties about God and evil that attracted Augustine to Manicheanism rested on the assumption that evil had to be a substance—some positive reality in its own right—and that this cosmic substance must be the source of evil in human wills. Neo-platonism changes Augustine's attitude to this question too. The natural universe has the limitations inseparable from its being material; but such limitations do not make the material universe evil in itself. Since everything comes from, and depends on, a perfectly good God, he argues, it has to be good: 'To You evil utterly is not—and not only to You, but to Your whole creation likewise, evil is not.' We imagine that some created things are evil because we notice that they conflict with other things—a flood destroys the work of many human beings. But though things conflict with each other, they do not conflict with the universe as a whole: 'God forbid that I should say: I wish these things were not.'

To account for moral evil Augustine refers to the rebellion of the human will against God. It is not the action of some reality independent of God, but the result of human decision. Augustine must still claim that the creation would not have been better without the existence of moral evil; and here his solution to the problem of evil runs into the usual difficulties. (Why, for instance, could God not have created human beings with free wills that did not make wrong choices? Even if some wrong choices are inevitable, why must they have the catastrophic results that they sometimes have?) Still, he can reasonably claim that Neo-platonism has opened possible positions that free us from the unattractive choice between the Manichean position and a crude version of Christianity.[36]

xii. *Neoplatonism and Christianity*

Augustine found that in the Neoplatonist books he never read about the Incarnation. He came to regard this as a serious gap, once he had reread Saint Paul, and especially the Letter to the Romans. Paul rejects the view of moral and spiritual growth that renounces the body and the moral and social concerns of ordinary life; in his view, such renunciation only increases conflict within the self. Augustine felt conflict all the more keenly the more he was attracted by Neoplatonism.

He agrees that Neoplatonic mysticism leads the soul to some awareness of ultimate reality. But he found that the Neoplatonist discipline allowed only fleeting glimpses of the goal. Rejection of the body did not prevent him from returning to the body most of the time. In so far as he took Manichean purification or Neoplatonic mysticism as a guide for his life, he rejected Christian claims about the incapacity of human beings to achieve their own good from their own resources: 'for I was not yet humble enough to take the humble Jesus as my God; nor had I come to know what his weakness would teach me.' He accepted the Incarnation once he realized his own incapacity.[37]

Augustine was struck by the moral demands of Christianity; for he had tried both Manichean and Neoplatonist measures for renouncing the flesh, or for separating his true self from it and treating it as an unwelcome appendage, and none of these measures had prevented him from being distracted by the demands of the flesh. But if Paul's demand had simply been a moral demand, it would have been as unrealistic as the counsels of Manichean and Neoplatonist perfection that Augustine had already tried. Paul's demand is different. It implies a person's acceptance of his own inability to achieve his own good.[38]

xiii. *Augustine's final outlook*

The Catholic faith that Augustine eventually accepted would have seemed unintelligible to the prophet Isaiah, and alien to Saint Paul; it is more similar to the historic Christianity familiar to us than to the faith of the New Testament. Augustine approached it through Manicheanism and Neoplatonism; and the version of Christianity he eventually accepted was deeply influenced by Greek philosophical ideas. Still, it remains 'foolishness to the Greeks'; it still rests on the doctrines of Creation and Incarnation from which, in the view of orthodox Christianity, all the least credible aspects of Christian theology inescapably follow.

It should not now be surprising that the last three books of the *Confessions* are devoted to an account of the nature and action of God in the Creation. For the Creation shows the nature of the God that Augustine discovers in the course of the *Confessions*. In the Creation God did something at some time, and changed things from the way they were before, because he wanted to. In Augustine's view, however, God is eternal, changeless, immaterial, and self-sufficient, and on these points he is like the ultimate reality of Neoplatonism. How could such a being act in time, and why should he want to change things if he needed nothing? If he made the world, why is the world as bad as it is?

Augustine insists that despite the difficulties of explaining how and why God created the world, he did create it, and, as Genesis says, 'it was very good'. It is neither an illusion nor an evil substance opposed to the good God. Though Augustine faces serious difficulties in explaining evil as the product of free human choice, he does not resort to the intuitively easier answers offered by cosmological dualism. He insists that the creator of the world and of human nature also sent his son to release human nature from the bad results of free choice; the Incarnation is the continuation and completion of the work begun in the Creation.

Since other people are a part of the creation, Augustine's belief in the God who created the material universe requires him to extend his concern for other people beyond the concerns of his earlier life. Manicheans and Neoplatonists rejected the concerns of ordinary social life in favour of small groups of the elite pursuing the life of renunciation of the flesh. Augustine spent much of the rest of his life, however, as a priest and a bishop, preaching to ordinary people and administering his diocese. In the organized teaching of the Church, Christian doctrine influenced people outside the educated classes—people largely untouched by the whole course of Greek philosophy.

Not everyone will agree that when Augustine returned to Catholic Christianity he made the right choice. From the point of view of Greek philosophy, his choice might appear to be a retreat, not an advance. Parmenides, Heracleitus, and their successors invite their audience to judge their arguments by reason, and Augustine sometimes seems to accept that standard; he wanted to be as sure of the truth of the Catholic doctrine as he was that $7 + 3 = 10$. The Church, however, did not even claim to meet his demand for rational proof, and did not remove his doubts by the sort of proof he initially wanted. Augustine's conversion might understandably seem to be a relapse into blind faith and superstition of the sort that the Presocratic naturalists tried to destroy. The anthropomorphic aspects of the Christian God, the hopeless obscurity of the Trinity and the Incarnation, and the anti-humanist tendency of the Christian doctrines of sin, grace, and faith—all these might seem to constitute an outlook that could commend itself only to blind faith despairing of human nature and rational inquiry.[39]

Augustine shares the aim of many other Fathers of the Church in wanting to show that the alleged contrast between Christianity and Greek philosophy rests on a mistake. Paul argues that the Christian doctrine of sin and grace makes sense to those who have taken the moral insights of Jewish and Greek ethics as seriously as they can. Similarly, Augustine argues that rational inquiry shows the need for faith. Rational inquiry shows us the possibility of conceiving God as an immaterial reality; and it shows us the possibility of a moral life free of conflict within ourselves and with other people; but it cannot show us how to achieve the ideals it offers us. Christianity shows, in Augustine's view, how to achieve what a philosopher can only hope for. For this reason he claims that Christianity comes not to destroy, but to complete.

Notes

Abbreviations

The following abbreviations are used frequently for authors and titles. Any other abbreviations should be intelligible from the context.

Ar.	Aristotle
DK	Diels, H., and Kranz, W., eds., *Die Fragmente der Vorsokratiker*, 10th edn., Berlin, 1952.
EN	Aristotle, *Nicomachean Ethics*
Gorg.	Plato, *Gorgias*
Il.	Homer, *Iliad*
Met.	Aristotle, *Metaphysics*
NEB	*New English Bible with Apocrypha*, Oxford and Cambridge, 1970.
OCD	Hammond, N. G. L., and Scullard, H. H., eds., *Oxford Classical Dictionary*, 2nd edn., Oxford, 1970.
Od.	Homer, *Odyssey*
ODCC	Cross, F. L., and Livingstone, E. A., eds., *Oxford Dictionary of the Christian Church*, 2nd edn. (revised), Oxford, 1983.
Phd.	Plato, *Phaedo*
Rep.	Plato, *Republic*
RSV	*New Oxford Annotated Bible with Apocrypha* (*Revised Standard Version*), New York, 1977.
Sextus, *AM*	Sextus Empiricus, *Against the Mathematicians*
Sextus, *P*	Sextus Empiricus, *Outlines of Pyrrhonism*
SVF	Von Arnim, H., ed., *Stoicorum Veterum Fragmenta*, 4 vols., Leipzig, 1905-24.
Thuc.	Thucydides

Chapter 1

1. Greek influences on later thought: Bolgar in Finley [1981], ch. 15.
2. There is no full history of Classical philosophy that can be recommended to readers of English. But Hussey [1972], Crombie

[1964], Ackrill [1981], Long [1974], and Wallis [1972], taken together, provide a good introductory account.

3. Some of the gaps in this book may be filled by reading Lloyd [1970] and [1973], and Sambursky [1960].

4. Some English translations are listed in the Bibliography under the Classical author's name. Many works are translated (some much better than others) in the Loeb Classical Library series (with facing Greek or Latin text); I cite these as 'Loeb' in the Bibliography. The Penguin Classics series contains a large number of Classical authors in translations (many of them good) into contemporary English — though some of them are too free to be suitable for the study of philosophical writers.

5. Boardman [1986] is a good survey of the whole Classical world, with useful bibliographies and chronological tables. For particular people and events *OCD* and *ODCC* are useful; I have not multiplied references to them.

Chapter 2

1. Introduction to Homer: Bowra [1972], Griffin [1980].

2. Xenophanes B 10 (for method of reference see 3 n. 4). See 3 § vii.

3. I refer to books of the *Iliad* by roman figures, and to books of the *Odyssey* by arabic figures.

4. Augustine: *Confessions* i. 14. Public recitation of Homer: Lycurgus, *in Leocratem* 102. See also [Plato], *Hipparchus* 228b, Cicero, *De Oratore* ii. 34, Plutarch, *Pericles* 13. 11.

5. See Plato, *Apology* 29b-d, Aristotle, *EN* 1116a21-b30, Lucretius, iii. 18-24 (cf. *Od.* 6. 41-6). Zeno the Stoic wrote an elaborate defence of Homer's consistency, *SVF* i. 274. Chrysippus the Stoic 'filled a whole book' with quotation and discussion of Homer and other poets, *SVF* ii. 907. Horace says that Homer gives a clearer and better description of what is morally good and what is useful than the philosophers give, *Epistles* i. 2. 1-4.

6. See Herodotus ii. 53; Xenophanes B 10-15; Heracleitus B 40, 42, 56-7, 106; Plato, *Rep.* 606e-607a.

7. Herodotus' estimate: ii. 53. A possible reference to Homer: *Homeric Hymn to Apollo* 165-72, Thucydides iii. 104.

8. Heroes: v. 392-4, xii. 443-9, xx. 285-7. Goodness: 17. 220-3 (cf. 13. 45-6, 18. 131-40); xx. 240-3. For *agathos* ('good') referring to the upper classes see i. 80, 15. 324. Heredity: xiv. 113, xxi. 106-8 (cf. vii. 107-14), 4. 611-14, 18. 275-80, 21. 335. See Theognis 183-96, 315-18, 429-38, 699-718, 865-9; Plato, *Meno* 95e; Adkins

[1960], 77. Paris: vi. 325-68, 518-29. Different views on Homeric ethics: Adkins [1960], ch. 3, Long [1970], Adkins [1971].

9. Achilles: xi. 783-4. Virtues: ii. 364-7, vii. 107-14, xiii. 235-7, xv. 641-4. Achilles: i. 412. Planning: xviii. 105-6. Aristotle on other-directedness: *EN* 1095b22-30, 1159a22-4.

10. Achilles: i. 254-8, ix. 104-13, 247-59. Hector: vi. 440-81, xii. 241-3, xxii. 220-32.

11. Achilles: xvi. 21-35, xxi. 74-113, xxiv. 39-54, 486-512. Supplication: xxiv. 477-9, i. 488-527, viii. 371, 9. 266-71, Griffin [1980], 24 f. Cyclops: 9. 172-6, 187-92, 287-95, 447-55.

12. Achilles: xix. 203-14. Hector: vi. 431-9, 459-63, xxii. 99-110.

13. Honour: ix. 315-22, 408-16, xviii. 95-126.

14. Suitors: 21. 320-35. Contrast Adkins [1960], 39. Hesiod: *Works and Days* 156-69, 294.

15. Thersites: ii. 211-77. The hero: xii. 310-28, Adkins [1960], 34-6.

16. Homeric gods (and Greek religion in general): Guthrie [1950], Lloyd-Jones [1983], chs. 1-2, Dodds [1951], chs. 1-2, Griffin [1980], 172-8, Burkert [1985], ch. 3.

17. The gods' aims: xxiv. 33-76, vi. 297-311, xxi. 210-52, i. 8-52.

18. Natural processes: xxi. 211-513; Amos 3:6; Vlastos [1975], 10-13.

19. Criticisms of the Homeric gods: 3 § xi., Plato, *Rep.* 379b-387c, 6 § xviii. Different aspects of Heracles: xviii. 115-19, 11. 601-26, Guthrie [1950], 235-41.

20. Divine happiness: i. 584-600, 6. 41-6.

21. Achilles: ix. 412-16.

22. Zeus's rise to power: xiv. 200-4, xv. 185-99, Hesiod, *Theogony* 453-731. Zeus's power: viii. 1-29 i. 5. The will of Zeus: xii. 230-43, xiii. 620-39, 1. 76-9.

23. Fates: xvi. 431-61, xxii. 167-85, xvi. 458-61, xxiii. 115-19.

24. Fate: 9 § v.

25. Justice: xvi. 384-93.

Chapter 3

1. Quotations from Aristotle, *Met.* 1000a9-20; *De Caelo* 298b25-9; *Met.* 983b20-1. On *phusis* see Vlastos [1975], 18-20. The naturalist philosophers are often called the 'Presocratics'—somewhat misleadingly, since some of the later ones were contemporaries of Socrates. Aristotle on Socrates and his predecessors: 7 § i–ii. Best introduction to the Presocratics: Hussey [1972]. Longer treatments: Guthrie [1962], i–ii, Barnes [1979]. Translated texts in: Kirk [1982]

Barnes [1987], McKirahan [1994]. Major cosmological issues: Furley [1987], [1989], ch. 18.

We can read Herodotus' complete history, and complete essays by the medical writers, but the other naturalists are known to us only in fragments, quotations, or paraphrases. The earliest main sources are Plato and, above all, Aristotle. The historical surveys by Aristotle's pupil Theophrastus are the sources of many of the later surviving accounts of the naturalists. The Stoics and Epicureans drew inspiration from favourite naturalists, the Stoics from Heracleitus and the Epicureans from the Atomists. Christians referred to naturalist criticisms of the pagan gods. In late antiquity, however, no major philosophical school studied the naturalists closely, and texts of their works became scarce. Simplicius (c. AD 500–40) mentions the scarcity of texts of Parmenides as a reason for transcribing lengthy passages in full (*Commentary on Aristotle's Physics* 144. 25–8).

2. On the scientific character of naturalist thought see Cornford in Furley [1970], ch. 2, and Vlastos [1995], vol. 1, chs. 1–5.

3. Ar. *Met.* 983b6–17. On unqualified becoming see 7 § iii.

4. Anaximander: DK 12 A 10, Ar. *Physics* 187a20–3. Thales (see Ar. *Met.* 983b19–984a5) proposed water as the origin and nature of everything. Presumably, he explained the phenomena by appeal to such processes as melting, condensation, and evaporation; but he does not seem to explain how solid matter could have emerged from water, if there was nothing but water in the first place. Anaximander's qualitatively indeterminate original stuff containing opposites answers this objection to Thales: opposites interact in different ways that are more likely to explain what we observe.

   I cite evidence on the naturalists either from the ancient source, if this is easily accessible (as for Aristotle), or especially worth noting; or, failing that, from DK. DK provides a number for each philosopher, and divides the evidence on him into indirect testimony (A) and supposed direct quotations (B); hence the reference given above refers to fragment A 10 of no. 12, Anaximander. Often I omit the philosopher's number. These references can be traced in other collections (see note 1).

5. Injustice: see DK A 14, B 2–3; Ar. *Physics* 203b10–14; DK A 9, B 1. Coming to be: Ar. *Phys.* 203b18–20.

6. DK 22 B 30.

7. The river: Plato, *Cratylus* 402I (cf. DK B 91). Transformation: Ar. *De Caelo* 298b29–33, *Physics* 253b9–21. The accuracy of Plato's

report is defended by Guthrie [1962], i. 488-92, and attacked by Kirk [1983], 194-7.

8. For these examples see DK B 51, 53, 60, 61, 67.

9. See Ar. *Eudemian Ethics* 1235a25-9, DK B 80, 54.

10. Herodotus includes oracles (i. 53); dreams (viii. 12, 17-18); divine retribution (viii. 106). To later readers the early historians seemed to treat their subject in a rather mythological way, with an uncritical attitude to unlikely or poorly attested stories: 'For when they say that those who openly told myths won a good reputation, they thought that they would also make their writing pleasant if they told in the guise of genuine history what they had never seen and had never heard—at least, not from people who knew anything; their sole aim was to write what would be pleasant and marvellous to listen to' (Strabo xi. 6. 3). This judgement identifies the epic influence in early historical writing; and it may well express our own reaction to parts of Herodotus' narrative.

    The best short introduction: De Ste Croix [1977]. Limits of Herodotus' naturalism: Lloyd [1979], 29-32.

11. Athenians: v. 78. Spartans: vii. 104. 4-5.

12. Egyptians: ii. 35. 2. Greeks: vii. 102. 1. Persians: ix. 132. 3 (cf. [Hippocrates], *Airs, Waters, Places* 24).

13. Plato attributes this naturalist attitude to Hippocrates of Cos: *Phaedrus* 270c-e (cf. *Protagoras* 311b, [Hippocrates], *Ancient Medicine* 22. 1-17). The authorship and dates of the treatises in the 'Hippocratic' Corpus are disputed. Introduction: Lloyd [1970], ch. 5; [1978], 9-60.

14. *Epidemics* i. 23, *Breaths* 2, *Airs, Waters, Places* 2. On *idea* see 5 § iii.

15. Sacred disease: *Sacred Disease* 1-2 (selections). On this treatise see Lloyd [1979], 15-29. On *nomizein* and *phusis* see 4 § xi.

16. Nature and chance: *Airs, Waters, Places* 22 and 6.

17. The Muses have seen what has happened, and tell the poet (Homer, *Il.* ii. 483-7, *Od.* 22. 347, 11. 363-8, 13. 487-9). But the Muses can sometimes tell the poet plausible lies as well as truth (Hesiod, *Theogony* 24-8). To distinguish true from false the poet has to rely on memory, the mother of the Muses (*Theog.* 50-4). Moreover, the test of accurate memory is tradition. Homer told traditional stories; if he had claimed to 'remember' from the Muses that Hector had killed Achilles and the Trojans had won the war, his story would not have been accepted. On the Muses and the poets see Snell [1953] ch. 7, Macleod [1983], 4-6.

18. Hecataeus: F1a in Jacoby [1923] (cf. Herodotus v. 36). Xenophanes: DK 21 B 10; Sextus Empiricus, *AM* i. 289, ix. 193. Heracleitus: Ar. *Eudemian Ethics* 1235a25-9; Diogenes Laertius ix. 1; DK 22 B 56-7, 106.

19. Anaximander: DK 12 A 27. Xenophanes: DK 21 A 32-3; cf. Ar. *Meteorologica.* 352b17-19. See also Herodotus ii. 12; Strabo i. 3. 4; Guthrie [1962], i. 387. Observation: Lloyd [1979], ch. 3; Vlastos in Furley [1970], ch. 3; Vlastos [1975], 84-7; Barnes [1979], 47-52.

20. Human origins: DK 12 A 30.

21. Maps: Herodotus iv. 36. 2, v. 49. 1, 50. 3. Cf. DK 12 A 6; Stobaeus i. 1. 11; Guthrie [1962], i. 387.

22. Rejection of assumptions: [Hippocrates], *Ancient Medicine* 1-2. Observational tests: Lloyd [1979], 24. References to possible experiments: Herodotus ii. 3 (cf. 10, 28); [Hippocrates], *Art* 13, *Heart* 8, *Sacred Disease* 14; Ar. *Meteorologica* 358b35-359a5, *Parva Naturalia* 470b22-4, 471a31-b5; Aristophanes, *Clouds* 144.

23. Heracleitus on *historia* and 'much learning' (*polumathiē*): B 129, B 40. Herodotus' caution: ii. 29, 99, vii. 152 (cf. ii. 123), iv. 195, iv. 42. *Historia*: 7 § ii.

24. The response of traditional beliefs to observational challenge: Lloyd [1979], 17-19. General laws: Heracleitus, DK 22 B 94.

25. Hume, *Inquiry concerning Human Understanding* viii, p. 86.

26. The *logos*: DK 22 B 50; Sextus Empiricus, *AM* viii. 129-34; DK B 89; Marcus Aurelius iv. 46. The senses: Sextus, *AM* vii. 126.

27. Justice: Homer, *Od.* 9. 112-15, 174-6; Hesiod, *Works and Days* 274-85; Plato, *Protagoras* 323a-d.

28. Xenophanes: DK 21 B 2. Pindar, *Isthmians* 3. 13-14. Solon: Plutarch, *Solon* 23. 3, 24. 5; Murray [1980], 192-7.

29. Solon: Ar. *Constitution of Athens* 2. 2 (trans. Moore [1983]). Bad laws: fr. 4 (West [1980]), 17-20, 30-1 (part in Woodruff [1995], 25). See Murray [1980], 179, 189.

30. Cleisthenes: Herodotus v. 66; Murray [1980], 254-8.

31. Solon: Ar. *Constitution of Athens* 5. 3, 7. 1, 9. 1. Heracleitus: B 43-4, 114.

32. Naturalist theology: Vlastos [1975], ch. 1.

33. Homer, *Il.* xvi. 385-92; Hesiod, *Works and Days* 213-47; Xenophanes B 11, 12, 14, 16; Sextus, *AM* i. 289, ix. 193; Heracleitus B 5, 14, 15, 96. According to Herodotus vi. 84, the Spartans claimed that their king Cleomenes went mad not because a god was punishing him, but because he had taken up the Scythian and un-Greek habit of drinking wine unmixed with water.

34. Thales: Ar. *De Anima* 411a7-8. Xenophanes: Ar. *Met.* 986b21-5, DK 21 A 11-12, 14-16, 23-6, B 32. [Hippocrates], *Sacred Disease* 1, 21. Heracleitus B 94, 32, 67.

35. Cf. Xenophanes B 23. Christian writers: Clement, *Stromateis* v. 109; *Protrepticus* 34; Origen, *contra Celsum* vii. 62.

36. The character of a god: Herodotus ii. 52-3; Xenophanes A 31, B 25-6; Heracleitus B 78, 83, 102, Plato, *Hippias Major* 289a-b.

37. Yahweh: Exodus 3: 13-15. Different views of God: 1 Samuel 5: 1-4, Exodus 7: 8-13, 1 Kings 14: 6-20, Psalms 96: 5, 19: 1-5, 22: 6-7, 89: 5-14, 104, Amos 9: 5-6, Job 38-41, Psalms 44: 23-6, 59: 4-5, 79, 40: 6-8, 17-23, 51: 15-17, Isaiah 40: 28.

38. Disruptive gods: Herodotus i. 32, iii. 40, vii. 46. A strange coincidence convinces Polycrates that he cannot avoid divine envy, iii. 42. Envy: vii. 10, v. 92, Homer, *Od.* 5. 118. Wisdom: iii. 108.

39. Xerxes: Herodotus vii. 11, 17, 18.

Chapter 4

1. Attendance at dramatic festivals: Plato, *Gorgias* 502b-d; Pickard-Cambridge [1968], 263-5. Aeschylus on Homer: Athenaeus, *Deipnosophistae* viii. 347e. Good translations of tragedies in Grene [1959]. Introduction: Taplin [1978], Lloyd-Jones [1983], chs. 4-6.

2. Cleisthenes: 3 § x. The Assembly and the generals: Thuc. ii. 65. 3, iv. 27-8. Ephialtes: Ar. *Constitution of Athens* 25. 2-4, Davies [1978], ch. 4. Conspiracy with Sparta: Thuc. i. 107. 4. The *Oresteia*: Dodds [1973], ch. 3, Macleod [1983], ch. 3.

3. Homeric motives. Iphigeneia: *Agamemnon* 265-7. Clytaemnestra: 1412-25, 1438-47. Aegisthus: 1577-1611. Orestes and Electra: *Choephori* 491-509. The Furies and Apollo: *Eumenides* 778-92. Zeus: *Ag.* 160-83. Furies: *Eum.* 490-516.

4. Responsibility: Homer, *Il.* xix. 86-9; Aeschylus, *Ag.* 1468-80, 1485-8, 1497-1508; Dodds [1951], ch. 1.

5. Solon believed that innocent descendants suffer for the crimes of their ancestors: see 13. 31-2 (West [1980]). Contrast Aeschylus, *Seven against Thebes* 653-719, 750-62. Cf. Herodotus iii. 42 (see 3 § xi). Results of divine justice: Aesch. *Persians* 800-31; Sophocles, *Trachiniae* 1276-8; Aesch. *Ag.* 180-3; *Cho.* 93541, 1065-76.

6. Orestes: *Ag.* 1633-5, *Cho.* 973, 1044-7, *Eum.* 585-613.

7. Implausible arguments: *Eum.* 566-741, 778-92, 794-807, 824-36, 848-69, 881-915. Common good: 895-915.

8. Heracleitus on law and justice: 3 § x.

9. Hidden order: DK 22 B 54. Both Leucippus (mid-fifth century) and Democritus contribute to the formation of the Atomic theory; but their contributions are not easily distinguished, and I speak for convenience of Democritus alone. See Kirk [1983], 403-6.

10. Conflicting appearances: Annas [1986], chs. 3-4. Equipollence: Sextus, *P* i. 10, 202. Contrast Theophrastus, *De Sensu* 69-70.

11. Heracleitus' solution: Sextus, *P* ii. 63. Heracleitus may not in fact have intended to violate the Principle of Non-Contradiction; but many of his successors took him to have violated it. Convention and reality: Sextus, *AM* vii. 135, 138.

12. Atoms and compounds: Ar. *Met.* 1042b9-15, Theophrastus, *De Sensu* 63.

13. Anaxagoras: Sextus, *AM* vii. 140. See Guthrie [1962], ii. 459; Barnes [1979], ii. 68-74. Atoms and sensations: Theophrastus, *De Sensu* 65-7.

   Democritus' atomic theory evidently resembles the 'corpuscular' conception of matter developed by seventeenth-century science and philosophy, partly under the influence of Greek atomism. See Sambursky [1960], ch. 5, Barnes [1979], ii. 40-2.

14. Leucippus: DK 67 B 2. Necessity: Plato, *Laws* 889b-c (see 3 § viii, 8 § vii). Democritus the laughing philosopher: Lucian, *Vitarum Auctio* 13. See also DK 68 A 21, Cicero, *De Oratore* ii. 255, Horace, *Epistles* ii. 1. 194, Guthrie [1962], ii. 387 n.

15. Determinism and materialism: see 7 § ix. 8 § vi. 9 § v.

16. Development of society: Aeschylus, *Prometheus Bound* 442-506; Diodorus Siculus, i. 8. 1-3, 9. See 8 § ix. Guthrie [1957], chs. 2-4.

17. Thucydides' first English translator, the philosopher Hobbes, says Thucydides pleased him above all the other authors he read: 'sed mihi prae reliquis Thucydides placuit', Hobbes [1839], i. p. lxxviii. Introduction to Thucydides: Brunt [1963], De Ste Croix [1972], 5-34. Thucydides and Democritus: Hussey [1985].

18. Human nature and Thucydides' history: Thuc. iii. 82. 2, i. 22. 4. Thucydides expresses his own views (i) in infrequent comments in the course of his narratives, and (ii) in a subset of the speeches whose general outlook (because of its coherence with (i)) can plausibly be ascribed to him (in contrast to the speeches that clearly represent a point of view that he does not accept).

19. On scarcity see Hume, *Inquiry into Morals* iii. 183. Freedom and rule over others: Thuc. i. 141. 1; Herodotus i. 210, Polybius v. 106. Hobbes on power: *Leviathan*, ch. 11 (see also chs. 13-14).

20. Social contract: Plato, *Rep.* 358e-359a (cf. Ar. *Politics* 1280a35-b11; 8 § ix; Guthrie [1962], iii, ch. 5). Equal compulsion: Thuc. v. 89.
21. Power and fear: Thuc. i. 23. 6, i. 88.
22. Revolution, war, and human nature: Thuc. iii. 82. 1-2, 84. 2.
23. Security: Thuc. i. 76. 2, v. 89, vi. 83. 2-4. Spartans: ii. 8. 4, iii. 57. 4, 68. 1, v. 104, 105. 4.
24. Pericles and Thucydides: i. 140. 1, ii. 60. 1, ii. 63. 2-3, 65. 9. Athenian democracy: ii. 65, iv. 27-8, v. 16. 1, vi. 24. 3. These views about democracy partly explain Thucydides' violently hostile portrait of the popular leader Cleon (who also probably caused Thucydides' exile after his military failure recorded in iv. 106. 3-4).
25. Mytilene: Thuc. iii. 36. 3. Hobbes: Hobbes [1975], 13. Cf. 'Is democratia ostendit mihi quam sit inepta et quantum coetu plus sapit unus homo' ('he showed me how foolish democracy is, and how much wiser one man is than a mob'), Hobbes [1839], p. lxxviii.
26. Justice as simple-mindedness: Thuc. iii. 83. 1; Plato, *Rep.* 348c, 400e.
27. Beneficiaries of justice: Plato, *Rep.* 343c, 367c; *Gorg.* 483b-484b (see 4 § xv).
28. Law: Aeschylus, *Eumenides* 885-91; Plato, *Protagoras* 337c-d; Antiphon, DK 87 B 44A, p. 349; Xenophon, *Memorabilia* i. 2. 39-46.
29. Senses and mind: DK 68 B 125; Sextus, *AM* vii. 137. The *skeptikos* and suspension of judgement: Sextus, *P* i. 8-10. See 8 § iii. Aristotle: *Met.* 1009b11-12. Scepticism: Annas [1986], Williams in Finley [1981], ch. 9. The main source is Sextus Empiricus.
30. Protagoras and Democritus: DK 68 B 156. The Measure: Plato, *Theaetetus* 152a. Relativity: *Theaetetus* 152d. (Appeal to *relational* properties (healthy for fishes, unhealthy for men, etc.) as support for *relativism* against objectivism involves a confusion; but the confusion is probably present in Protagoras.) On Protagoras see Guthrie [1962], iii. 181-92. The main source is Plato's *Theaetetus*; see McDowell [1973], Levett [1990].
31. Treatment of the dead: Herodotus iii. 38.
32. Variation: Sextus, *P* i. 148-63; Ar. *EN* 1094b14-16, 1134b18-27. The sceptic's attitude: Sextus, *P* i. 17.
33. Protagoras: Plato, *Theaetetus* 167c, 172b; *Protagoras* 325c-326e.
34. *Oligoi* = 'few'; hence oligarchy = rule by the few, more particularly by the rich. Democracy and oligarchy: Ar. *Politics* iv. 4.
35. Athenian democracy: Jones [1957], chs. 3, 5. Destruction of Greek democracy: De Ste Croix [1981], 300-26. The Romans in Athens: Ferguson [1911], 455. Alcibiades: Thuc. vi. 89. 6.

36. Addressing the Assembly: Aeschines, *in Timarchum* 23; Demosthenes 18. 170; [Xenophon], *Constitution of Athens* 1. 6 (the 'Old Oligarch'; see Moore [1983]). Gorgias: Plato, *Gorg.* 452e–453a; Diodorus Siculus xii. 53 (quoted by Jebb [1893], i. p. cxxv).

The formal study of rhetoric began in Sicily after the fall of the tyrants in the 460s (Cicero, *Brutus* 46). Pericles is supposed to have been the first to 'bring a written speech into court—his predecessors improvised' (*Souda* s. v. Pericles, quoted by Jebb [1893], i. p. cxxviii); and the popular leader Cleon is supposed to have begun the use of ostentatious techniques of intonation and gesture, Ar. *Constitution of Athens* 28. 3. The debates reported in Thucydides (though probably the speeches are the historian's own compositions) suggest Athenian sophistication. Contrast Thuc. i. 86, iv. 84. 2 on Spartans. The Thirty Tyrants (see 4 § xv) made it illegal 'to teach the discipline of speech-making', Xenophon, *Memorabilia* i. 2. 31.

37. The Greek word *sophistês* (cognate with *sophos*, 'wise') just means 'expert', not necessarily with any unfavourable suggestion. See Guthrie [1962], iii, ch. 3. Sophistic teaching: Plato, *Hippias Major* 285c–d, *Protagoras* 347a. General education (*paideia*): *Apology* 24d–25a, *Protagoras* 318d–319a, 324d–326e, *Meno* 91a, 92e. Attitudes to sophists: *Protagoras* 314e–315a; *Meno* 91b–92c. Sophists contrasted with rhetoricians: *Gorg.* 465b–c. Less democratic cities received the sophists' educational claims rather dubiously, *Hippias Major* 284b, 285d–e.

Evidence on the sophists is collected in DK and translated in Sprague [1972], and in Woodruff [1995]; Plato's dialogues are a major source. A brief survey: Dodds [1973], ch. 6.

38. Antiphon: Thuc. viii. 68. 1. The identity of this Antiphon with the sophist is disputed (see DK 87 A 2); see Morrison in Sprague [1972]. Andron: Plato, *Gorg.* 487c, Craterus 342 F5 (in Jacoby [1923], iii. b), Rhodes [1982], 19 n.

39. Charmides and Critias: Plato, *Charmides* 153c, 154b; Lysias xii. 53; Xenophon, *Hellenica* ii. 3. 2, *Memorabilia* i. 2. 12, ii. 49, Rhodes [1982], 429f. Critias' play, the *Sisyphus* (sometimes ascribed to Euripides; DK 88 B 25): Sextus, *AM* ix. 54. Chaerephon: Plato, *Apology* 21a, *Charmides* 153b.

40. Defence of democracy: Thuc. vi. 38. 5–39. 2. Defence of conventional morality: Anonymus Iamblichi = DK 89 § 6. Attack on law and democracy: Xenophon, *Memorabilia* i. 2. 45, Plato, *Gorg.* 483c–d, 484a.

41.   The dangers of injustice: Anonymus Iamblichi (see n. 40) § 7.

Chapter 5

1.   See *Laches* 187e–188a; *Gorg.* 481c. The historical Socrates: Lacey in
      Vlastos [1971a]; Vlastos [1991], chs. 2–3.

      There are four major sources of evidence on Socrates (who wrote
      no philosophical works himself): (1) Aristophanes (? *c*.450–*c*.385),
      in the *Clouds*, aimed (with incomplete success) to be funny; he
      did not try to be accurate, and he betrays malice as well as
      misunderstanding. (2) Xenophon (*c*.428–*c*.354) was a politically
      conservative soldier, with intellectual interests and limited philo-
      sophical acumen. His 'Socrates' gives conventionally respectable
      moral and political advice. (3) It is fairly widely agreed that the
      earliest group of Plato's (428–347) dialogues (*Apology*, *Crito*,
      Euthyphro, *Laches*, *Charmides*, *Ion*, *Hippias Minor*, *Lysis*, *Eu-
      thydemus*; the *Protagoras* and *Gorgias* to some extent) is intended
      to represent the historical Socrates, and that the 'Socrates' in the
      'middle' diologues (*Meno*, *Hippias Major*, *Cratylus*, *Phaedo*, *Sym-
      posium*, *Republic*) and 'late' dialogues (*Parmenides*, *Phaedrus*, *The-
      aetetus*, *Sophist*, *Statesman*, *Timaues*, *Philebus*, *Laws*) is intended
      to present Plato's own views without implying that the historical
      Socrates shared them. The early dialogues are generally short, con-
      versational, often humorous, and largely concerned with ethics.
      The middle and late dialogues are longer, and include more varied
      topics, much more epistemology and metaphysics, and much more
      exposition (especially in the *Laws*, one of the dialogues in which
      'Socrates' is not the main character). (4) Aristotle supports this
      division, since he takes the 'early' group of Plato's dialogues, but
      not the others, to describe Socrates' views; see 6 § v. These early
      dialogues are probably a reliable guide to Socrates' views. The
      dating of Plato's dialogues: *OCD* s. v. Plato, Vlastos [1991], 46.

2.   The sophists: 4 § xiv, *Meno* 91b–92e.

3.   Young men: *Charmides* 155d–e. Critias: Aeschines, *in Timarchum*
      174. The speech was delivered in 345; the remark would not help
      his case unless he could expect the story to be widely believed and
      familiar. On the Thirty see 4 § xv. Alcibiades on democracy: 4 §
      xiii.

4.   The prosecution: *Apology* 19b, 23d, 24d. Socrates' trial: Finley
      [1968], ch. 5.

5.   Some of the Athenian public readily accepted Aristophanes' charge
      (*Clouds* 365–411, 614–28) that naturalist speculations rejected Zeus

in favour of some nonsense about mechanical forces controlling the world. An Athenian who offended the city's gods could be expected to provoke divine anger against the whole city (cf. the beginning of Homer's *Iliad* and Aeschylus' *Agamemnon*). Many Athenians might believe such an explanation of their defeat in the Peloponnesian War.

6. Cosmology: *Apology* 19d. Religion: 26d. Corruption: 29d–30b.

7. Facing death: *Apology* 28b–29a. The Thirty: 32c–d. Divine command: 28d–29a. Threat of disobedience: 29c–30c. Obedience: *Crito* 50c–51c, Kraut [1984]. Arguments: *Crito* 46b.

8. Laches: *Laches* 190b–c. Euthyphro: *Euthyphro* 4b–e, 5c–d. Socratic arguments: Robinson in Vlastos [1971a], ch. 4; Vlastos [1994], ch. 1.

9. Single account: *Laches* 191c–192b; *Euthyphro* 6d–e. Pattern, form: *Euthyphro* 5d–e, 6e; *Meno* 72a–e. *Idea*: 3 § vi.

10. Imitation: *Meno* 92e.

11. Disputes: Thuc. iii. 82. 4.

12. Socrates' disavowal of knowledge: *Charmides* 165b–c; *Euthyphro* 5c; *Lysis* 223b; *Gorg.* 509a.

13. Laches: *Laches* 191a–c, 193d.

14. Jellyfish: *Meno* 80a. Daedalus: *Euthyphro* 11b–d. Seeking truth: *Charmides* 166d; *Gorg.* 486d–e.

15. Piety and the gods: *Euthyphro* 10a–11b.

16. Prophets: Isaiah 1: 11–17; Micah 6: 6–8; Psalm 50. Sacrifices: Plato, *Rep.* 365d–366a.

17. For Plato's development of this theme, perhaps inspired by Socrates, see 6 § xviii.

18. Kant, *Foundations*, Ak. p. 408. On Christian ethics see 11 § iii.

19. Piety: *Euthyphro* 11e–15e. Bravery: *Laches* 194c–197e.

20. Unity of virtues: *Laches* 198a–199e. Training for bravery: 190c–d. Puzzle: 199e–200c; but cf. *Protagoras* 360d. Reactions: Isocrates, *Helen* 1.

21. Self-interest and happiness: *Euthydemus* 278e, 280b. On *eudaimonia* see 7 § x. Self-interest and justice: *Crito* 48b. Cf. *Apology* 28b–d, 41c–d; *Gorg.* 470e, 504e–505b, 507c; 6 §§ xii–xiv.

22. Socrates on immortality: see 6 § x.

23. Socratic techniques: *Rep.* 539b–c.

24. It is in fact highly unlikely that Aristophanes himself intends the *Clouds* to defend traditional morality, which he portrays in mocking and satirical terms.

25. Aristotle: *Parts of Animals* 642a30, 7 §§ ii–iii. Cicero: *Tusculan Disputations* v. 10. Milton: *Paradise Regained* iv. 272–80. See Guthrie [1962], iii. 417–25.

Chapter 6

1. Plato's life and political views: *Epistles* vii. 324d, 325c-326a. The seventh of the letters attributed to Plato is our main source for his biography (and especially for the journeys to Sicily, the political significance of which is obscure and disputed); it is probably spurious, but likely to be right on the points mentioned in the text.

   Books on Plato: Kraut [1992], esp. ch. 1; Crombie [1964]; Gosling [1973]: Irwin [1995]. On Socrates and Plato see 5 § i.

2. Plato's distortion of Socrates: a brief statement in Robinson [1969], 85 f., and a fuller statement in Popper [1966], i. 194-7, 305-13.

3. Self-examination and cross-examination: *Apology* 38a; *Crito* 46b-c; *Gorg.* 480d-e, 508e-509a.

4. The priority of definition: *Meno* 71a-c. Meno's question: 79e-80e.

5. The slave's progress: *Meno* 82b-d; 82e, 84a-b (confidence); 83a-e (puzzlement); 84d-85b (success). Sincerity: 83d.

6. True beliefs: 85c.

7. Previous knowledge: 85d-86a. On recollections see Vlastos [1995], vol. 2, ch. 11; Fine in Kraut [1992], ch. 6.

8. Knowledge and belief: 85c, 98a (cf. *Euthyphro* 11c-d). Socrates: *Gorg.* 454c-e, 465a. See Annas [1981], ch. 8, Cross [1964], ch. 8.

9. Scepticism: see 4 § x.

10. Definition, form, and standard: *Meno* 71b, 72c; *Euthyphro* 6d, 6e. The correct names for things will reflect the real properties that they share (*Cratylus* 387d).

11. Reality of forms: *Phd.* 65d, *Cratylus* 439c. Opposites: *Phd.* 74a-c; *Hippias Major* 293a-b. Stability: *Phd.* 78c-d, *Rep.* 485b. Separation: *Symposium* 211b. Aristotle: *Met.* 987a32-b10, 1078b9-1079a4, 1086a32-b11. The Theory of Forms: Cherniss in Vlastos [1971b], i, ch. 2; Vlastos [1973], chs. 2-3; Annas [1981], ch. 9.

12. '*F* and not *F*': *Laches* 192c; *Charmides* 161a; *Rep.* 331c-332a.

13. Heracleitus: 3 § ix on senses, and 3 § iv on flux. Senses: *Rep.* 523a-525a, 479a-c. Flux: *Phd.* 78d-e. Compresence and flux are more plausibly applied to properties or types of (e.g.) actions or objects than to particulars; Plato probably means that bright colour makes some things beautiful and other things ugly, rather than committing himself to the claim that every particular bright-coloured thing is both beautiful and ugly.

14. Independent existence probably captures what Aristotle intends by 'separation'; but Plato hardly uses the term, and it is not clear that he uses it in this sense for the relation between Forms and sensible things (see Fine [1993], ch. 3).

15. Apparent evidence of self-predication: *Phd.* 74e-75a; *Protagoras*

330c-d; *Symposium* 211a-b. Aristotle: see 7 § iv. Plato's *Parmenides* raises some of the difficulties about Forms and self-predication; see 128e-135a, and esp. 132a-b (the 'Third Man'; see Vlastos [1973], ch. 4).

16. See 3 § iv (Heracleitus); 4 § xii (Scepticism and conventionalism).

17. Sun, Line, and Cave: *Rep.* 507a-521c, 531c-534e, Annas [1981], ch. 10, Fine in Everson [1990], ch. 5.

18. Prisoners: 515c-e. Turning the soul: 518d.

19. Assumptions: *Phd.* 100a, 101d; *Rep.* 510b-511a; *Meno* 86c. Their use is especially characteristic of mathematicians: *Rep.* 510b-e, 533b-c.

20. Dialectic: 511b-d, 533a-b, 534b-d. Plotinus on the Line: 10 § vi.

21. Conflicting appearances: 4 § iv, x, xii.

22. Circles: see 9 § ii.

23. Socrates: *Apology* 29d-30b; *Crito* 47e-48a. Immortality:*Apology* 40c-41c; *Crito* 54b-c. [*Alc*]. 129a-130e (probably not by Plato) develops Socrates' views in a dualist direction.

24. Dualism: *Phd.* 64c, 79a-81b. On the *Phaedo*: Gallop [1975], Bostock [1986].

25. Recollection: *Phd.* 72e-76e. Death: 64c-68b. Virtue: 68c-69d.

26. Socrates' soul: *Phd.* 115c-e. Senses: 65a-66a, 66b-d.

27. Sensual desires: *Phd.* 66a, 94b-e. The soul, as Plato conceives it in the *Phaedo*, does not include all those states that we would call 'mental' or 'conscious'. Irrational desires and sense-impressions are conscious and mental; but Plato attributes them to the body, not to the soul.

28. Plato seems to see some of the objections to the view he takes in the *Phaedo*. See *Rep.* iv. 608d-612a, *Phaedrus* 245c-246d. But he does not abandon his dualism.

29. Benefits of injustice: *Rep.* 343c, 360e-361d. Questions about justice: 367e. Socrates: see 5 § vii. Thrasymachus: 4 § xi.

30. The reply to Thrasymachus begins with a description of the best sort of city—best because it is designed to secure the welfare both of each group within it and of the whole (420b-421c). The virtues of the city are the states that achieve these ends; and the parallel states in an individual soul, achieving the good for the whole soul and for its parts, will be the virtues of the soul.

31. Conflict of desires: *Rep.* 439b. The same sort of argument supports Plato's belief in a third part, the 'emotional' or 'spirited' part, associated with anger and with feelings of honour and shame (439e-441c).

32. The senses: *Rep.* 602c-603a. Rational part: 442c, 588b-c.

33. The virtues: *Rep.* 442b-d. Justice: 433c-d, 442e-443b, 444e-445b.

34. Types of justice: Sachs in Vlastos [1971b] ii, ch. 2; Vlastos [1973], ch. 5; Irwin [1995], ch. 15.

35. Ordinary justice: *Rep.* 442e–443a. Real interests: 7 § xii.

36. Love of Forms: *Symposium* 210a–212a; *Phaedrus* 249d–256e. Nonpersonal objects of love: *Symposium* 209a–e. The same term *kalon* corresponds to both 'admirable' (as applied, e.g., to actions and people) and 'beautiful'. Platonic love: Vlastos [1973], ch. 1.

37. Loving the Forms: *Rep.* 490b. Propagation: *Symposium* 208a–c, 211e–212a. Immortality is denied to us as the complex of desires, memories and so on that we have in our bodily life, even if it is available for us as pure intellects. If this is what the *Symposium* means, it need not conflict with the doctrine of immortality in the *Phaedo*.

38. Government: *Rep.* 500d, 519c, 520e–521a, Kraut [1973]; Kraut [1992], ch. 10.

39. Socrates' political views: *Crito* 52d–53a; *Protagoras* 319b–d; *Gorg.* 517b–519a. Philosopher-rulers: *Rep.* 473d–e (cf. *Protagoras* 357d–e; *Meno* 99e–100a).

40. Class struggle: *Rep.* 422e–423a, 586a–b. Democracy: *Gorg.* 517b–519d, 521d–522a; *Rep.* 557e–558c, 488a–490a, 493a–d. Rhetoric: *Gorg.* 464b–465c.

41. The philosophers' knowledge: *Rep.* 519b–521b. Education: 416d–417b, 462–5. Selection: 415a–c. Women: 451b–457b, 540b. The ideal state: Annas [1981], ch. 7; Vlastos [1995], vol. 2, ch. 10.

42. Lower classes: 463a–b, 590c–591a.

43. The 'liberal' argument is clearly expounded and criticized by Williams [1972], 20–6. See also 4 § xiv on Protagoras.

44. The decline of rhetoric: Tacitus, *Dialogues* 37–41.

45. Teleology: *Phd.* 96d–99c; *Rep.* 508d–509b, 517b–c. Action and purpose: *Phd.* 98c–d, 99a–b. See 4 § v, 7 § vii.

46. The craftsman: *Timaeus* 27e–30b, 48c (cf. *Cratylus* 390b–c; *Rep.* 596b). Goal-directed order: *Laws* 889a–890a. Mind as cause: 891c–899d.

47. Divine perfection: *Timaeus* 29e. Homeric gods: *Rep.* 377b–392a. The wandering cause: *Timaeus* 48a–b.

48. The Sceptical Academy: Long [1974], 88–90; Sedley in Barnes [1980], 10–12. Dogmatic Platonism: Dillon [1977], ch. 1.

49. Mathematics: *Rep.* 522e–525e. Limitations: 510c–511d. Plato's use: Vlastos [1975], ch. 3.

50. Bentham [1839], 135.

Chapter 7

1. Socrates: *Met.* 987a29–b7, *Parts of Animals* 642a30. Nature: *Parts of Animals* i. 5. Good introductions to Aristotle: Ackrill [1981]; Barnes [1982]. Longer discussions of several aspects of this thought: Lear [1988]; Irwin [1988].
2. The *Timaeus* and biology: 6 § xviii.
3. Development of Aristotle's thought: Ross and Owen in Barnes [1975], i, chs. 1–2.
4. Experience: *Generation and Corruption* 316a5–10; *Prior Analytics* i. 30. Plato: *Phd.* 99d–e.
5. *Historia*: *Parts of Animals* 646a8–12, 3 § vii.
6. Aristotle and his school also compiled a list of winners at the games in Delphi and Olympia, to fix a more reliable chronology. See the list in Barnes [1984], 2387. On the lost constitutions see fragments in Barnes, 2453–8.
7. Herodotus: *History of Animals* 523a16–29; *Generation of Animals* 756b6. Natural motion: *De Caelo* i. 2, iv. 1, Sambursky [1960], ch. 4, Dijksterhuis [1961], 24–32. Bees: *Generation of Animals* 760b28–33. Some of Aristotle's 'observations', e.g. *Parva Naturalia* 459b28–460a33, are strangely inaccurate.
8. Common beliefs: *Topics* 104a3–15. Dialectic: *Topics* i. 2. Method: *EN* 1145b2–7. First principles: *Topics* 101a36–b4.
9. Change: *Physics* 189b39–190a21, 190a31–b17. *Physics* i–ii: Charlton [1970].
10. Here the Greek word is *anthrôpos* (Latin *homo*) = 'man' = 'human being'. A different Greek word *anêr* (Latin *vir*) = 'man' = 'adult male'. The use of 'human being' to translate the second-substance term *anthrôpos* would mislead us about the grammatical character of Aristotle's term.
11. First substance: *Categories* 2a11–14, 4a10–13. Second substance: 2b29–3a6. Non-substances: *Categories* 4. See Ackrill [1963]. On Aristotle's conception of substance see Witt [1989].
12. Separation and self-predication: 6 § vii. Third Man: *Met.* 1038b35–1039a3; cf. *Topics* 178b36–179a10. Reduplication: *Met.* 990a34–b8.
13. Matter = *hulê*, lit. 'wood'; see *Physics* 191a7–12; Plato, *Philebus* 54b–c.
14. The bronze and the statue: *Physics* 245b9–12, *Met.* 1033a16–23.
15. On Heracleitus see 3 § iv. For Aristotle's reply about the river see *Generation and Corruption* 321b16–32. Cf. 8 § vi.
16. Anaxagoras: DK B 17. Matter as substance: *Physics* 193a9–12, 17–21.
17. Causes: *Physics* 194b16–195a3, Ackrill [1981], ch. 4. The Greek *aition* (hence 'aetiological') corresponds to both 'cause' and 'explanation'. I will use both terms as they seem suitable. 'End' or

'goal' = Greek *telos*, Latin *finis*; hence the labels 'final cause' or 'teleological explanation' for this type of causation. Not all four causes are always appropriate. The (universal) triangle has a formal cause, stating its definition, but no efficient cause (since it does not come into being), and no final cause (since it is not made to promote any goal or end).

18. Form as essence: *Physics* 193a30–b21. Final causes: *Physics* 198b32–199a8. Plato: 6 § xviii, Sorabji [1980], chs. 9–11.

19. He does not believe that natural species ever came into being at all; they have always existed, *Generation of Animals* 731b32–732a2.

20. Plato on definition: 6 § v.

21. Democritus: *De Anima* 406b17–22, 24–5. On *Phaedo* 98d–99b see 6 § xviii. Further agreement with Plato: *De Anima* 407b27–408a28, *Phd.* 85e–95a.

22. Soul as form: *De Anima* 412a3–28, 412b10–413a3, 403a24–b7. Constituents: *Met.* 1041b11–33. See 9 § iii. Unity: *De Anima* 412b6–8. Sometimes the thing that has the form, sometimes the form itself, is said to be the substance. Dead bodies: 412b20–2; cf. *Parts of Animals* 640b30–641a5. See Ackrill [1981], ch. 5; Irwin in Everson [1991], ch. 4.

23. Aristotle himself argues for the non-material character of intellect, in *De Anima* iii. 4.

24. Constitutive and eliminative atomism: 4 § v.

25. Human responsibility: 4 § viii, 9 § v.

26. Self-love: *EN* 1168b15–19. See 5 § viii, 6 § xii.

27. On the relations between *eudaimonia* and happiness see Ackrill in Rorty [1980], ch. 2; Kraut [1979].

28. Addition: *EN* 1097b16–20. Virtue: 1095b31–1096a2; cf. 1153b19–21. Cf. *Rep.* 361b–d. Socrates: 5 § vii. Pleasure: 1174a1–4.

29. Function: *EN* 1097b22–1098a20. See Nagel in Rorty [1980], ch 1.

30. The mean: *EN* 1106a14–b28. Aristotle does not imply that we should have only moderate feelings or appetites; on the right occasion the virtuous person should be extremely pleased or extremely angry.

31. Courage: *EN* 1115b7–24. Temperance: 1119a11–20. Wisdom: 1140a25–8.

32. Self-sufficiency: *EN* 1097b7–11.

33. Friendship: *EN* 1156b7–12.

34. Plato's state: *Politics* 1261a15–b15, 1263a40–b14.

35. The state: *Politics* 1280b29–1281a4.

36. Menial labour: *Politics* 1328b34–1329a2, 1329a24–6. Slavery: 1254b16–1255a3. Women: 1260a9–24.

37. Contemplation: *EN* x. 6–8; Plato, *Rep.* 520c. The gods: 1177b26–1178a8. Invulnerability: 1177a20–b1, 1178a23–b7. Human nature: 1178b5–7. The claim that contemplation is not the whole of happiness is highly controversial; see Hardie [1980], ch. 16; Kraut [1989].

38. Self-sufficiency: *EN* 1097b14–15.

39. Yeats, 'Among School Children', in Yeats [1950]. On the criticism of Aristotle by Atticus the Platonist see Dillon [1977], 248–50.

40. Successors: 10 § i.

41. Hume, *Inquiry concerning Human Understanding* i, p. 7.

42. Ptolemy, *Almagest* i. 7; Cohen [1958], 125; Lloyd [1973], 116.

Chapter 8

1. Hellenistic philosophy in general: Sedley in Barnes [1980], ch. 1; Long [1974]; Annas [1993] (on ethics). Long [1987] is excellent; it contains many of the texts cited in this and the next chapter, and its commentary is a reliable guide to the problems. A good shorter collection: Inwood [1988].

2. An inscription bearing the Delphic advice to know oneself (cf. Plato, *Charmides* 164c–165b) has been found in Afghanistan. See Walbank [1981], 61, Austin [1981], 314f.

3. See Acts of Apostles 14: 11, Jones [1940], 285–90. The later use of 'pagan' (Latin *pagus*, village) for non-Christians indicates this division between city and country.

4. Septuagint: Barrett [1956], 208–16; *ODCC* s. v. Aristeas.

5. Polybius ix. 28–9; Walbank [1981], 91f.

6. Polybius xviii. 14. 6–7. Political life: Jones [1964].

7. Alexandria and Athens: Lloyd [1973], chs. 1–2. Education: Jones [1940], 220–4.

8. Horace, *Epistles* ii. 1. 156–7 (referring to literature).

9. Cephalus: Plato, *Rep.* 330d–e. Security: Diogenes Laertius x. 141. Fame: contrast Plato, *Symposium* 208c–d. Competition: Lucretius ii. 39–54, iii. 1053–75. Underlying fear of death: iii. 1053–6, 1068.

10. Purpose of studying nature: Lucretius ii. 58–60 Diogenes Laertius x. 143. On *phusiologia* see 3 § i.

11. Scepticism: 4 § xii, 6 § ix, 9 § ii.

12. Criterion: Sextus, *P* ii. 14–16; ii. 18–20. The most extreme Sceptics were the Pyrrhonians, following Pyrrhon (*c*.365–270). The Academic Sceptics took a more moderate line; see 6 § xix, 10 § i, Annas [1986]. Our evidence for this Hellenistic scepticism is largely derived from the later compilation by Sextus Empiricus (see Annas [1994]). I use

'Sceptic' and 'Sceptical' with initial capitals for members of doctrines of these schools; I use small initial letters to refer more generally to this philosophical tendency. On Sceptics and Stoics see Striker, Annas, and Barnes in Everson [1990].

13. Tranquillity: Sextus, *P* i. 12, 25–9. Epicurus: Diogenes Laertius x. 146.

14. Senses: Diogenes Laertius x. 146–7; Sextus, *AM* viii. 9; Diogenes Laertius x. 52. Descartes: *Meditation* i.

15. Epicurus on conflicting appearances: Taylor in Barnes [1980], ch. 5. Dreams etc.: Plato, *Theaetetus* 158b–e.

16. Lucretius, ii. 112–41, 308–32, 826–33.

17. Empirical equivalence: Diogenes Laertius x. 87, 91, 94.

18. Senses: 3 § viii, 7 §§ ii–iii, xv.

19. Soul: Lucretius iii. 417–829.

20. Compounds: Diogenes Laertius x. 69; Lucretius i. 670–1. See 3 § iv, 7 § v.

21. Gods: Plato, *Laws* 899d–900b. Design: Cicero, *De Natura Deorum* i. 43; Lucretius v. 195–234, 1161–1240.

22. Perceptions of gods: Sextus, *AM* ix. 43–6, Lucretius v. 1169–82. The gods' location: Lucretius v. 146–55, 75–8, Cicero, *De Divinatione* ii. 40.

23. Divine happiness: Diogenes Laertius x. 123, Lucretius iii. 1827, Homer, *Od.* 6. 42–6, Ar. *EN* 1178b8–23. Plato: 6 § xviii.

24. Determinism: see 3 § ix.

25. Aristotle: *EN* 1111a22–4. Fate: Diogenes Laertius x. 134.

26. Aristotle: *EN* 1110a14–18, 1113b3–21.

27. Swerve: Lucretius ii. 251–93; Furley [1967]; Long [1987], 106–12.

28. See 9 § v.

29. Pleasure: Diogenes Laertius x. 126; Cicero, *De Finibus* i. 30; Ar. *EN* 1172b9–25.

30. Sensual pleasure: Diogenes Laertius x. 142; 6 § xiv (Callicles).

31. Virtues: Diogenes Laertius x. 132, 148.

32. Justice: Diogenes Laertius x. 141, 150–1; 4 § vii, 6 § 12. Evolution of society: Lucretius v. 958–61, 988–1027. See 4 § vi, 7 § xiii.

33. See 7 § 10.

34. Death: Diogenes Laertius x. 124; cf. 125–6, Lucretius iii. 830–68. See Nagel [1979], ch. 1.

35. Virtues: Cicero, *De Finibus* ii. 69–71.

36. Some Epicureans try to meet the objection about friendship, by claiming that the wise person will find pleasure in the company of his friend, apart from any further instrumental benefits (Cicero, *De Finibus* i. 65–70). But it is hard to see how, on purely Epicurean grounds, such pleasure can be justified.

37. On Epicureans in politics see 9 § x.

Chapter 9

1. The extent of Stoic knowledge of Aristotle is still disputed. See Long [1974], 9f., Sedley in Barnes [1980], 5. For Stoic texts and excellent discussion see Long [1987]. On the different leading Stoics and the development of Stoicism see Sandbach [1975], chs. 7-8. Zeno (344-262), Cleanthes (331-232), and Chrysippus (c.280-207) are the three founders of the Stoic school; but though the Stoic system developed considerably in the century or so covered by their careers, I have not tried to distinguish their individual contributions.

2. On the senses of *logos* see 3 § x on Heracleitus (a major influence on Stoicism).

3. See Plutarch, *De Communibus Notitiis* 1036b, *De Stoicorum Repugnantiis* 1059b, Diogenes Laertius iv. 62, Sextus, *AM* vii. 159.

4. Sextus, *AM* vii. 151-2, 248-60 (esp. 257 on an appearance compelling assent), 401-11.

5. Infinite regress: 8 § iii. Related objections about circularity: 6 § ix.

6. System in Stoicism: Diogenes Laertius vii. 40. See further Annas in Barnes [1980], ch. 4.

7. Form and *pneuma*: Diogenes Laertius vii. 134, 138-9; Plutarch, *De Stoicorum Repugnantiis* 1053f-1054b; Sambursky [1960], ch. 6.

8. See Cicero, *Academica* i. 39. For (1) and replies to it see Plato, *Sophist* 247d-249b.

9. One might, however, try a further defence of (2) by appeal to the systematic considerations underlying the reply to Scepticism (§ ii).

10. Letters and syllable: Ar. *Met.* vii. 17, 7 § viii.

11. Aristotle on form: 7 § viii.

12. The world as an animal: Cicero, *De Natura Deorum* ii. 22. *Pneuma*: Plutarch, *De Stoicorum Repugnantiis* 1053b, Diogenes Laertius vii. 148-9; Virgil, *Aeneid* vi. 724-32.

13. Cleanthes: Stobaeus, *Eclogae* i. 1. 12. The Stoics' view is close to that of Heracleitus; see 3 § xii. Like him, they depart rather far from traditional views of the gods. But, unlike him, they prefer to stress their acceptance of the traditional gods, suitably conceived.

14. See 8 § vii. The end of Hume's *Dialogues* echoes (perhaps ironically) the end of Cicero's *De Natura Deorum*. See Kemp Smith [1935], 77f. On Epicurus see Hume, *Dialogues* x and *Inquiry concerning Human Understanding* xi.

15. See Plutarch, *De Communibus Notitiis* 1049f-1051b.

16. Determinism: Sextus, *AM* ix. 200-3; Plutarch, *De Communibus Notitiis* 1056b-c; Alexander, *De Fato* 22 (good discussion in Sharples [1983]). Zeus and fate: Epictetus, *Enchiridion* 53; Seneca, *Epistles* 107. 10.

17. The Lazy Argument: Cicero, *De Fato* 28-30. Assent: see § ii above, Cicero, *De Fato* 39-43, Alexander, *De Fato* 13.

18. Praise and blame: Alexander, *De Fato* 35, 37.

19. An ancient parallel to 'epicure': Horace, *Epistles* i. 4. 15-16.

20. Appeals to nature: 4 § xv, 8 § ix.

21. Development of reason: Diogenes Laertius vii. 85-6, Cicero, *De Finibus* iii. 16-26.

22. Happiness: 7 § x. Virtue and happiness: Cicero, *Tusculan Disputations* v. 80-2, Diogenes Laertius vii. 127. Socrates: Cicero, *Paradoxa Stoicorum* 4. Virtue as the only good: Cicero, *De Finibus* iii. 42-8.

23. This objection seems to be well aimed at the Cynics, disciples of Socrates (of whom Diogenes (*c*.400-*c*.325), 'Socrates gone mad', is the most notorious; Diogenes Laertius vi. 54) who take his conception of virtue and happiness to what they regard as its logical conclusion. Since the Cynics accept Socrates' claim that the good person cannot be harmed, they live in complete indifference to everything besides virtue (5 § vii). Zeno the Stoic was a pupil of Crates the Cynic (*c*.365-285) (Diogenes Laertius vi. 91, vii. 2), and was influenced by Cynic ethics.

24. Indifferents: Diogenes Laertius vii. 102, 104; Sextus, *AM* xi. 59-64; Cicero, *De Finibus* iii. 50-8.

25. Criticisms: Cicero, *De Finibus* iii. 41; iv. 40-8, 78.

26. In the *De Finibus* ('On the ends', i.e. on different views of the ultimate good) Cicero presents the Stoic arguments to show that virtue is identical to happiness, and that everything besides virtue is irrelevant to happiness. In the *De Officiis* ('On duties') he presents a detailed account (derived from the Stoic Panaetius) of practical ethics, expressing the Stoics' concern with preferred indifferents.

27. The basis of society: Cicero, *De Finibus* iii. 62-70; *De Officiis* i. 11-23; *De Legibus* i. 28-34; ii. 11. Early Stoicism: Diogenes Laertius vii. 32-4, 188; Sextus, *P* iii. 200. Later views: Cicero, *De Officiis* i. 21-2, 114; ii. 73.

28. On philosophy and political life in Rome see Griffin in Barnes [1989], ch. 1. The desire for withdrawal from politics and war, and for the tranquil and undisturbed condition of private life, is at least congenial to Epicurean views (though evidently not confined to Epicureans); see

Horace, *Epodes* 16, Virgil, *Eclogues* 1. Stoic sentiments in Horace: *Odes* i. 23. 1–8; iii. 3. 1–8. On Virgil see e.g. *Aeneid* vi. 724–32 (on the doctrines discussed in § iv above). See Clarke [1956], ch. 6.

29. See Epictetus, *Discourses* iii. 24. 84–94; *Enchiridion* 7, 15. Socrates: *Discourses* iii. 23. 32, iv. 1. 159–69; *Enchiridion* 33. 12.

30. This process of forming a complete monarchy out of the (officially) shared rule of Emperor and Senate continued through the first century AD ; it is described and deplored by the historian Tacitus in his *Annals*. In this conflict between Emperor and Senate some Stoics distinguished themselves in the opposition to the Emperor. Under Augustus Stoicism had been officially welcomed and encouraged. But under his successors, in particular Nero (AD 54–68) and Domitian (81–96), Stoics were often, and reasonably, suspected of opposition to imperial policy; see Brunt [1975]. The prominent Stoic Seneca (*c*.4 BC–AD 65) was a high official under Nero, but eventually fell from favour, and committed suicide. The outlook required for a successful career as a favourite of the Emperor came to seem incompatible with the Stoic virtues.

31. Suicide: Diogenes Laertius vii. 130; Cicero, *De Finibus* iii. 60–1.

32. Emotions: Cicero, *Tusculan Disputations* iv. 28–32; *De Finibus* iii. 35; Epictetus, *Enchiridion* 5.

33. Sympathy: Lactantius, *Divinae Institutiones* vi. 10; Milton, *Paradise Regained* iv. 299–308.

34. Universal nature: Diogenes Laertius vii. 87–9; Cicero, *De Finibus* iii. 31, iv. 14. Playing one's part: Cicero, *Tusculan Disputations* i. 118; Epictetus, *Enchiridion* 17; Marcus Aurelius, ii. 9.

35. Fates: Seneca, *Epistles* 107. 10, 'ducunt volentem fata, nolentem trahunt'.

36. Will of Zeus: Plutarch, *De Stoicorum Repugnantiis* 1050a.

37. See, e.g., the Stoic defence of divination: Cicero, *De Divinatione* i. 82–7.

38. Epicurean political activity: Momigliano [1941]. Stoics: Brunt [1975], Sandbach [1975], ch. 9.

39. Romans 1: 18–23; Acts 17: 27–8; Psalm 19: 1, 7; Justin, *Apology* ii. 10, 13.

40. St Ambrose's *De Officiis* is closely modelled on Cicero's work of the same name.

Chapter 10

1. Andronicus: Plutarch, *Sulla* 26. 1–2; Strabo xiii. 1. 55. Both passages suggest that he also tried to distinguish genuine from spurious

works of Aristotle; probably they greatly exaggerate the general ignorance of Aristotle before Andronicus' edition. His edition was probably produced *c.*40 BC. Greek commentaries on Aristotle: Sorabji [1990].

2. Later Platonism: 6 § xix. Study of Aristotle: 8 § i; Merlan in Armstrong [1967], 114–23 (quite one-sided). Middle Platonists: Dillon [1977]; more briefly, Merlan in Armstrong [1967], ch. 4, Wallis [1972], ch. 2.

3. Porphyry, *Life of Plotinus* 14 (in Armstrong [1966], which is the only reliable translation). Brief accounts of Plotinus: Armstrong [1967], chs. 12–16; Wallis [1972], ch. 3; Emilsson in Everson [1991], ch. 8; O'Meara [1993].

4. The hypostases: v. 2. 1. *Hupostasis* in later Greek philosophy has roughly the sense of *ousia*, 'substance', in Aristotle (see 7 § iv), though it becomes more specialized in some contexts. On Plotinus' use see Atkinson [1983], 55–8. I use initial capitals for the names of the Plotinian hypostases, and small initial letters in remarks about soul etc. in general, rather than in their specific Plotinian role.

5. The two paths: Plato, *Rep.* 518b–c, 532a–b.

6. Leading back to the One: v. 1. 1. 23–5; Porphyry, *Life of Plotinus* 2. 26–7.

7. Only three hypostases: ii. 9. 2–3.

8. Matter and change: ii. 4. 1. 1–2; ii. 4. 6. 14–20; ii. 4. 8; ii. 4. 10–12; iii. 6. 6–7.

9. Subject and properties: ii. 4. 6.

10. Matter and the senses: v. 5. 1. 17–20; iii. 6. 7. 33–41; iii. 6. 13. 38–55. See Berkeley, *Siris* § 316 (one of several favourable references to Plotinus); Sorabji [1983], 290–4.

11. Democritus: 4 § v.

12. The status of matter: ii. 4. 14; ii. 4. 16. 3; ii. 5. 4. 11–12; ii. 5. 5. 25–6.

13. Beauty: Plato, *Symposium* 210–11 (see 6 § xv); Plotinus i. 6, esp. i. 6. 2. 17–18.

14. Form and soul: ii. 6. 2. 14–15; ii. 7. 3.

15. Plato on soul: 6 § xi.

16. Experiences in one soul: iv. 9. 2; iv. 8. 3–4; iv. 3. 6. 15–17.

17. Time, change, and soul: iii. 7. 11. 43–5; iii. 7. 11. 58–9; iii. 7. 13. 23–30; cf. Plato, *Timaeus* 37d–38b. Plotinus assumes correctly that we become aware of time because of the temporal sequence of our experiences; and we can say how much time something takes

by comparing the sequence of our experiences with some other sequence of regular change—the movements of the clock or of the heavens. But he seems to argue from the claim that these are conditions for our awareness of time to the conclusion that they are conditions for the existence of time. This argument is unsound. See Sorabji [1983], ch. 6. Still, Plotinus might be entitled to claim that we have no reason to believe in the reality of time once we disbelieve in the reality of the material universe.

18. Forms and intellect: Plato, *Parmenides* 132b-c; Plotinus v. 5. 1. 42-9; v. 4. 2. 44-8; v. 6. 1; v. 9. 5. 10-20; v. 9. 6. 1-3.

19. Intellect dependent on Forms: v. 5. 2. 1-12; v. 9. 5. 14-19; v. 9. 5. 29-35; vi. 5. 7. 1-6; vi. 5. 10. 38-42. Recollection: see 6 § iii.

20. Plurality: v. 3. 11.

21. Intuitive knowledge: i. 8. 2. 8-20; iv. 4. 12. 1-30; iii. 7. 3. 16-18; vi. 9. 4. 1-11; Sorabji [1983], 152-6. Plotinus derives the contrast from Plato, *Rep.* 511c-d, though it is probably not what Plato intends; see 6 § viii.

22. The One: v. 3. 12; vi. 8. 8. 12-19; vi. 9. 5. 24-46. See Plato, *Parmenides* 137c-142a. The Good beyond being: v. 5. 6. 8-22; vi. 7. 21-2. See Plato, *Rep.* 509b. On the Neoplatonist interpretation of the *Republic* and the *Parmenides* see Dodds [1928], Hardie [1936], 112-30.

23. Intellect and its objects: v. 5. 1. 51-69.

24. Love and beauty: i. 6. 6. 13-33; i. 6. 7. See Aristophanes' humorous suggestion, Plato, *Symposium* 190c-192e. Plotinus takes this desire for union with the object of love even more seriously than Plato did. Berkeley: *Siris* § 358.

25. Emanation: iii. 2. 1. 20-7; iv. 3. 9. 14-19; v. 1. 6. 19-25; iii. 8. 10; v. 1. 6. 28-40.

26. One, Intellect, Soul: ii. 9. 3. 8; v. 1. 6. 38-40; v. 1. 7. 5-8; ii. 9. 1; v. 1. 7. 39-48.

27. Audacity: v. 1. 1. 4-9; iii. 7. 11. 14-19; iv. 8. 4. 10-22. These activities of the soul cannot readily be attributed to the Plotinian hypostasis in its own right (hence I have not capitalized 'soul'). Nor, however, can the soul that engages in them be completely separate from the hypostasis; it is presumably an aspect of the hypostasis. Further obscurities in Plotinus' view emerge here.

28. Self-assertion: iv. 8. 5; iv. 8. 6; iv. 3. 13. In formulating this difficulty about the 'descent' of the soul, Plotinus refers back to Plato. For Plato seems to treat the embodiment of the soul both as a regrettable imprisonment and as part of the wise and benevolent design of the universe (iv. 8. 1. 27-51).

29. Matter and evil: ii. 4. 11. 16–25; i. 8. 3. 31–40; i. 8. 14. 41–50.

30. Influence of the body: v. 1. 1. 1–23.

31. Matter and evil: iii. 2. 2. 1–45; ii. 3. 18; i. 8. 7; i. 8. 15. 1–9. Stoics: 9
     § iv. Gnostic sects upheld cosmological dualism; some identified
     the evil force with the God of the Old Testament, also identified
     with Plato's Demiurge, and identified the good force with the God
     of the New Testament. They appeal to the apparent other-
     worldliness of Plato's *Phaedo* to support their own attack on the
     sensible world (ii. 9. 6. 10–28). Plotinus argues, appealing to the
     Timaeus, that they have completely misunderstood Plato (ii. 9. 6.
     43–53). On Gnosticism see *ODCC* s. v.; Armstrong [1967], 243–5.

32. Attention to the whole: iii. 2. 14. 7–20; iii. 2. 16. 28–52; iii. 2. 15.
     See also Plato, *Laws* 817b–d; Marcus Aurelius xii. 36.

33. Blame: iii. 2. 16. 1–11. Stoics: 9 § v.

34. Soul and Intellect: iv. 8. 8; v. 1. 10. 5–18; vi. 2. 22. 28–33; i. 4. 10.
     24–34.

35. Body and soul: iv. 4. 18. 8; iv. 7. 8(5); iv. 7. 8(4). 14; iv. 7. 9–10; iv.
     3. 20.

36. Body 'affecting' soul: i. 8. 15. 13–28; iv. 3. 26. 1–14; iii. 6. 1. 1–24;
     iii. 6. 3. 1–25; iii. 6. 4. 1–37. Cf. 9 § iii. 'We': i. 1. 7. 7–24; i. 1. 9–10;
     ii. 3. 9. 11–32; vi. 4. 14. 16–31; iv. 4. 18. 11–21.

37. Attachment to the body: i. 1. 9. 1–16; iii. 6. 2. 22–33, 54–68. Virtues:
     i. 1. 10. 11–14; i. 2. 2–3; i. 2. 6. 12–28; i. 6. 6 (cf. Plato, *Phd.* 69b–c).

38. Contemplation: i. 4. 7–10. See 7 § xiv. External harms: i. 4. 13–14.

39. Detachment from the body: ii. 9. 15. 34–40; ii. 9. 18. 1–14.

40. Responsibility: iii. 1. 7; iii. 1. 10. 4–15; iii. 2. 10; iii. 2. 17. 13–17.
     See 8 § viii, 9 § v.

41. Philo and Christian thought: Chadwick in Armstrong [1967], chs.
     8–11.

Chapter 11

1. Stoic influence: see Ecclesiastes; Wisdom 7: 22–8: 10; 9: 9; 11: 17; 4
    Maccabees 1: 1–3: 18, 13: 1–18. (4 Maccabees is most easily avail-
    able in RSV.) Philo: 10 § x. Though many pious Jews resisted any
    cultural or religious assimilation to the Hellenistic world (see
    esp. 1 Maccabees 1: 1–2: 42), Jewish thinkers continued to think
    in partly Greek terms, and some Gentiles took an interest in
    Judaism—sometimes a strong enough interest to lead to their
    conversion. See Acts 6: 1, 9; 8: 27–40; John 12: 20. Paul received
    a Rabbinic education in the Gentile city of Tarsus and in Jerusalem
    (cf. Philippians 3: 5). See Momigliano in Finley [1981], ch. 11.

History of the early Church: Chadwick [1967]. Useful collections
of sources: Barrett [1956], Stevenson [1957], Bettenson [1963].
ODCC is very useful. The most generally useful translations of the
Bible are RSV and NEB (in editions containing the Apocrypha, on
which see RSV Introduction or *ODCC*).

2. Paul: 1 Corinthians 1: 23-4. A sceptical Greek view: Lucian, *De
Morte Peregrini* 13. A Christian reply: Justin, *Apology* i. Law and
prophets: Matthew 5: 17.

3. Tertullian: *De Praescriptione Haereticorum* 7. Origen: *contra Celsum* iii. 38, 44 (followed by Origen's reply). See further Armstrong
in Finley [1981], ch. 12.

4. Suetonius, *Claudius* 25 (cf. Acts 18: 2) may imply that there were
Christians in Rome in AD 49. They were certainly persecuted by
Nero after the fire in Rome in 64 (Tacitus, *Annals* xv. 44), and
Christian tradition maintained that St Peter and St Paul died in
this persecution (Eusebius, *Ecclesiastical History* ii. 25). Paul on
teachings of Christ: 1 Corinthians 7: 10-12, 25; 11: 25; 15: 3.

5. The tradition describing St Mark as 'the interpreter of Peter' (Eusebius, *Ecclesiastical History* ii. 39) implies that Mark had at least
acquired some of the material for his book by 66. St Luke's book,
'Acts of Apostles' (no definite article in Greek) was probably written before Paul's death (which is not mentioned, but would have
been suitable to mention if Luke had known of it); and in the
preface Luke refers to his account of Christ's life and teaching
(Acts 1: 1).

6. John's Gospel must have existed before the early second century,
the probable date of a papyrus fragment of the Gospel (which is
also the earliest known manuscript of any of the NT; see *ODCC*
s. v. Rylands). On the formation of the NT Canon see Eusebius,
Ecclesiastical History iii. 24-5.

7. Worship: Justin, *Apology* i. 65-7. Doctrine and ministry: Clement,
1 Corinthians i. 44. 1; Eusebius, *Ecclesiastical History* iv. 22. 2-3.
Edict of Milan: Lactantius, *De Mortibus Persecutorum* 48. On the
so-called 'Nicene Creed' (perhaps from 381) see *ODCC* s. v.

8. Christian preaching: Acts 3: 12-26; 7: 2-53; 10: 34-43. The prophets: Isaiah 1: 10-20; Amos 5: 18; Joel 1: 14-22; Malachi 4: 1-6;
Luke 3: 7-17.

9. Ritual offences: see the beginning of the *Iliad* and of Aeschylus'
Agamemnon; 1 Samuel 13: 8-14; 14: 37-45; 15: 9-35. Moral as
opposed to ritual offences: Hosea 6: 6; Micah 6: 6-8; Jeremiah 7:
22-3; Isaiah 1: 11-15; Amos 2: 6-7; Psalms 40: 6-8; 50: 7-23; 51:
16-19. See 5 § v.

10. Priority of the moral law: Matthew 15: 1-20; Luke 6: 1-11, 11: 42;
    Matthew 22: 35-40; Luke 10: 27; Leviticus 19: 18; Deuteronomy 6:
    5.

11. Jesus: Matthew 19: 1-22; Mark 2: 15-17; Luke 18: 9-14. Paul:
    Philippians 3: 6; 1 Timothy 1: 15; Romans 3: 23. (NEB is especially
    useful for reading Paul's letters, though less close to the Greek than
    RSV.)

12. Perfection: Matthew 5: 21, 27, 31, 33, 38, 43, 48.

13. Love of neighbour: Leviticus 18: 9; Luke 10: 36-7. Hardness of
    heart: Matthew 19: 9; Romans 7: 12.

14. Demands of perfection: Matthew 19: 21. When Paul measures him-
    self against the command 'You shall not covet', he thinks of the
    underlying principle, not the more convenient rule embodied in the
    Decalogue: contrast Romans 7: 7 with Exodus 20: 17.

15. Consciousness of sin: Romans 3: 20; Luke 18: 9.

16. Satan: Milton, *Paradise Lost* i. 258-63. Cf. Augustine, *Confessions*
    ii. 6. Plato, *Gorg.* 483e-484a is perhaps the closest anticipation.

17. Justification (i.e. acquittal): Romans 8: 3-4. Baptism: John 3: 3;
    Romans 6: 3; 2 Corinthians 5: 17. The Eucharist: John 7: 53.
    Redemption: Romans 3: 24-5.

18. Moral integrity: Hebrews 4: 15; 2: 18; cf. Luke 4: 1-13.

19. New creation: 2 Corinthians 5: 17. The Spirit: John 3: 5; Romans
    8: 5. Will and action: Philippians 2: 12.

20. Pride: Romans 3: 27. Grace and faith: 3: 24, 28; 7: 24.

21. See Romans 6: 1: 'Are we to remain in sin, so that grace may be
    multiplied?'

22. Perfection: Matthew 5: 48; 19: 21; 1 Corinthians 9: 24-7; Philippians
    4: 12-16. Failure: Luke 17: 7-10. Hope: Ephesians 2: 12. Love and
    the law: Romans 13: 8-10.

23. Fullness of God: Colossians 1: 17, 19; 2: 9. Word of God: John 1:
    1-14; 1 John 1: 1-10. God's word creates the heavens and the earth,
    by his definite commands (Psalms 33: 6; 104: 7). The Stoics think of
    the *logos* not as a series of definite commands, but as the immanent
    reason that maintains the world in its order; see 9 § iv. This Stoic
    view influences Wisdom 7: 22-8: 1, 9: 1-2, 11, 17-20. St John
    combines these different conceptions of the Logos. Messiah: Mark
    1: 34, 43; 5: 19, 43; 7: 36; 8: 30; John 6: 14-15, Luke 24: 21. Son of
    God: Matthew 4: 3; 16: 16; Mark 14: 61; Luke 22: 70. Strongest
    claims: Mark 2: 7; John 8: 58 (cf. Exodus 3: 14); 14: 9.

24. Reconciling: 2 Corinthians 5: 19. Emptying: Philippians 2: 7.

25. Holy Spirit: John 14: 16. The activity of the Spirit: Genesis 1: 1;
    John 3: 5-8. Stoics: 9 § iii.

26. *Hupostasis* and *ousia*: 10 § ii. The Trinity: Kelly [1977], chs. 9-10, Prestige [1952], chs. 8-11. Controversies: Stevenson [1957], 340-68.
27. Augustine: *De Trinitate* ix. 1-8, x. 17-19.
28. Chalcedon: Bettenson [1963], 73.
29. On Augustine see Chadwick [1986]; Markus in Armstrong [1967], chs. 20-7. Bourke [1974] is a useful selection.
30. Deathbed baptism: *Confessions* i. 11. The Scriptures: iii. 5.
31. Wreckers: iii. 3. Cicero: iii. 4. Manicheans: iii. 6. This sect (supposedly founded by the third-century Persian sage Mani) represented themselves as more authentic Christians than the 'semi-Christians', as they called the ordinary Catholics (Augustine, *contra Faustum* i. 3). They continued some of the leading themes of Gnosticism; See 10 § x. Stoics: 9 § iv.

    Cosmological dualism can be traced back to the struggle of the opposites in Anaximander and other Presocratics, and to earlier Iranian sources. It is not prominent in the Old or New Testaments (cf. Genesis 3: 4; Job 1: 6-13; Daniel 10: 13; Jude 9; Revelation 12: 7). But it may easily attract a Christian believer; see Satan in Milton's *Paradise Lost*.
32. Manichean diets for recycling light: iii. 10.
33. Slackness: v. 7, 10. Criticism of Manichean beliefs: iv. 3, v. 3-7, vii. 6 (astrology). Nebridius: vii. 2; Augustine, *Acta cum Felice* ii. 22. Incorruptibility: vii. 4; cf. Isaiah 40: 28.
34. God as material substance: v. 10; vi. 3. Incarnation: v. 10. St Ambrose, the bishop of Milan, taught Augustine to interpret the Old Testament 'spiritually', in an allegorical sense, to avoid some of its cruder apparent implications (v. 14). Probably he introduced Augustine to the 'books of the Platonists' (i.e. Neoplatonists) translated into Latin by Victorinus (vii. 9, viii. 3). Plotinus and Plato: Augustine, *contra Academicos* iii. 41.
35. The parallel with the Trinity cannot be exact; an orthodox Christian could hardly suggest that the Second and Third Person are in some way illusory, or ultimately less real than the First.
36. Natural evil: vii. 13. Evil wills: vii. 16.
37. The Incarnation: vii. 9. Paul: vii. 21. Mysticism: vii. 17, ix. 10. Humility: vii. 18.
38. Moral demands: viii. 12; Romans 13: 13.
39. Parmenides: see DK 28 B 7. Heracleitus: 3 § ix. Augustine on reason and faith: vi. 4; vi. 5; vii. 5; viii. 1; viii. 7.

Bibliography

This is simply a list of the works cited in the Notes. More specific suggestions for further reading on particular topics are given in the Notes.

The date after the author's name refers to the original publication of the work; the work is cited from the most convenient source, from which the place of original publication may be discovered.

Works by more than one author are cited in the Notes by the name of one author.

Translations and editions are listed under the name of the ancient author.

Ackrill [1963]: *see* Aristotle.

Ackrill, J. L. [1981] *Aristotle the Philosopher*, Oxford.

Adkins, A. W. H. [1960] *Merit and Responsibility*, Oxford.

Adkins, A. W. H. [1971] 'Homeric values and Homeric society', *Journal of Hellenic Studies*, 91 (1971), 1–14.

Aeschylus, tr. in *Complete Greek Tragedies*, D. Grene and R. Lattimore eds., 4 vols., Chicago, 1959.

Alexander, tr. R. W. Sharples, *Alexander of Aphrodisias on Fate*, London, 1983.

Annas, J. [1981] *An Introduction to Plato's Republic*, Oxford.

Annas, J. [1993] *The Morality of Happiness*, Oxford.

Annas [1994]: *see* Sextus.

Annas, J., and Barnes, J. [1986] *The Modes of Scepticism*, Cambridge.

Aristophanes, *Clouds*, tr. and ed. A. H. Sommerstein, Warminster, 1982.

Aristotle, *Works of Aristotle* (complete tr.), ed. J. Barnes, 2 vols., Princeton, 1984.

Aristotle, *Athenian Constitution*, tr. and ed. J. M. Moore, in *Aristotle and Xenophon on Democracy and Oligarchy*, 2nd edn., London, 1983.

Aristotle, *Athenian Constitution*, ed. P. J. Rhodes, Oxford, 1982.

Aristotle, *Categories and De Interpretatione*, tr. and ed. J. L. Ackrill, Oxford, 1963.

Aristotle, *Nicomachean Ethics*, tr. T. Irwin, Indianapolis, 1985.

Aristotle, *Physics i–ii*, tr. and ed., W. Charlton, Oxford, 1970.

Armstrong [1966]: *see* Plotinus.

Armstrong, A. H., ed. [1967] *The Cambridge History of Later Greek and Early Mediaeval Philosophy*, Cambridge.

Atkinson, M. J., ed. [1983] *Plotinus: Ennead v 1*, Oxford.

Augustine, *The Essential Augustine* (selections), tr. and ed. V. J. Bourke, Indianapolis, 1974.

Augustine, *Confessions*, tr. E. B. Pusey, London, 1907.

Austin, M. M. [1981] *The Hellenistic World*, Cambridge.

Barnes, J. [1979] *The Presocratic Philosophers*, 2 vols., London.

Barnes [1984]: *see* Aristotle.

Barnes, J. [1987] *Early Greek Philosophy* (tr.), Harmondsworth.

Barnes, J., Schofield, M., and Sorabji, R., eds. [1975] *Articles on Aristotle*, 4 vols., London, 1975–9.

Barnes, J., Burnyeat, M. F., and Schofield, M., eds. [1980] *Doubt and Dogmatism*, Oxford.

Barnes, J., and Griffin, M., eds. [1989] *Philosophia Togata*, Oxford.

Barrett, C. K., ed. [1956] *The New Testament Background*, London.

Bentham, J. [1839] *Deontology*, ed. A. Goldworth, Oxford, 1983.

Berkeley, G., *Siris*, in *Collected Works*, A. A. Luce and T. E. Jessop, eds., vol. 5, Edinburgh, 1953.

Bettenson, H., ed. [1963] *Documents of the Christian Church*, 2nd edn., Oxford.

Boardman, J., Griffin, J., and Murray, O., eds. [1986] *Oxford History of the Classical World*, Oxford.

Bostock, D. [1986] *Plato's Phaedo*, Oxford.

Bourke [1974]: *see* Augustine.

Bowra, C. M. [1972] *Homer*, London.

Brunt, P. A. [1975] 'Stoicism and the Principate', *Papers of the British School at Rome*, 43 (1975), 7–35.

Brunt, P. A. [1963] Introduction, in *Thucydides* (tr. B. Jowett, ed. Brunt), New York.

Burkert, W. [1985] *Greek Religion*, Oxford.

Chadwick, H. [1967] *The Early Church*, Harmondsworth.

Chadwick, H. [1986] *Augustine*, Oxford.

Charlton [1970]: *see* Aristotle.

Clarke, M. L. [1956] *The Roman Mind*, London.

Cohen, M. R., and Drabkin, I. E., eds. [1958] *A Source Book in Greek Science*, Cambridge, Mass.

Crombie, I. M. [1964] *Plato: the Midwife's Apprentice*, London.

Cross, F. L., and Livingstone, E. A., eds. *Oxford Dictionary of the Christian Church*, 2nd edn. (revised), Oxford, 1983.

Cross, R. C., and Woozley, A. D. [1964] *Plato's Republic*, London.

Davies, J. K. [1978] *Democracy and Classical Greece*, London.

De Ste Croix, G. E. M. [1972] *The Origins of the Peloponnesian War*, London.

De Ste Croix, G. E. M. [1977] 'Herodotus', *Greece and Rome*, 24 (1977), 130–48.

De Ste Croix, G. E. M. [1981] *The Class Struggle in the Ancient Greek World*, London.

Descartes, R., *Meditations*, in *Philosophical Writings of Descartes*, tr. J. Cottingham *et al.* (2 vols., Cambridge, 1985).

Diels, H., and Kranz, W., eds., *Die Fragmente der Vorsokratiker*, 10th edn., Berlin, 1952.

Dijksterhuis, E. J. [1961] *The Mechanization of the World Picture*, Oxford.

Dillon, J. M. [1977] *The Middle Platonists*, London.

Dodds, E. R. [1928] 'The *Parmenides* of Plato and the origin of the Neoplatonic One', *Classical Quarterly*, 22 (1928), 129–42.

Dodds, E. R. [1951] *The Greeks and the Irrational*, Berkeley.

Dodds, E. R. [1973] *The Ancient Concept of Progress and Other Essays*, Oxford.

Everson, S., ed. [1990] *Companions to Ancient Thought, 1: Epistemology*, Cambridge.

Everson, S., ed. [1991] *Companions to Ancient Thought, 2: Psychology*, Cambridge.

Ferguson, W. S. [1911] *Hellenistic Athens*, London.

Fine, G. [1993] *On Ideas: Aristotle's Criticism of Plato's Theory of Forms*, Oxford.

Finley, M. I. [1968] *Aspects of Antiquity*, London.

Finley, M. I., ed. [1981] *New Legacy of Greece*, Oxford.

Furley, D. J. [1967] *Two Studies in the Greek Atomists*, Princeton.

Furley, D. J., and Allen, R. E., eds. [1970] *Studies in Presocratic Philosophy*, i, London.

Furley, D. J. [1987] *The Greek Cosmologists*, vol. 1, Cambridge.

Furley, D. J. [1989] *Cosmic Problems*, Cambridge.

Gallop [1975]: *see* Plato.

Gosling, J. C. B. [1973] *Plato*, London.

Grene [1959]: *see* Aeschylus.

Griffin, J. [1980] *Homer on Life and Death*, Oxford.

Guthrie, W. K. C. [1950] *The Greeks and their Gods*, London.

Guthrie, W. K. C. [1957] *In the Beginning*, London.

Guthrie, W. K. C. [1962] *A History of Greek Philosophy*, 6 vols., Cambridge, 1962–81.

Hammond, N. G. L., and Scullard, H. H., eds., *Oxford Classical Dictionary*, 2nd edn., Oxford, 1970.

Hardie, W. F. R. [1936] *A Study in Plato*, Oxford.

Hardie, W. F. R. [1980] *Aristotle's Ethical Theory*, 2nd edn., Oxford.

Herodotus, tr. A. De Selincourt, Harmondsworth, 1954.

Hippocrates, tr. W. H. S. Jones (Loeb), 4 vols., London, 1923–31.

Hippocrates, tr. *Hippocratic Writings*, ed. G. E. R. Lloyd, Harmondsworth, 1978.

Hobbes, T. [1839] *Opera Latina*, ed. W. Molesworth, vol. 1, London.

Hobbes, T., *Leviathan*, London, 1651 (and many editions).

Hobbes [1975]: *see* Thucydides.

Homer, *Iliad*, tr. R. Lattimore, Chicago, 1951.

Homer, *Odyssey*, tr. R. Lattimore, New York, 1967.

Hume, D., *Inquiries concerning the Human Understanding and concerning the Principles of Morals*, ed. L. A. Selby-Bigge, 2nd edn., Oxford, 1902.

Hume, D., *Dialogues on Natural Religion*, ed. N. Kemp Smith, Oxford, 1935.

Hussey, E. L. [1972] *The Presocratics*, London.

Hussey, E. L. [1985] 'Thucydidean history and Democritean theory', in *Crux*, P. A. Cartledge and F. D. Harvey eds. (London, 1985), 118–38.

Inwood, B., and Gerson, L. P., tr. [1988] *Hellenistic Philosophy: Introductory Readings*, Indianapolis.

Irwin, T. H. [1988] *Aristotle's First Principles*, Oxford.

Irwin, T. H. [1995] *Plato's Ethics*, Oxford.

Jacoby, F., ed. [1923] *Die Fragmente der Griechischen Historiker*, Berlin and Leiden, 1923–58.

Jebb, R. C. [1893] *The Attic Orators*, 2 vols., London.

Jones, A. H. M. [1940] *The Greek City*, Oxford.

Jones, A. H. M. [1957] *Athenian Democracy*, Oxford.

Jones, A. H. M. [1964] 'The Hellenistic age', *Past and Present*, 27 (1964), 1–22.

Kant, I., *Foundations of the Metaphysics of Morals*, tr. L. W. Beck, Indianapolis, 1959.

Kelly, J. N. D. [1977] *Early Christian Doctrines*, 5th edn., London.

Kemp Smith [1935]: *see* Hume.

Kirk, G. S., Raven, J. E., and Schofield, M. [1983] *The Presocratic Philosophers* (tr. and comm.), 2nd edn., Cambridge.

Kraut, R. [1973] 'Egoism, love, and political office in Plato', *Philosophical Review*, 82 (1973), 330–44.

Kraut, R. [1979] 'Two conceptions of happiness', *Philosophical Review*, 88 (1979), 167–97.

Kraut, R. [1984] *Socrates and the State*, Princeton.

Kraut, R. [1989] *Aristotle on the Human Good*, Princeton.

Kraut, R., ed. [1992] *Cambridge Companion to Plato*, Cambridge.

Lear, J. [1988] *Aristotle: the Desire to Understand*, Cambridge.

Levett [1990]: *see* Plato.

Lloyd, G. E. R. [1970] *Early Greek Science*, London.

Lloyd, G. E. R. [1973] *Greek Science after Aristotle*, London.

Lloyd [1978]: *see* Hippocrates.

Lloyd, G. E. R. [1979] *Magic, Reason and Experience*, Cambridge.

Lloyd-Jones, H. [1983] *The Justice of Zeus*, 2nd edn., Berkeley.

Long, A. A. [1970] 'Morals and values in Homer', *Journal of Hellenic Studies*, 90 (1970), 121–39.

Long, A. A. [1974] *Hellenistic Philosophy*, London.

Long, A. A., and Sedley, D. N. [1987] *The Hellenistic Philosophers*, Cambridge.

McDowell [1973]: *see* Plato.

McKirahan, R. D. [1994] *Philosophy before Socrates*, Indianapolis.

MacKenna [1962]: *see* Plotinus.

Macleod, C. W. [1983] *Collected Essays*, Oxford.

Milton, J., *Complete Poems and Major Prose*, ed. M. Y. Hughes, New York, 1957.

Momigliano, A. D. [1941] Review in *Journal of Roman Studies*, 31 (1941), 149–57.

Moore [1983]: *see* Aristotle.

Murray, O. [1980] *Early Greece*, London.

Nagel, T. [1979] *Mortal Questions*, Cambridge.

New English Bible with Apocrypha, Oxford and Cambridge, 1970.

New Oxford Annotated Bible with Apocrypha (*Revised Standard Version*), New York, 1977.

O'Meara, D. J. [1993] *Plotinus: an Introduction to the Enneads*, Oxford.

Pickard-Cambridge, A. W. [1968] *The Dramatic Festivals of Athens*, Oxford.

Plato, *Collected Dialogues* (almost complete tr.), E. Hamilton and H. Cairns, eds., Princeton, 1961.

Plato, *Euthyphro, Apology, Crito, Meno, Phaedo*, tr. G. M. A. Grube, Indianapolis, 1981.

Plato, *Gorgias*, tr. and ed. T. Irwin, Oxford, 1979.

Plato, *Phaedo*, tr. and ed. D. Gallop, Oxford, 1975.

Plato, *Republic*, tr. G. M. A. Grube, Indianapolis, 1974.

Plato, *Theaetetus*, tr. J. McDowell, Oxford, 1973.

Plato, *Theaetetus*, tr. M. J. Levett, ed. M. F. Burnyeat, Indianapolis, 1990.

Plotinus, tr. A. H. Armstrong, 7 vols., London, 1966–88.

Popper, K. R. [1966] *The Open Society and its Enemies*, 2 vols., 5th edn., London (1966; 1st edn. 1944).

Prestige, G. L. [1952] *God in Patristic Thought*, 2nd edn., London.

Rhodes [1982]: *see* Aristotle.

Robinson, R. [1969] *Essays in Greek Philosophy*, Oxford.

Rorty, A. O., ed. [1980] *Essays on Aristotle's Ethics*, Berkeley.

Sambursky, S. [1960] *The Physical World of the Greeks*, 2nd edn., London.

Sandbach, F. H. [1975] *The Stoics*, London.

Sextus Empiricus, tr. R. G. Bury (Loeb), 4 vols., London, 1933–49.

Sextus Empiricus, *Outlines of Scepticism*, tr. J. Annas and J. Barnes, Cambridge, 1994.

Sharples [1983]: *see* Alexander.

Snell, B. [1953] *The Discovery of the Mind*, Oxford.

Sorabji, R. [1980] *Necessity, Cause, and Blame*, London.

Sorabji, R. [1983] *Time, Creation, and the Continuum*, London.

Sorabji, R., ed. [1990] *Aristotle Transformed*, London.

Sprague, R. K., ed. [1972] *The Older Sophists* (tr. and comm.), Columbia, S.C.

Stevenson, J., ed. [1957] *A New Eusebius*, London.

Taplin, O. [1978] *Greek Tragedy in Action*, London.

Thucydides, tr. R. Crawley, London, 1876.

Thucydides, tr. T. Hobbes, ed. R. Schlatter, New Brunswick, 1975.

Vlastos, G., ed. [1971a] *The Philosophy of Socrates*, Garden City.

Vlastos, G., ed. [1971b] *Plato*, 2 vols., Garden City.

Vlastos, G. [1973] *Platonic Studies*, Princeton.

Vlastos, G. [1975] *Plato's Universe*, Seattle.

Vlastos, G. [1991] *Socrates: Ironist and Moral Philosopher*, Cambridge.

Vlastos, G. [1994] *Socratic Studies*, Cambridge.

Vlastos, G. [1995] *Studies in Greek Philosophy*, 2 vols., Princeton.

Von Arnim, H., ed., *Stoicorum Veterum Fragmenta*, 4 vols., Leipzig, 1905–24.

Walbank, F. W. [1981] *The Hellenistic World*, London.

Wallis, R. T. [1972] *Neoplatonism*, London.

West, M. L., ed. [1980] *Delectus ex Iambis et Elegis Graecis*, Oxford.

Williams, B. [1972] *Morality*, New York.

Witt, C. [1989] *Substance and Essence in Aristotle*, Ithaca.

Woodruff, P., and Gagarin, M., tr. [1995] *Early Greek Political Thought from Homer to the Sophists*, Cambridge.

Yeats, W. B., *Collected Poems*, London, 1950.

Index

The index includes dates for the main historical figures and
sources mentioned in the text and notes.

philosopher, 105; and pleasure, 135, 158, 160; self-sufficient, 141; and tranquillity, 149

happiness and fortune, 134, 141, 174, 197: in Epicurus, 159, 161; in Stoicism, 174

happiness and virtue: in Aristotle, 134, 136; in Plato, 103; in Socrates, 80; in Stoicism, 173, 175, 179

Hecataeus (*fl.* 500 BC), historian: on tradition, 29

Hector, 9, 11

Hellenistic philosophy, and Aristotle, 143

Hellenistic world, 145

Heracleitus (*fl. c.*500 BC), naturalist: v. Aristotle on change, 125; on conflicting appearances, 48; criticisms of, 43; on gods, 38; on identity, 154; law and justice, 37, 47; opposites, 59, 94; Plato on, 91; on rational argument, 220; on senses and reason, 33, 47, 91; on Zeus, 52

hero, in Homer, 8, 15

Herodotus (? *c.*484–*c.*420 BC), historian, 26-8: Aristotle on, 120; on cosmic justice, 41; ongods, 39, 40, 45; on history, 26, 31; on nature and convention, 60; on observation, 30

Hesiod (*c.*750 BC), epic poet, 12, 20

Hippocrates (? *c.*470–*c.*400 BC), medical writer, 28: and empiricism, 31; on gods, 39

historia, 31, 120

history, 226; Herodotus on, 31; and naturalism, 26, 55

Hobbes, Thomas (1588-1679), political philosopher: v. Aristotle, 143; on democracy, 56; on power, 53; and Thucydides, 229, 230

Holy Spirit, in Christianity, 212

Homer (? *c.*750 BC): and Augustine, 215; in education, 63; ethics, 11, 65, 147; on gods, 30, 112, 156, 169, 217, 224; and Herodotus, 26; on honour, 62; on human nature, 55; importance of, 6; on justice, 36; on morality and religion, 77; v. naturalism, 22; and observation, 153; on responsibility, 45; and tragedy, 44; and virtue, 7; on

Zeus, 16, 180

honour: in democracy, 62; in Homer, 8, 10, 18

Horace (65 BC–AD 8), poet, 147, 176, 223

human good, *see* happiness

human nature: in Aristotle, 137; in Christianity, 206; in Epicurus, 158; and Homeric hero, 55; and naturalism, 53; in Plato, 102; in Plotinus, 196; in Stoics, 173

Hume, David (1711-76), sceptic: on Aristotle, 143; on determinism, 33; on religion, 170; 241; and Stoicism, 183

hypostasis: in Augustine, 218; in Christianity, 212; in Plotinus, 185, 218, 244

identity: Aristotle on, 125; Epicurus on, 154; Heracleitus on, 24, 125, 154

immortality: Aristotle on, 141; Epicurus on, 154; Plato on, 98, 105, 236; Socrates on, 81

indifferents, in Stoicism, 174, 176, 177

intellect, in Plotinus, 190, 194

Jesus Christ (*c.*7 BC–*c.* AD 30): divine and human nature of, 213; and ethics, 205, 207, 208; humanity of, 211; incarnation, Augustine on, 217-20; and perfectionism, 206; person of, 210; redemption by, 208; work of, 208

John, Gospel of, 204, 246

justice: Aeschylus on, 46; Aristotle on, 137, 138; in city and soul, 103; and common good, 47, 57, 106; definition of, 91; and democracy, 64; Epicurus on, 159, 161; and gods, 38, 42; Hebrew prophets on, 205; and Homer, 13, 36, 45; human and cosmic, 66; and law, 37, 41, 47; Plato on, 103; Plotinus on, 198; and political division, 107; problems of, 101; and scepticism, 60; and self-interest, 55, 65, 80, 101, 108; and social contract, 53, 101, 159; Socrates on, 70-1, 77, 79, 82; Solon on, 36, 38; in soul, 103; Stoicism on, 175; Thrasymachus on, 101; Thucydides on, 56, 73

OXFORD

MORE OXFORD PAPERBACKS

This book is just one of nearly 1000 Oxford Paper-
backs currently in print. If you would like details of
other Oxford Paperbacks, including titles in the
World's Classics, Oxford Reference, Oxford
Books, OPUS, Past Masters, Oxford Authors, and
Oxford Shakespeare series, please write to:

UK and Europe: Oxford Paperbacks Publicity Man-
ager, Arts and Reference Publicity Department,
Oxford University Press, Walton Street, Oxford
OX2 6DP.

Customers in UK and Europe will find Oxford
Paperbacks available in all good bookshops. But in
case of difficulty please send orders to the Cash-
with-Order Department, Oxford University Press
Distribution Services, Saxon Way West, Corby,
Northants NN18 9ES. Tel: 01536 741519; Fax:
01536 746337. Please send a cheque for the total cost
of the books, plus £1.75 postage and packing for
orders under £20; £2.75 for orders over £20. Customers outside the UK should add 10% of the cost
of the books for postage and packing.

USA: Oxford Paperbacks Marketing Manager,
Oxford University Press, Inc., 200 Madison Av-
enue, New York, N.Y. 10016.

Canada: Trade Department, Oxford University
Press, 70 Wynford Drive, Don Mills, Ontario M3C
1J9.

Australia: Trade Marketing Manager, Oxford University Press, G.P.O. Box 2784Y, Melbourne 3001,
Victoria.

South Africa: Oxford University Press, P.O. Box
1141, Cape Town 8000.

OPUS

A HISTORICAL INTRODUCTION TO THE PHILOSOPHY OF SCIENCE

John Losee

This challenging introduction, designed for readers without an extensive knowledge of formal logic or of the history of science, looks at the long-argued questions raised by philosophers and scientists about the proper evaluation of scientific interpretations. It offers an historical exposition of differing views on issues such as the merits of competing theories; the interdependence of observation and theory; and the nature of scientific progress. The author looks at explanations given by Plato, Aristotle, and Pythagoras, and through to Bacon and Descartes, to Nagel, Kuhn, and Laudan.

This edition incorporates an extended discussion of contemporary developments and changes within the history of science, and examines recent controversies and the search for a non-prescriptive philosophy of science.

'a challenging interdisciplinary work'
New Scientist

OPUS

TWENTIETH-CENTURY FRENCH PHILOSOPHY

Eric Matthews

This book gives a chronological survey of the works of the major French philosophers of the twentieth century.

Eric Matthews offers various explanations for the enduring importance of philosophy in French intellectual life and traces the developments which French philosophy has taken in the twentieth century from its roots in the thought of Descartes, with examinations of key figures such as Bergson, Sartre, Marcel, Merleau-Ponty, Foucault, and Derrida, and the recent French Feminists.

'*Twentieth-Century French Philosophy* is a clear, yet critical introduction to contemporary French Philosophy. . . . The undergraduate or other reader who comes to the area for the first time will gain a definite sense of an intellectual movement with its own questions and answers and its own rigour . . . not least of the book's virtues is its clarity.'
Garrett Barden
Author of *After Principles*

PHILOSOPHY IN OXFORD PAPERBACKS
THE GREAT PHILOSOPHERS
Bryan Magee

Beginning with the death of Socrates in 399, and following the story through the centuries to recent figures such as Bertrand Russell and Wittgenstein, Bryan Magee and fifteen contemporary writers and philosophers provide an accessible and exciting introduction to Western philosophy and its greatest thinkers.

Bryan Magee in conversation with:

A. J. Ayer	John Passmore
Michael Ayers	Anthony Quinton
Miles Burnyeat	John Searle
Frederick Copleston	Peter Singer
Hubert Dreyfus	J. P. Stern
Anthony Kenny	Geoffrey Warnock
Sidney Morgenbesser	Bernard Williams
Martha Nussbaum	

'Magee is to be congratulated . . . anyone who sees the programmes or reads the book will be left in no danger of believing philosophical thinking is unpractical and uninteresting.' Ronald Hayman, *Times Educational Supplement*

'one of the liveliest, fast-paced introductions to philosophy, ancient and modern that one could wish for' *Universe*

Oxford
Paperback
Reference

THE OXFORD DICTIONARY OF PHILOSOPHY

Edited by Simon Blackburn

* **2,500 entries covering the entire span of the subject including the most recent terms and concepts**

* **Biographical entries for nearly 500 philosophers**

* **Chronology of philosophical events**

From Aristotle to Zen, this is the most comprehensive, authoritative, and up to date dictionary of philosophy available. Ideal for students or a general readership, it provides lively and accessible coverage of not only the Western philosophical tradition but also important themes from Chinese, Indian, Islamic, and Jewish philosophy. The paperback includes a new Chronology.

'an excellent source book and can be strongly recommended . . . there are generous and informative entries on the great philosophers . . . Overall the entries are written in an informed and judicious manner.'
Times Higher Education Supplement

A Very Short Introduction

CLASSICS

Mary Beard and John Henderson

This *Very Short Introduction* to Classics links a haunting temple on a lonely mountainside to the glory of ancient Greece and the grandeur of Rome, and to Classics within modern culture—from Jefferson and Byron to Asterix and Ben-Hur.

'This little book should be in the hands of every student, and every tourist to the lands of the ancient world . . . a splendid piece of work'
Peter Wiseman
Author of *Talking to Virgil*

'an eminently readable and useful guide to many of the modern debates enlivening the field . . . the most up-to-date and accessible introduction available'
Edith Hall
Author of *Inventing the Barbarian*

'lively and up-to-date . . . it shows classics as a living enterprise, not a warehouse of relics'
New Statesman and Society

'nobody could fail to be informed and entertained—the accent of the book is provocative and stimulating'
Times Literary Supplement

POLITICS

Kenneth Minogue

Since politics is both complex and controversial it is easy to miss the wood for the trees. In this Very Short Introduction Kenneth Minogue has brought the many dimensions of politics into a single focus: he discusses both the everyday grind of democracy and the attraction of grand ideals such as freedom and justice.

'Kenneth Minogue is a very lively stylist who does not distort difficult ideas.'
Maurice Cranston

'a dazzling but unpretentious display of great scholarship and humane reflection'
Professor Neil O'Sullivan, University of Hull

'Minogue is an admirable choice for showing us the nuts and bolts of the subject.'
Nicholas Lezard, *Guardian*

'This is a fascinating book which sketches, in a very short space, one view of the nature of politics ... the reader is challenged, provoked and stimulated by Minogue's trenchant views.'
Talking Politics

ARCHAEOLOGY

Paul Bahn

'Archaeology starts, really, at the point when the first recognizable 'artefacts' appear—on current evidence, that was in East Africa about 2.5 million years ago—and stretches right up to the present day. What you threw in the garbage yesterday, no matter how useless, disgusting, or potentially embarrassing, has now become part of the recent archaeological record.'

This Very Short Introduction reflects the enduring popularity of archaeology—a subject which appeals as a pastime, career, and academic discipline, encompasses the whole globe, and surveys 2.5 million years. From deserts to jungles, from deep caves to mountain-tops, from pebble tools to satellite photographs, from excavation to abstract theory, archaeology interacts with nearly every other discipline in its attempts to reconstruct the past.

'very lively indeed and remarkably perceptive . . . a quite brilliant and level-headed look at the curious world of archaeology'
Professor Barry Cunliffe,
University of Oxford

A Very Short Introduction

BUDDHISM

Damien Keown

'Karma can be either good or bad. Buddhists speak of good karma as "merit", and much effort is expended in acquiring it. Some picture it as a kind of spiritual capital—like money in a bank account—whereby credit is built up as the deposit on a heavenly rebirth.'

This Very Short Introduction introduces the reader both to the teachings of the Buddha and to the integration of Buddhism into daily life. What are the distinctive features of Buddhism? Who was the Buddha, and what are his teachings? How has Buddhist thought developed over the centuries, and how can contemporary dilemmas be faced from a Buddhist perspective?

'Damien Keown's book is a readable and wonderfully lucid introduction to one of mankind's most beautiful, profound, and compelling systems of wisdom. The rise of the East makes understanding and learning from Buddhism, a living doctrine, more urgent than ever before. Keown's impressive powers of explanation help us to come to terms with a vital contemporary reality.'
Bryan Appleyard

A Very Short Introduction

JUDAISM

Norman Solomon

'Norman Solomon has achieved the near impossible with his enlightened very short introduction to Judaism. Since it is well known that Judaism is almost impossible to summarize, and that there are as many different opinions about Jewish matters as there are Jews, this is a small masterpiece in its success in representing various shades of Jewish opinion, often mutually contradictory. Solomon also manages to keep the reader engaged, never patronizes, assumes little knowledge but a keen mind, and takes us through Jewish life and history with such gusto that one feels enlivened, rather than exhausted, at the end.'
Rabbi Julia Neuberger

'This book will serve a very useful purpose indeed. I'll use it myself to discuss, to teach, agree with, and disagree with, in the Jewish manner!'
Rabbi Lionel Blue

'A magnificent achievement. Dr Solomon's treatment, fresh, very readable, witty and stimulating, will delight everyone interested in religion in the modern world.'
Dr Louis Jacobs, University of London